Contesting Historical Divides
in Francophone Africa

Contesting Historical Divides
in Francophone Africa

Edited by

Claire H. Griffiths

University of Chester Press

First published 2013
by University of Chester Press
University of Chester
Parkgate Road
Chester CH1 4BJ

Printed and bound in the UK by the
LIS Print Unit
University of Chester
Cover designed by the
LIS Graphics Team
University of Chester

A catalogue record for this book is available from the British
Library

ISBN 978-1-908258-03-8

CONTENTS

v

Contents

LIST OF ILLUSTRATIONS

ACKNOWLEDGEMENTS

We are sincerely grateful to the General Editor of the University of Chester Press, Dr Sarah Griffiths, for her patience, flexibility and invaluable assistance during the editing of this volume. We also would like to thank our colleagues in the Print Unit and in the Graphics department at the University of Chester who worked so quickly and helpfully to print the books and produce the maps and cover design.

While this volume has been subject to peer review by experts in the field, any academic errors or misconstructions remain entirely the responsibility of the authors. We would like to express our gratitude here for the time and support given by subject experts who participated in this procedure. The result is a volume smaller than originally envisaged but, we trust, all the more coherent in its theme and convincing in its argument. We are also grateful to the contributors whose submissions were not selected after peer review for the final collection presented here.

Finally we would like to acknowledge the immense debt those of us who have undertaken extensive periods of fieldwork owe to our research collaborators in Francophone Africa and the Indian Ocean islands, without whom our projects and investigations could not achieve a fraction of what they set out to accomplish. The generosity of our many fieldwork colleagues is very deeply appreciated by us all.

PREFACE

The research presented in this volume was conducted in several countries in the region we call Francophone sub-Saharan Africa and in the islands of the south-west Indian Ocean. Many months, and in some cases years, of fieldwork in Francophone Africa and French overseas territories lie behind each of the territorial studies and overviews.

We hope that the result, combining desk research with extensive evidence from the field, crossing several disciplinary divides, notably between literature, politics, history and sociology, will provide a useful and interesting addition to the considerable body of research that has been published, and is still being published, in the wake of the fiftieth anniversary of independence in the French African colonies.

The University of Chester re-launched its Press as an academic publishing venture in 2010 at the time the Francophone Africa research group – and this book project – were at their inception. In an era when the need for universities actively to support and nurture new and innovative research is growing, the role of university presses in promoting academic scholarship is crucial. We are very pleased to take this opportunity to participate in the launch of the University of Chester Press with this volume.

INTRODUCTION

CONTESTING HISTORICAL DIVIDES IN FRANCOPHONE AFRICA
Post-Slavery, Post-Colonial, Post-Imperial?

Claire H. Griffiths

As historians, cultural theorists and social scientists continue to grapple with the legacy of a history of Francophone Africa inherited from the former colonising powers, the chapters in this book engage with new historiographies of the region still developing during the post-independence era. Postcolonial historians from Cheikh Anta Diop to the present have pioneered new political geographies and histories of Africa that recast the roles and redefine the agents of history, uncovering new perspectives and enabling new connections to be established between Africa's present and its past. As we remove historical divides, we reveal traces of past traumas in economies where men, women and children are working for no wages in cocoa plantations, domestic service and indentured labour in countries that were once under French colonial rule. Indeed, the economic realities of development in the postcolonial period present a multiplicity of connections with the centuries of foreign occupation. This collection of essays explores some of the contemporary manifestations of these political, social, educational and cultural legacies in the countries that were once part of the French African and Indian Ocean Empire.

The conflict in Mali that began in early 2012 had drawn the attention of the world to the former colonies of French West Africa by the time this volume went to press. On 11 January 2013 France intervened militarily in northern Mali to restore Timbuktu and other key gains of the Tuareg and subsequent Islamist insurgency to the Malian government. This recent

Fig. 1. Map of Francophone Africa.

example of France's Africa policy, immediately televised and communicated through social media around the world, met with little surprise. When the integrity of a nation created by France and returned to Africa at independence is threatened, the former colonial power, regardless of political complexion, will lead or will be expected to lead an international response. This was demonstrated through military action in Mali and then through deliberate military inaction in the Central African Republic weeks later when the rebels finally ousted François Bozizé from the presidential palace in

2

Bangui. Does this mean France still rules in West Africa? If not, what are the limits of the colonial *acquis* in the postcolonial world? These have been the issues that have occupied the authors of this book.

The eight essays published in this volume emerged from work presented at an interdisciplinary research colloquium marking the fiftieth anniversary of political independence in Francophone West Africa held at the University of Chester in September 2010.[1] The unifying theme of that research day was a multiple interrogation of Francophone Africa since independence under the title *Post-Slavery? Post-Imperial? Post-Colonial? Contesting Historical Divides in Francophone Africa.*

This volume continues that questioning of the timelines and terminologies associated with postcoloniality and independence. While "post-imperial" and "post-colonial" constitute the organising themes of almost all contemporary rewritings of the history of the region, a word is reserved in this preliminary chapter for the first of these interrogations which is, as we write, entering the frame in which change, modernity, progress and development are increasingly being explored, historiographically, in the sub-regions that were once French Africa. While the fieldwork in postcolonial slavery studies is, relatively speaking, in its infancy, the potential value of this research category to social, political, legal and cultural research in and on the region is emerging. The re-apparition of this line of enquiry well over a century and a half after legal abolition, along with other new research categories in the social and historical sciences, owe much to the impact of postcolonial thought on historiographical research methodologies. These developments are effectively beginning to reframe and expand the conceptual limits of the research disciplines and categories in which African Studies are conducted, as well as revising and in some cases overturning the substantive content of established research–based knowledge on the region. As an emerging field of research, slavery studies provides an example of the ways in which contemporary research methodologies have to traverse not just timelines but also disciplinary lines. Legal as well as labour histories need revisiting as evidence attesting to the various forms of slavery that continued to operate in the region before and after the colonial/postcolonial historical divide are set against the legislative history of abolition, from the mid-nineteenth century through to the anti-slavery laws of the early twentieth century. Contemporary research now reveals that notwithstanding the legislation, chattel slavery in the region continued through to the twenty-first century, when finally, in the glare of international press coverage, another stage in legal abolition was reached with the criminalisation of this form of enslaved labour in 2003 in Niger. Recent cases testifying to the continuation of this practice post-abolition have reached the Ecowas court, providing further proof that the term "post-slavery" can still not be applied with conviction to the region in 2013. Indeed, as this research category gathers momentum and impacts on other social science and legal disciplines, evidence of a recent growth in slavery – from child labour in the cocoa plantations of the region to human trafficking into Europe – will help cast a new light on the impact of internal and exogenous transnational factors, such as the re-emergence of neoliberalism and the globalisation of markets, on the development of postcolonial Africa. The incompleteness of the knowledge base in postcolonial slavery studies, due in no small part to the inadequacy of current information gathering methods, are witness to the case that these transversal categories are in an early stage of development, and, regardless of their intrinsic and potential value, have yet to make a significant impact on the multidisciplinary field of contemporary African Studies.

However, at the other end of our historical continuum, back in the founding decades of the imperial project in French Africa, the newer transversal research categories, such as gender studies and slavery studies, are serving to refresh and reveal new perspectives on legal, economic, social and labour history. Frederick Cooper (1979) and more latterly Alice Conklin's work on defining the parameters, incidence, legalisation and abolition of the forms of slavery in the former French colonies has led the way in this field. As Conklin has noted, "one of the most paradoxical features of the French colonial system in West Africa was administrative-sanctioned recourse to forced labour, which the Government General made no effort to conceal" (Conklin, 1998, p. 437).

In Chapter 1 Jonathan Derrick foregrounds the role forced labour played in French Africa and its fundamental contribution to the imperial enterprise at a time almost a century after the practice was rendered illegal, albeit under another name. His argument concurs with other current research published elsewhere attesting to the key role of slave labour in the groundnut industry during the second half of the nineteenth century. As Mohammed Bashir Salau has recently written citing Bernard Moitt,

> Senegal acquired slaves from the French Sudan ... and by the first years of the twentieth century, slave labor was extensively used in the major production centers ... partly because the French had serious reservations about dismantling slavery (Bashir Salau, 2011, p. 120).

Likewise Martin Klein's research has been demonstrating the centrality of slave labour to industrial production in the making of French Africa through the nineteenth century, though noting a decline after 1905 at the point when the French introduced labour legislation that outlawed the public practice of slavery on the large estates. Others are locating a major shift in the dependence on slave labour in the last quarter of the nineteenth century as a result of war and conflict in the region (Klein, 1998, p. 121). Derrick returns us to the issue of how unfree labour developed under French control in French Africa in the post-slavery era as he traces the growth of *la corvée* in the interwar period noting that in both *Afrique équatoriale française* and *Afrique occidentale française* forced labour reached "epidemic proportions" in the Second World War.[2] A third era of anti-slavery activity led to abolition being tabled on the agenda for the 1944 Brazzaville conference and finally legal abolition was achieved in 1946 thanks to efforts in the French National Assembly by the future president of the Ivory Coast (Derrick, p. 38).

While slavery studies, gender studies and other newer fields continue the long process of building bridges into older disciplinary research bases, the question of whether the Francophone African space is "post-imperial" or "post-colonial" has been generating a considerable body of published research over the past three decades, culminating in the recent peak of publications around the fiftieth anniversary.[3] To what extent the region has shaken off its imperial and colonial legacy is a question addressed by a number of these publications. The question has also provided the core theme addressed by all the contributors to this volume. While the focus of the chapters presented here is directed towards the political, social and cultural agenda of the region in these early decades of the twenty-first century, all engage with the multiple legacies of French and British imperialism and colonialism.

Introduction

Over and above the collective purpose to interrogate assumptions inherent in the term "postcolonial", what binds all the essays of this volume together is a clear and common investigative purpose to focus on uncovering new evidence from less widely researched examples or clarifying misapprehensions about the state of postcoloniality in Francophone Africa.

In Chapter 1, Jonathan Derrick deconstructs a key term in the French colonial project to reveal the intended and effective limits of "assimilation" policy in French West Africa. As he explains,

> Talk at the time [in the 1920s and 30s] of the colonies becoming part of "Greater France" was just talk. On their side Africans sought French education for their own reasons, then as later, and one may question how many ever really wanted to become Frenchmen (Derrick, pp. 23–24).

The discussion goes on to remind us of the future president, Léopold Sédar Senghor's thoughts on the matter of French education delivered during a period in the short life of the Popular Front government when far more attention was being paid to social and educational issues in the colonies than was the case either before or after the Blum regime. Senghor argued at this time for the need to develop African language use particularly at the first levels of education in French Africa (Derrick, p. 34). Not much heed was paid then to these words, nor indeed in the seventy-five years since that advice was offered.

During this period the use of African languages in education has barely extended beyond elementary education. It is not without some relevance to this enquiry into the state and nature of postcoloniality in Francophone Africa that the keynote speech delivered by the Kenyan writer and academic, Ngũgĩ wa Thiong'o, to the African Studies Association of the UK Biennial Conference in 2012 explored the same issue Senghor had addressed some seventy-five years earlier. Evidence drawn from a show of hands at the lecture revealed that not one among the hundreds of Africanist scholars crammed into a huge lecture theatre to hear this talk entitled "Africa in the Language of Scholarship" that evening was producing and publishing his or her research monographs in an African language. The point did not require any labouring – it was clear in that show of hands and the myriad other examples offered by Ngũgĩ that so long as the intellectual life of Africa is conducted through the vehicle of the two principal colonial languages, English and French, we must continue to question what stage decolonisation has reached in Africa.

The exploration of the myths and misconceptions about what made French colonialism in Africa distinct from other European colonial missions is continued in the second chapter where David Perfect and Martin Evans "take the long view" in their investigation of "the colonial past and how it shapes the present" in the Senegambia region of West Africa (Perfect and Evans, p. 59). The transnational dimension of colonisation comes into focus as Perfect, a specialist on Gambian political history, and Evans, providing analysis from the Senegalese side, discuss how Britain and France contributed to the construction of colonial Senegambia as official control fluctuated between the two powers throughout most of the late seventeenth and eighteenth centuries. This chapter highlights both the commonality and specificity of the colonial practices of the two superpowers of the day. Their common purpose provides a textbook example of the exogenisation of economic infrastructure and trading patterns which decimated the traditional African economic landscape during European colonisation. As they note, even in a region as economically rich and diverse as Senegambia, "both colonies had much greater trading links with their respective metropoles than with each other or with other African countries" (Perfect and Evans, p. 66), noting that where indigenous trade survived and flourished it became illegal.

The political legacy of the French and British activities in the region is borne by the current generations of Joola and other ethnic groups who occupy the war-torn region of southern Senegambia separated by the Anglo-French Convention of 1889. The ongoing impact of this colonial agreement is testified by the longest-running civil war in postcolonial African history. The Casamance conflict not only sets up significant obstacles to cross-border diplomacy between the political elites of the two countries implicated in the war and exacts a heavy toll on the local populations, it also impacts on future populations as development projects are abandoned. "Both sides continue to play out roles set for them well over a century ago" conclude the authors.

Chapter 3 brings the Casamance conflict to centre stage as Martin Evans examines the notion of historiography – or interpretations of historical records – as a political tool in the hands of the parties to the conflict. Mobilisation to a cause and justification for violent intervention are vocalised in competing narratives that evoke the curious spectacle of an African liberation movement claiming independence on the grounds of a colonial precedent. Evans explores the Casamance separatist claims that their region was governed as a separate entity under an agreement reached at the Berlin Conference of 1884–1885. This highly disputed claim has, as Evans will explain, involved at some points the highest offices of the French state, even at one point the president of the Republic in the person of François Mitterrand who commissioned a report into the findings, the results of which are measured in this chapter against the separatists' claims.

As the absence of African language-based research continues to hamper the development of African Studies, Evans's chapter along with others in this volume makes a contribution to efforts to include more local voices and opinions in research projects. In this case Evans has enriched the information in his chapter with commentary provided in African languages and recorded and translated with the help of a local interpreter-assistant. His accounts of the contested histories of Casamance reveal how the residents of Balantacounda in central Casamance tell a different story of the evolution of the Casamance from residents of other regions, proving if proof were still required that histories are as geographically sensitive as they are politically charged.

In Chapter 4 the discussion of the colonial legacy extends beyond mainland Africa to investigate postcolonial relations between France and its former and current island possessions in the south-west Indian Ocean. The history of this colonial and now partially postcolonial archipelago as told in this chapter reveals new understandings of the workings of the contemporary republican state after the empire. Following on from Derrick's analysis of French colonial rule in Africa in Chapter 1, Massey also dismisses simplified narratives of assimilation and direct rule that still hold some purchase in contemporary discussions of French policy in the overseas territories. As Massey's analysis demonstrates, the complexity of French colonial and neocolonial strategy in Africa and beyond is exemplified in the political history of the Comoros archipelago.

Introduction

Over and beyond the extraordinary tales of state-sponsored assassination and corruption that litter this history, Massey reveals underlying traits that position this group of islands firmly in the class of "business as usual" for French African policy. The history of the secessionist movements in the Comoros archipelago have some traits in common with the Casamance example explored in Chapter 4, while carrying an additional layer of complexity in the radically different political statuses of the islands that make up the archipelago.

While contributing new knowledge to the field of Francophone African politics by focusing on this little-known area, the chapter also offers fresh evidence supporting established understandings of that policy, noting "France's enduring priorities in its dealings with its former colonies and overseas territories: status, strategic necessity and an abiding impulse to preserve its cultural legacy" (Massey, p. 130). The essay provides an explanation of what led to the unrest of the final years of the twentieth century and the rupture of the Comorian Union and detailed insights into how relative political stability is being maintained in the twenty-first century. This stands as an intriguing example of how divide and rule can still be played out in the colonies without any apparent attempt at concealment. Referring to the island of Maoré (or the department of Mayotte as it is called in France) Massey notes that in the face of opposition from the UN "Maoré is under French occupation" while having the constitutional status as France's 101st department (Massey, pp. 130, 135). The failure of this tropical paradise island to reap the benefits of the explosion in mass tourism in the Indian Ocean[4] becomes clear as Massey charts the ramifications of late colonial rule in a largely postcolonial world.

11

In Parts 1 and 2, the main focus of the discussion lay in the colonial and foreign policies shaping the relationship between France and empire, both former and current. In the following section the target of the analysis moves from politics to policy, and from state to society. In Chapter 5, the author argues that while gender policy is clearly a discrete area of political activity in postcolonial Africa, this field reveals an underlying dynamic that connects development policy in the region with its colonial past. In addition, this area of social intervention reveals how external powers operate in the development field in Francophone Africa today. While most of the chapters in this volume will chart the most recent history of the region, Griffiths's discussion draws from sociological history from the period before the coloniser settled on African soil, using this to challenge the common conflation of postcolonial with modernity and progress. By focusing on gender relations in the sub-region in the period from pre-colonial to postcolonial and the impact of state intervention (through social policy) on these relations, Griffiths uses this example of European social engineering to engage with broader issues of historical and historiographical research on Africa. In this context, she stresses the dangers of studying women as a socio-historical sub-group, and locating them in the discrete category of "women's history" in Africa, if this separation then serves to disguise or cover up the interplay of gender relations and social dynamics that have shaped that still largely untold history. The discussion will go on to suggest that such a separatist approach also runs the serious risk of failure to challenge the philosophical underpinnings of a European historical project that created an absence of women in the historical archive of Africa. Such categories as "women's history" may address a knowledge gap but they may also fail to engage with the faulty methodology that generated this and other gaps in our understanding of how Europe configured its colonial "subaltern".

Griffiths's exploration of our historical knowledge of gender relations in former French colonies provides the disturbing revelation that some contemporary French scholarship on gender in Africa has more in common with the colonial configuration of the subjugated African woman than some earlier French research undertaken in the interwar period and in the decade before independence (much of which has disappeared from view).[5] The historical divides being contested in this chapter are explored within a framework that questions assumptions about what "post-coloniality" means from a social perspective. Positivistic notions of progress and development are set against historical evidence of regression, social exclusion and marginalisation in the modern era. On this socio-historical journey from pre-colonial to late colonial times and beyond, we see growing levels of gender-based social disintegration and disadvantage. The chapter concludes with fresh evidence of the "recolonisation" of the social development field in the years after the departure of the French.

Both Chapters 5 and 6 highlight the predominance of transnational foreign interests currently engaged in social development politics in the region, and the central role played by the agencies of the Bretton Woods institutions. In Chapter 6, Brenda Garvey provides further evidence of the role the UN has been playing in framing the socio-educational debate in postcolonial Francophone Africa. She traces the current engagement with pre-school education in Senegal to the UN global education summit held in Dakar in June 2000 just months after Abdoulaye Wade had seized power from Abdou Diouf in the presidential elections held earlier that year. However she notes that though pre-school education entered the policy-making arena in the region primarily thanks to its prominence on the UN agenda,[6] the way in which this education has developed in Senegal has failed to attract the funding this international interest promised. Suggesting the absence of funding may be linked to the content of the pre-schooling on offer, she describes the "bottom-up" policy making process that led to the current *Case des Tout-Petits* experiment in nursery education in Senegal. The absence of presidential intervention in the policy area presents similarities with the social policy area explored in Chapter 5. In both cases incoming presidents adopted a high profile in setting the social policy agenda – in the pattern of centralised states – and then ceased to follow through at the implementation stage. Readers familiar with French social policy-making in the modern era will see parallels here in the place occupied by policy fields in the policy-making hierarchy. This is revealed by the degree of presidential time and interest they inhabit outside the slogans accompanying national political agenda setting at election time.

In this case, the slogans focused on the need to re-introduce African language use and culturally relevant education to Senegalese schooling. The description Garvey provides of the pre-school curriculum shows how far the schools are from reaching that stated aim (Garvey, p. 192). She examines the use of Wolof in nursery education and, again in parallel to the previous chapter, uncovers a colonising dynamic in contemporary social policy. While clearly contesting colonial language use in formal education in Senegal, the *Case des Tout-Petits* experiment appears to find itself now caught in a re-colonising momentum. Nevertheless her conclusions, based on a comparison with other countries

14

in the region, suggest some positive outcomes from this educational experiment in Senegal.

The research symposium which provided the inspiration for this volume set itself an ambitious agenda to uncover or create new links across disciplines in the field of Francophone African Studies. It also set itself the challenge to build up links between established and emerging research. The last section of the book incorporates two of the early career projects which were at the time of the symposium at doctoral stage.

In Chapter 7, Alice Burgin discusses the film *Ndeysaan* (The Price of Forgiveness) by Mansour Sora Wade in the modern aesthetics of *négritude* operating in postcolonial Francophone African culture. The investigation sets out to answer questions about how a philosophical movement "challenging colonial hegemony" and born of a colonial experience can continue to operate in the twenty-first century as a vehicle of "cultural affirmation". Indeed the author questions whether *négritude* persists in contemporary Francophone African cultural production as an expression of "anachronistic nativism" to use Denis Ekpo's term (2010), and thereby contests the notion of a reframing of *négritude* in the post-1960 era.

In the character of Maxoye, we see "the recurring construct of African woman in *négritude* philosophy" (Burgin, p. 212). This was and is "a motivational force constructed … in the passive", Burgin argues citing Ajayi (1997). It is this characterisation of womanhood that appeared to underlie the *revalorisation* programme launched for women by the first president of Senegal and founder of the *négritude* movement, Léopold Sédar Senghor. The programme failed to follow through on the President's independence declarations to restore the African woman to her rightful place with tangible results of empowerment, as discussed in Chapter 5. The figure of Maxoye speaks to a *négritude* claim of African woman as "untouched by colonialism, who is natural and nurturing" (Burgin, p. 213). Readers may conclude that this configuration presents closer similarities with European gender roles dominant during the colonial era and beyond, rather than norms and practices prevailing in the vast and diverse territories of pre-colonial Africa.

The chapter exemplifies the philosophical and methodological developments being made in postcolonial studies today, to which this volume seeks to contribute, challenging the traditional binaries spelled out in the volume's title and acknowledging the evolving "multi-valenced" relationships and identities that populate and traverse the geopolitical space we call Francophone Africa.

In the last chapter of the book Sarah Burnautzki tests the limits of French literary universalism in the field of Francophone African creative writing. Posited as colour blind and egalitarian, Burnautzki seeks to reveal in her essay a normative "ethnification" of Francophone African literary production, an argument that contests claims of a funda-mental reconfiguration of political and economic interests in the French literary system in the post-independence era. As she notes, "these processes of literary "ethnification" are not easily distinguishable in the Francophone context" (Burnautzki, p. 231), so what follows in this chapter is a careful uncovering and naming of the cultural othering as it is operating in African literature published in French.

Burnautzki raises a point of particular salience to this collection of essays: that France has been sheltered to an unusual degree from hugely important intellectual and theoretical developments during the post-independence era. Notably, and quoting Antoine Compagnon (2000), she argues

16

that the politics of cultural "exceptionalism" has resulted in France being marginalised from an international dialogue of theories (Burnautzki, p. 236). Consequently paradigmatic shifts of central importance to current cultural production and research in postcolonial Francophone Africa have only very recently been re-imported into French intellectual and cultural life.[7]

The position of Caribbean theorists in mitigating this marginalisation, from a middle ground between Anglo-Saxon multiculturalism and French universalism, adds a further layer of geo-cultural diversity to the discussion in this chapter.

Conclusion

The coming together in one volume of eight studies interrogating the same theme of Francophone African postcoloniality from their own disciplinary perspectives has created some unusual connections and revealed parallels that aspire to inform both the discrete field of enquiry and the broader debate. Throughout this volume we encounter the same political dynamic driving centre-periphery relations that remain "committed to constructing a homogeneous dominant culture" as Burgin notes citing Shore (2001). Evidence of a former colonial power articulating a discourse of development and cooperation that both sponsors a degree of political autonomy and privileges the cultural, political and economic interests of the former coloniser is visible in all the essays in this collection. The nature of the evidence is very diverse but we hope that the collective impact of that evidence will be all the more compelling.

Notes

1. The fiftieth anniversary has clearly served as a timely opportunity to re-read, revisit and update the histories of the region as well as to push back the frontiers of the disciplines engaged in this research. This colloquium was one of hundreds of conferences, symposia and gatherings organised across the world in 2010 to mark this occasion. In common with some and unlike others it gave us the opportunity to engage critically with notions of an imperial past and a postcolonial present. As Eva Hausteiner (2011) noted in her review of Jane Burbank and Frederick Cooper's *Empires in world history* "Speaking of empires in the past is widely accepted, but imperial structures as recurring and even contemporary political phenomena are still highly debated. The endeavor of bringing empire back in as a transhistorical concept of heuristic value, complementing existing notions of political order, such as the nation-state, and going beyond the analysis of imperia*lism*, is far from concluded." This debate has returned to the top of the academic agenda in the recent wake of the anniversaries of British and French decolonisation in Africa.

2. The issue of re-enslavement post-abolition has also recently come to the fore in American slavery studies with the award of the Pulitzer prize to Douglas A. Blackmon for his 2012 work entitled *Slavery by another name: The re-enslavement of Black Americans from the Civil War to World War II*. London: Icon Books.

3. Not unexpectedly many of the publications that have come out of the fiftieth anniversary academic events cover some of the regions discussed in the present volume, though none covers the combination of themes

and specific areas explored here. There are too many outputs to mention here, both published and forthcoming. Readers may find the bibliography *1960–2010: African independence fifty years on* compiled by Teresa Vernon (British Library) and Anne Worden (University of Portsmouth Library) helpful in this regard. http://frenchstudieslibrarygroup.files.wordpress.com/2012/08/annual-review-issue-8-2011-12-current1.pdf pp. 48–52.

4. While the Maldives and the Seychelles have seen "remarkable increases in their visitor numbers" according to ETNGlobal Travel Industry the political unrest in the archipelago has created an unwelcome environment for tourism: http://www. eturbonews. com /30693/tourism-assessment-Indian-Ocean-Region (retrieved on 19 January 2013).

5. Denise Paulme's work was translated in the early 1960s at the University of California at Berkeley as *Women of tropical Africa* and subsequently incorporated into American social science scholarship on the region.

6. It should be noted that pre-school Koranic education is widespread in Senegal – and indeed in the other countries of the region where Islamic colonisation took root.

7. The irony is that so much of postcolonial theorising draws heavily from French postmodernism and poststructuralist theory which have not succeeded in overturning the dominance of an earlier Enlightenment-inspired universalistic intellectual philosophy that has for centuries been shaping so much of French education and research.

References

Ajayi, O. (1997). Negritude, feminism, and the quest for identity: Re-reading Mariama Bâ's *So Long a Letter*, *Women Studies Quarterly: Teaching African Literatures in a Global Literary Economy, 25*(3&4), 435–452.

Bashir Salau, M. (2011). *The West African slave plantation: A case study*. Basingstoke: Palgrave Macmillan.

Blackmon, D. A. (2012). *Slavery by another name: The re-enslavement of Black Americans from the Civil War to World War II*. London: Icon Books.

Compagnon, A. (2000). L'exception française, *Textuel, 37*, 41–52.

Conklin, A. (1998). Colonialism and human rights. A contradiction in terms? The case of France and West Africa, 1895–1914, *The American Historical Review, 103*(2), 419–442.

Cooper, F. (1979). The problem of slavery in African Studies: Review article, *Journal of African History, 20*(1), 103–125.

Ekpo, D. (2010). Introduction: From negritude to post-Africanism, *Third Text: Critical Perspectives on Contemporary Art and Criticism, 24*(2), 177–187.

Hausteiner, E. M. (2011). Review of *Empires in world history: Power and the politics of difference*, by J. Burbank & F. Cooper (Princeton, NJ: Princeton University Press, 2010), in *Ethics & International Affairs, 25*(4), 484–486.

Klein, M. A. (1998). *Slavery and colonial rule in French West Africa*. New York: Cambridge University Press.

Shore, C. (2001). The cultural policies of the European Union and cultural diversity. In Tony Bennett (Ed.), *Differing diversities: Transversal study on the theme of cultural policy and cultural diversity*. Strasbourg: Council of Europe.

PART 1

CONTESTING THE PAST:
REVISITING HISTORIES OF FRENCH AFRICA

CHAPTER 1

LOOKING BACK TO "FRANCE OF 100 MILLION INHABITANTS": ROOTS OF THE PRESENT IN COLONIAL FRENCH AFRICA

Jonathan Derrick

It is now fifty years since the majority of France's colonies in Africa gained independence. They are still called "Francophone" countries, and although this now accepted term is not ideally right for countries with their own languages, whose people mostly speak French either as a second language or not at all, those countries' ties with France are as strong as ever. While the use of Arabic modifies the picture in North Africa, in sub-Saharan Africa the position of French as an official language and the language of education is unassailable – even in the one country (Guinea) which chose its own way ahead by opting for independence in opposition to France in 1958 – and education in French has expanded enormously in the past half century, despite widespread problems of the quality of schooling. Millions of people from Francophone Africa, including probably many hundreds of thousands from south of the Sahara, live in France and help their homelands through remittances. Most governments in Africa have close ties with France that are vital to their foreign policies.

In Francophone Africa, as in the whole continent, the present is obviously shaped by the colonial past. The present-day states are based on colonies carved up a century ago by Europeans, having no resemblance to pre-colonial states, with a few exceptions such as Madagascar and Morocco. Despite all that has been said and written about the problems of states with artificial borders, those states with their borders remain: examination of border disputes goes back to

European treaties of the 1890s. This is manifestly true of all Africa, but is there some special way in which French colonialism affects the present in the former French possessions? This is a perception among some Africans from non-Francophone areas, who see their Francophone fellow Africans as very attached to France not only politically (through links that have led to armed French interventions in African affairs) and economically (through heavy dependence on French aid) but also psychologically: French-educated people are seen as very French or very France-oriented. Did France in fact impose a lasting cultural and mental hold over Francophone Africa, of a special sort by comparison with Anglophone Africa in particular? This may seem possible at first glance, because of the common perception of "assimilation", or creation of "black French-men", as French colonial policy.

This paper looks at the roots of the present in the period which was, all over Africa, the peak period of colonialism: the 1920s and 1930s, when colonial rule was firmly established after early conquest and resistance and not yet seriously challenged by nationalism. That was when Britain, France, Portugal and Belgium applied colonial policies in full, without complications caused by world wars. The colonial powers could then act, not just react. That is a good period for studying colonial rule, France's included. It is argued here that French rule did lead to some spread of education in French, and to some Africans acquiring advanced French culture and a special feature of France's colonialism, French citizenship; but it did not aim, as some suggested, to turn the majority of Africans into Frenchmen, and did not make – at that time – any moves to integrate colonies with France itself. Talk at the time of the colonies being or becoming parts of a "greater France" was just talk. On their side, Africans sought

French education for their own reasons, then as later, and one may question how many ever really wanted to become Frenchmen.

What was "Assimilation"?

The idea of "France of 100 million inhabitants" was uttered by the journalist and novelist Pierre Mille[1] in the early years of France's occupation of its new colonial empire (largely conquered, like the other African colonial empires, between 1880 and 1910). It was repeated at the time of the great Colonial Exhibition at Vincennes in 1931. At the opening ceremony the Minister of the Colonies, Paul Reynaud, declared, « *La France a maintenant 100 millions d'habitants, une superficie de 11 millions de kilomètres carrés, 35 000 kilomètres de côtes, 700 000 kilomètres de routes et 70 000 kilomètres de rail.* »[2]

The exhibition was to impress the French public with the French empire (though the Italian, Dutch and Portuguese empires had their stands), and the phrase "France of 100 million inhabitants" was intended to proclaim France's grandeur. If any listeners thought it indicated a deliberate policy to fully transform the colonies in Africa and elsewhere from colonies into actual parts of France, they were mistaken.

There were misapprehensions about French colonial policy, due partly to the role of a particular man standing with the President and the Colonies Minister Reynaud on the rostrum at Vincennes: Blaise Diagne, deputy for Senegal and Deputy Minister of the Colonies. The Four Communes of Senegal (Dakar, St Louis, Gorée and Rufisque) had had a deputy in the Third Republic National Assembly since the nineteenth century; Diagne was the first Senegalese of pure African descent to hold that post, elected in 1914; he then secured an extension of French citizenship to more inhabitants of the Four Communes, during the First World

War when he also became famous for organising the recruitment of an extra 63,000 African troops for the French army in 1918. The prominence that this African achieved in the colonial order then, and as Deputy Minister of the Colonies later, was considered remarkable. So it was; but it did not justify all that was said at that time, and later, about a French policy of "assimilation" in the colonies.

This essay cannot go further without an examination of what the often misunderstood word "assimilation" actually means. In colonial contexts it has three main meanings:

First, *cultural assimilation*: the teaching or imposition, and absorption, of the culture of the colonising country among colonised subjects, especially – after the end of slavery – through the education system. While a degree of cultural assimilation was imposed through slavery in the New World, in colonial Africa later full-scale cultural assimilation involved education up to secondary level at least, on the model of the colonising country's education system.

Second, *personal legal assimilation*: the granting to colonial subjects, or some of them, of the rights of citizens of the colonising country, up to and including full French citizenship in the case of French colonies. This was often thought to require cultural assimilation as a precondition, but it was separate. In addition, the right to vote was separate from citizenship, even when both were highly restricted.

Third, *administrative assimilation*: turning a territory from a conquered colony into a legal part of the colonising country itself.[3]

This last form of assimilation did not necessarily involve personal legal assimilation for the people of the territory concerned. At the time under review, the inter-war era, the only part of Africa that was assimilated into France administratively was Algeria, or rather the northern, populated part of Algeria (excluding the Saharan territories); this was considered to be three French departments, Algiers, Oran and Constantine. But the Muslim Arab and Berber majority in Algeria did not have the rights of French people, which were enjoyed (in full citizenship) by the European settlers. The majority remained subjects (*sujets*), governed by special colonial arrangements such as the *Indigénat*, the system of summary justice started in Algeria in 1881 and later extended to French Black Africa. Even when a minority of Muslim Algerians were given the vote, they remained without citizenship and full citizen's rights.

Apart from the special case of Algeria, no part of French-ruled Africa was considered a part of France in the inter-war era. Occasional talk of "France of 100 million inhabitants" did not indicate policies intended to make Dahomey a part of France just like Seine-et-Oise. This was not even considered, even as a long-term aim, by any Third Republic French government. The basic aim of France, as of other colonising countries in Africa, was a very simple one, to go on governing Africa.[4]

As they did this, a certain amount of education on Western lines was spread under all the colonial regimes, including the French, by the government and by Catholic and Protestant missions. It included some secondary schooling, and Africans acquired the language and a good deal of the culture of the colonising country. This was what some at the time called "assimilation", and it was the real or supposed position of French-educated Africans in the French colonial order that lay behind some of the beliefs uttered, then and later, about French colonisation. The word *assimiler* was indeed used above all by the French themselves, but particular notions involving the word were uttered by British commentators studying the British and French colonial systems. Comparative studies of those systems were and still are reasonable and useful, because France and Britain between them ruled most of Africa. But today the differences seem less and the common features more obvious than they did in the colonial era.

During that era Margery Perham, writing in *The Times* about French Cameroun in 1933 after a visit there, wrote:

> Whereas British policy is concerned with the tribal masses, seeking to guide them through a slow integrated transition, the French system accommodates, above all, the *assimilé* … In British Africa the *assimilé* (for we assimilate in spite of ourselves) finds himself in a position socially and politically ambiguous, not without pathos at the moment but potentially dangerous for the future. In French Africa he is automatically incorporated as a collaborator in a work which, though it may fail to motivate us, is conceived on large and noble lines. The promise of social equality alone is enough to make French Africans forgive their rulers for any faults we may read into their administration (Perham, 1933).[5]

Perham was of course addressing an empire-ruling readership, and the phrase "We assimilate in spite of ourselves" reveals a colonial view of Africans as clay in European rulers' hands. But others, too, have talked of French "assimilation" in this way, as if France had a peculiar knack for producing cultural clones in Africa.[6] The views about contrasting British and French cultural impacts need to be thoroughly re-examined. In fact neither France nor Britain, nor Portugal, created African elites. They (or, more often in early years, missions aided by them) created schools, and Africans, after initial hesitation in some areas, willingly sent their children to those schools. This was because the colonial rulers and business firms needed African staff, and Africans were keen to have those jobs. Thus the official colonial language had to be the language of education.

"The French," Margery Perham wrote, "consciously aim at developing a gallicised native *élite* of government employees, clerks and planters".[7] In fact they just needed a certain number of Africans to do jobs requiring some education. A clerk in a government office in Dakar obviously knew French well; was he therefore "gallicised"? The assumptions behind such terms need to be examined.

Of course junior African staff literate in the colonial language were needed all over Africa. They were an important element in Africa's growing Western-educated communities.[8] But Africans sought Western education well beyond the governments' intentions, often going to Europe or the USA from the nineteenth century – especially from British West and South Africa, but also from French Africa (the Belgians prevented it almost completely). Africans, when they had the opportunity, saw their way ahead as lying through Western schooling in the colonial tongue, a link with the modern world beyond. Western education was not and is not an imposition on Africa. Certainly it followed colonial occupation which was very much an imposition, but it was adopted by Africans as the best way ahead for themselves.

Making African education similar to that in the colonial *métropole* was not an imposition, either. The French rulers certainly insisted on education being in French; in Cameroun, for example, this led to lengthy disputes in the 1920s with missions which wanted to continue a good deal of schooling in local languages. But there was another party involved in that dispute and in similar questions elsewhere: the African parents and pupils. Since education in the colonial language was the best way to qualifications needed for employment, especially government employment, Africans wanted it to be education of the – by Western colonial standards – best quality.

Africans who had such education in British colonies were, notoriously, treated with contempt and ridicule by British officials at the height of the colonial era. Perham's main point in the article quoted above was that Western-educated Africans were more accepted by the French than by the British. This was a common view at the time. It was linked to a perception that racism in personal relations (as distinct from theoretical belief in racist ideas) was less prevalent among the French; this was widely true in France itself, at least, as African American visitors found. But the perceptions of the French as being without racism were partly derived from the position of French Caribbean colonial officials in Africa (mentioned by Perham). These people could indeed rise to the top of the French colonial service, like Félix Eboué from French Guiana, who became Governor-General of French Equatorial Africa (AEF). They did so by completely identifying with France, not with the Africans (Eboué helped enforce French rule at its worst in AEF), but it is true that no Black Jamaican could have succeeded so well in the British colonial service. Commentators in the colonial era were also greatly impressed by the career of Diagne. But unlike him (a politician from the one small area where politics was possible for Africans) and the Caribbean officials, nearly all Western-educated Africans in government service were relegated to defined subordinate posts.

Perham wrote "The *assimilé* demands and obtains special consideration, and can distinguish himself in all those spheres where the rulers allow native partnership – government service, councils of notables and co-operative societies". But these were limited possibilities in the lower grades. In this respect, and many others, the British and French colonial systems had much in common. In both systems a change came at the time when imperialist advance moved beyond the small coastal areas already under European rule to occupy vast new areas. In the coastal areas where British rule had begun earlier – Sierra Leone Colony, Gold Coast Colony, Lagos and The Gambia – it had been light-handed colonial rule, where Africans had considerable freedoms and opportunities and could rise to very senior positions in government service. This ended about the turn of the twentieth century, when a new sort of colonial rule, with more crude and blatant white domination and African submission, was spread, and even in areas of earlier-established colonial rule Africans were relegated to junior positions. It was similar in French Africa, where the privileges of a few thousand Africans in the Four Communes were not extended to any other area conquered by France.

There was however an important difference: those privileged Senegalese, called the *Originaires*, had French citizenship and/or the vote. This exceptional situation, the legacy of nineteenth-century developments, was maintained through the efforts of Diagne who, taking advantage of the war situation in 1915 and 1916, secured the passage of laws declaring all the *Originaires* to be French citizens.[9] Their rights had been threatened because of the new colonial methods imposed by France as by Britain. In the French case these inspired the decree of 1912 on citizenship in French West Africa (AOF). Like similar decrees relating to other colonial territories, this laid down stringent conditions for citizenship, including a high degree of French education and culture and – very important for Muslims in Senegal as in Algeria – acceptance of French law as applying in all matters, including those where a practising Muslim would want Islamic law to apply. Until 1946, only minute numbers of Africans were able to acquire French citizenship: 2,136 in French West Africa (AOF) by 1936. The vast majority, as was intended, remained *sujets*.

Much has been written on the debate in France, early in the era of colonial conquest, about the relative merits, in colonial policy towards Africans, of assimilation and "association". The latter term was used to mean granting some recognition to African societies, traditions and cultures so as better to use some Africans, such as chiefs, as subordinate agents of colonial rule. It has been shown that, whatever was said in theoretical debate, in actual practice the policy called "association" was imposed by colonial necessity in the greater part of AOF and AEF, where rural masses, without any Western education or influence at first, could not have been governed like the Four Communes. As one writer on the unreal assimilation versus association debate has said, "If a policy of assimilation had been possible in Martinique or in Canada, such was hardly the case in the new regions under French control in the late nineteenth century."[10] In practice the French, like the British, felt obliged to take African societies as they were, within limits, and enforce submission through them.

However, the French did not adopt anything like the full doctrine of Indirect Rule perfected and applied by Lugard, and this difference was noted and studied at the time. The difference was visible; French sub-Saharan Africa had nothing like the Northern Nigeria set-up, where an Emir's traditional government was ostentatiously maintained and strengthened while the chief British official in his capital, ultimately holding the real power, was called a "Resident". There was indeed a parallel in French Morocco, where Lyautey as Resident-General developed ideas and practice similar to Lugard's. But in Madagascar the French abolished a powerful monarchy, and in AOF and AEF most of the major African states were broken up and the few important traditional rulers left in place, including notably the Morho Naba in Upper Volta, had few or no formal administrative or judicial powers. And many French officials, at first, applied this policy deliberately, seeing African kings and chiefs as like France's *ancien régime*.[11]

But after early zeal in sweeping away the African Louis XVIs, French officials in AOF tried to bolster the authority of chiefs so as to use them as intermediaries in enforcement of their rule.[12] At the same time, in the 1920s and 1930s, French colonial officials such as Robert Delavignette (appointed director of the *École Coloniale*, the French colonial service training college, in 1937) and Henri Labouret carried out research into African societies and encouraged others to do so;[13] one scholar comparing the two colonial systems suggests that the ideas of Labouret and Margery Perham in the 1930s had a good deal in common.[14] Not all their colleagues shared such a positive view of African tradition, and the move towards greater reliance on chiefs was due mostly to practical considerations; some of those called *chefs* had no traditional right to rule (like the Warrant Chiefs appointed by the British in Nigeria among the Igbos; once again, the differences in colonial practices were not so great). But whether they had that or not the chiefs under French rule, as under the British Indirect-Rulers, were given considerable *de facto* power in their localities. The French still did not make a supreme virtue of Indirect Rule as the British did, but although the difference was real, to describe it as a contrast between assimilation and Indirect Rule is wrong. Africans whose traditions and culture were disrupted under French rule were not given new modern or Western institutions in their place, they were not assimilated. For any large-scale effort at cultural assimilation, Western education would have been needed, and until the 1940s the amount provided was trifling.

In 1935 AOF had 62,300 pupils in primary schools, AEF 15,877, less than 0.5% of the total population (a higher proportion, but still very low, of the school-age population) in each case.[15] There were proportionately more children at school in French Cameroun and French Togo, but there the League of Nations Mandate provisions obliged France to allow more mission schooling. Generally French official dislike of Christian missions hampered the spread of education, for which the government's own funds were very limited.

Those funds for education were limited because, as Conklin says in her important study of AOF in the early colonial era, French policies then "make clear that the new Government General rejected the notion that part of its civilizing mission was to make Africans into Frenchmen".[16] For the small minority who received some modern schooling, the diplomas granted by African schools were local ones with no standing in France. For the even smaller minority who had secondary education in AOF, only two schools in Senegal awarded an equivalent of the *baccalauréat*,[17] and these did not include the famous École William Ponty – located first on the island of Gorée and then at Sébikotane on the mainland of Senegal – where African junior officials, teachers and *médecins africains* (assistant doctors without full medical qualifications) were trained. A study of that school (where many future African politicians went) has concluded that "Much as the French intended, most Ponty graduates are not 'Black Frenchmen' but Black Africans with a deep if somewhat reluctant admiration for France."[18]

Those relatively privileged people, and others, sought education for their own reasons. It was seen as necessary for them to improve their situation, and the French culture acquired was a useful tool for that purpose. All or nearly all would have agreed with Léopold Senghor that they should aim "to assimilate, not to be assimilated". On their side the French authorities wanted only a limited number of Western-educated Africans, and sometimes had doubts about making Africans' education similar to that in France. A conference held at the time of the 1931 Exhibition approved and advocated adapted education (« *la vieille anecdote des élèves noirs récitant une leçon sur leurs ancêtres les Gaulois n'est plus qu'une légende* », it was declared there).[19] In AOF, "rural popular schools" were introduced in 1934, to teach villagers in a way adapted and useful to rural life and avoid producing more Western-cultured school leavers.[20]

"Adapted" education was a constant concern of the British colonialists also, and everywhere Africans responded with deep suspicion of what they saw as second-rate education being proposed for them. Senghor, revisiting Senegal after his studies in France, said in a meeting on 4 September 1937 that the education system should not use French only but should start by teaching in African languages; by agreeing to some extent with the official policy, he aroused opposition among the Senegalese elite, though his idea did not in fact exclude full French metropolitan standards at secondary and higher levels. But, as he showed soon afterwards in an address to a meeting in Paris on 26 September 1937 (attended by Delavignette, Labouret and Professor Paul Rivet among many others), he understood that this opposition was due to suspicion of government intentions.[21] Africans, it must be stressed again, then and later, wanted Western education to be equivalent to what Europeans received.

This episode is revealing about the real, as opposed to the mythical, French cultural policy in Africa at that time. It puts the *négritude* movement, started by Senghor and other literary people in France at that same time, in perspective. The movement challenged French cultural arrogance that denied any value in African traditional culture, and it had cause, as such arrogance was general (the very word « *évolués* », used officially for Western-educated Africans, was revealing). But Senghor acknowledged that some Europeans, including ethnologists, had promoted knowledge of Black civilisation. In fact French colonial officials had already begun to study African cultures with positive interest, as noted above. As for Africans under French rule, they wanted more and more French education, while retaining their own languages and culture as Senghor, a Serer of Senegal, himself did. *Négritude* was never a popular movement, most Africans did not need its ideas. They could, if given the opportunity, be Ewes or Bamilekes or Baoulés, speaking and even writing their people's languages, and also highly cultured French-language graduates, even French citizens.[22]

The hostile colonialist feelings about "educated natives" were particularly marked, sometimes pathological, among the British, but they were not absent from French officials, whatever Perham thought. Relations were particularly poor between the French and those Africans who had begun to receive Western schooling before French rule arrived – the Dualas of Cameroun and the Malagasies. Early anti-colonial movements were particularly strong among those peoples,[23] and spread among some others too (in Dahomey for example) in the 1920s and 1930s, increasing French suspicion of educated Africans.[24] What to do with the *évolués*, widely seen as a problem or even a threat, was a theme of considerable official correspondence.[25]

Some Frenchmen responsible for government of the colonies did want Africans – in limited numbers – to have the most complete French culture including secular Republican principles. In Madagascar this was an aim of Victor Augagneur, the left-wing Governor-General from 1905 to 1910, who encouraged among other things Freemasonry which was so important in the Third Republic and in its Ministry of the Colonies in particular (Eboué and Diagne, for example, were Masons). One of the Malagasy disciples of this special sort of assimilation was Jean Ralaimongo, a teacher who served as a volunteer in the French forces in the First World War, as over 200,000 Africans did (mostly not volunteers). But Ralaimongo went on to found, in Paris in 1919, an association for promoting full French citizenship for all Malagasies. This was not what his French mentors or any French officials wanted. To give citizenship and citizens' rights, without the existing conditions laid down, to millions of people who did not even know French would alter the colonial order enormously. It would be a thousand-fold extension of the principle conceded exceptionally, and to the regret of many French people, for the *Originaires* of Senegal. Writers on this Malagasy movement describe it as being a movement for "assimilation"; so it was, in the third sense listed above, but certainly not in the usually understood (cultural) sense.[26]

Obviously the French reaction to Ralaimongo's demand was very unfriendly, though the demand continued to be made in Madagascar in the 1920s and 1930s, and was echoed by some other Africans. The Popular Front government of 1936–1937 made some changes in the criteria for French citizenship, but they remained very difficult to fulfil, especially for Muslims. For Muslim Algerians even a small extension of the right to vote (not citizenship) under the Blum-Viollette bill of 1936 was dropped under pressure from the French-Algerians. Some other Popular Front measures did benefit Africans, such as restrictions on forced labour, but there was no question then of ending colonial rule or even planning its end.

So France entered the Second World War with its empire intact and seemingly secure, no government or party in France questioning it, while in sub-Saharan Africa there was no agreed policy to attach the colonies closer to France administratively, though that idea and others were debated; no policy or intention to give more power to Western-trained elites or (still less) to grant a degree of African self-government, suggested only by lone voices;[27] only a small amount of Western education available for Africans, already too much and too completely French for some colonialists' liking; and only a very small number of Africans allowed to become French citizens, the ultimate "black Frenchmen". Lord Hailey's *African Survey* still felt able to say, even in the 1956 edition, that in the inter-war period:

> the underlying assumption [of French policy] remained that, on a long view, the future of the overseas territories must be one of eventual integration with France in a larger political unit … The pursuit of the concept of integration was in particular a marked feature of educational policy (Hailey, 1957, p. 209).[28]

If that had been true, what happened after the war would have been less extraordinary. But Hailey gave no proof of it, it was not correct, and the post-war developments were in truth extraordinary.

The Unique Interlude of the French Union
Following the Brazzaville Conference where General de Gaulle presided in January 1944, two major processes of change were carried out by the French colonial rulers. The first was the easing or abolition of many of the impositions from which Africans had suffered for decades, notably forced labour (which had been on an intense scale during the war, under both Free French and Vichy French rule) and the *Indigénat*. The second was the election of African represent-tatives to the post-war Constituent Assemblies and then, after the second Assembly had adopted the constitution of the Fourth Republic, to the French National Assembly. The two processes went together; although the constitution adopted by the first Constituent Assembly in Paris was rejected in a referendum, two African politicians among its members secured decisive laws abolishing forced labour – the Houphouet-Boigny Law of 11 April 1946 – and granting French citizenship to all Africans – the Lamine-Gueye Law of 7 May 1946; these laws were maintained in force after the second Constituent Assembly approved a new constitution, backed by a referendum and brought into force in October 1946.[29]

There followed twelve years in which the African colonies of France were considered legally to be parts of the French Republic, which in turn was joined by two "associated territories" (Cameroun and Togo, former Man-dated Territories now turned into United Nations Trust Territories) and "associated states" (envisaged as Morocco, Tunisia, and the states of Indo-China) in the French Union (the word "empire" was officially abolished, like the word "colony"). African deputies sat in the French National Assembly and in the 1950s several of them (Senghor, Félix Houphouet-Boigny of Côte d'Ivoire, Modibo Keita of the then French Soudan) were members of French governments. The French Union was unique; a leading French scholar says it « *ne répondait à aucun type déterminé d'union du droit international* ».[30] It contrasted strongly with developments in British Africa at the same time, and also with the situation in the French empire in 1939, when any suggestion of what was to come after 1944 would have seemed fantastic – above all because France had not prepared the ground for a large population of "black Frenchmen".

Portugal had turned its colonies, legally, into "Overseas Provinces" in 1930, while it also granted a few Africans privileges depending on full cultural assimilation, with *assimilados* as scarce as African French *citoyens* were before 1946. But the comparison with the French Union cannot be taken far because Portugal itself, as well as the "Overseas Provinces", was under a dictatorship. In the French Union there was genuine democratic support, in both France and Africa, for the new arrangements. All French parties supported them at first, and when Africans rapidly formed their own parties these also supported the continued French connection, including the biggest party, the Rassemblement Démocratique Africain (RDA) founded at Bamako in 1946 and headed by Houphouet-Boigny. At first the African leaders' published agenda did not include even self-government, much less independence.

Perhaps this is not too difficult to explain. If comparisons are made (as they have been, reasonably) with British-ruled Africa, one should recall that while British West Africa had had nationalist parties since the 1920s, Kwame Nkrumah's call for "Self-Government Now" was something new in 1947. For Africans everywhere, one can safely assume, the priority was improvement in their daily lives, and in French territories this was brought about on a large scale by the reforms of 1944–1946. The citizenship granted to Africans under the Lamine-Gueye Law was for most a special category of citizenship, of *citoyens de statut local*, with the attendant legal rights left vague, but an African under French rule could for some years say the modern equivalent of *civis romanus sum*. There was a big expansion of education, including provision of hundreds of scholarships for Africans to study in France (where only a minute number had studied pre-war). France had granted this and a good deal more, under pressure, so why not expect France to grant yet more, under more pressure, and accept continued French rule in that hope? Some Africans had always been impressed by parts of French culture and thinking, notably the Declaration of the Rights of Man, even when they had been flagrantly contradicted in colonial practice by *corvée* labour and summary justice; they could have been impressed more now that those abuses had ended.

The concessions made to Africans left a lot to be desired. The citizenship was not full French citizenship, and the number of voters choosing the first African deputies in Paris was very small; extensions of the franchise were granted later, but slowly and grudgingly. Even with a wider franchise, African constituencies were much more populous than French ones, and so African representation was far from being on equal terms; this successfully avoided what the president of the second Constituent Assembly, the veteran Radical politician Edouard Herriot, spoke of as a terrible danger, France becoming "the colony of its former colonies".[31] That was one demonstration of French politicians' concern to keep the new deal for Africans within strict limits. It went much further; the day to day administration of African territories remained essentially the old colonial sort after the college training the officials who still held most power was renamed the *École Nationale de la France d'Outremer* (ENFOM); French authority was often asserted violently, not only against armed insurrection as in Madagascar in 1947, but also against the RDA, a constitutional party accepting the French connection but allied for a few years to the Communists, who were seen as a major menace by successive French governments (as in the inter-war years, but with more obsessive concern in the Cold War). Yet African leaders for long wanted the French Union to continue. The RDA responded to repression, very severe in Côte d'Ivoire, by breaking with the Communists in 1951 and working more closely with the French government. African leaders served in French governments fighting the Algerian revolution started in 1954, and defended French rule at the UN.

Even when the Loi-Cadre introduced by Gaston Defferre, Minister of Overseas France, in 1956 led to a considerable degree of self-government with African elected represent-atives and part-African governments in each territory in the following year, it was not initially obvious that this was a prelude to independence. The full story of how this in fact happened, of the Franco-African politics of the 1940s and 1950s and the lively Franco-African scene of 1950s Paris, has been told elsewhere.[32] The question for this paper is, why did the French Union come and go in just fourteen years?

In actual fact the African political participation in the French Union turned out to be a preparation for indepen-dence, a means to an end. How many saw it that way, and from what date, one cannot tell. But a closer look at the origins of the French Union shows that it always had that potential. It is often recalled that the Brazzaville Declaration excluded any idea of "self-government", using the English word; but that is not the whole story. In the run-up to

Brazzaville the Commissariat for the Colonies wrote that the two essential ideas of the Conference were first, « *Elever les Africains à la responsabilité la plus complète dans le cadre et par le progrès de leurs coutumes et de leurs institutions propres* » and second, « *La personnalité des pays français d'outre-mer doit s'affirmer à l'intérieur d'une fédération où métropole et possessions seraient associés sur un pied d'égalité.* »[33] De Gaulle himself said later in 1944, « *la politique française consiste à mener chacun de ces peuples à un développement qui lui permette de s'administrer et plus tard de se gouverner lui-même.* »[34] And the preamble to the Fourth Republic Constitution declared, « *fidèle à sa mission traditionnelle, la France entend conduire les peuples dont elle a pris la charge à la liberté de s'administrer eux-mêmes et de gérer pratiquement leurs propres affaires* ».[35] If words have any meaning, those words mean African self-government. Certainly there was the paternalist implication of a necessary (unspecified) period of guidance, the Constitution did not include de Gaulle's words « *se gouverner lui-même* » and did not provide for a federation, and French people may always have meant self-government under some overarching French authority; but a wide degree of self-government was the officially declared aim.

Following Brazzaville, there were elected Territorial Assemblies in each of the *territoires d'outremer* (colonies), with African majorities. Their powers were limited, but these were in fact a preparation for local politics in each territory. And local politics was quickly organised by the RDA and other parties, which in a few years were elaborately established over each territory; they were in some cases already the real power at the local level, as far as people's everyday life was concerned, by the later 1950s (notably the PDG (*Parti Démocratique de Guinée-Rassemblement Démocratique Africain*) in Guinea).[36] African deputies in Paris had electoral support in particular territories and acted as those territories' spokesmen.[37] As it turned out, African self-government under the leadership of parties was as well prepared in French as in British territories. In both, the territories established in the colonial carve-up were the new states in preparation, even though one French territory, Upper Volta, had been abolished for budgetary reasons in 1932 and only reconstituted in 1948, twelve years before independence. All that is said about independent states having no unity except that derived from artificial colonial borders is reinforced by the case of Upper Volta. But it now seems clear that self-government and then independence in countries defined by those borders were on their way from the 1940s.

The idea of autonomy for "overseas territories" spread in the 1950s, while in France the *Fédération des Etudiants de l'Afrique Noire en France* (FEANF) came to demand full independence.[38] In Africa the *Union des Populations du Cameroun* (UPC) dissented from the position of the RDA of which it had been a constituent party, and called for full independence. The special position of French Cameroun and French Togo, for which the UN had power to intervene to encourage decolonisation, made it more difficult to continue the subordination of Africans to France in the rest of French Africa. Considering all this, and events such as the advance towards Ghana's independence in 1957, the Cold War (in which both the USA and the USSR favoured decolonisation), and Bandung and the Non-Aligned Movement, it seems in retrospect amazing that anyone could have expected the French Union to continue. In fact many did, even after partial self-government under the Loi-Cadre of 1956, but did they really expect that a real federation of equals, in which France and Dahomey would be equal members like California and

Rhode Island, could emerge? Or that Africans would accept anything short of that for any length of time?

The much used and much misunderstood word "assimilation" was often applied to the French Union, but while personal legal assimilation was partly achieved, administrative assimilation was not provided by declaring the ex-colonies "integral parts" of the Republic (with, under the Constitution, no right ever to leave it); they were not made groups of French departments like Algeria, the government of Gabon remained utterly different from that of Alpes-Maritimes. As for cultural assimilation, Africans were now better placed to insist on full alignment of their schooling with French metropolitan education, a demand which might seem to reveal enthusiasm for being French: but it was in fact made to ensure Africans had full equality and opportunities, so that it was called "decolonisation of education".[39] Anyway that word "assimilation" matters less than another word already mentioned: self-government. The Brazzaville Declaration rejected that English word, but the reality of self-government was a stated aim, and Africans paved the way for it. The term "assimilationist nationalism" has been used to describe a movement to improve Africans' situation through equal rights with the French[40] – which, if fully achieved, would end colonialism altogether. Hubert Deschamps, a senior colonial official (Governor of Côte d'Ivoire and then of Senegal 1941–1943) who recalled having gone on believing in "assimilation" when France had generally rejected it, wrote in 1963 that with the French Union the colonial system, « *avant de mourir, avait jeté son dernier feu assimilateur* »; but, he added, that came too late, and the French Union was in fact a preparation for independence.[41] It did indeed turn out to be so, and it may be suggested that this was many Africans' real aim all along. As

44

Tony Chafer suggests, "African leaders … adopted the language of assimilation, not because they wanted to become French, but because their priority was equal rights for Africans and they saw this as a stepping stone to acquiring greater control over their own affairs and eventual African emancipation."[42]

Chafer has rightly criticised "a tendency to assume that the 'Frenchness' of the political leaders of French West Africa – the fact that they spoke French and were deeply imbued with French culture – rendered their pro-French political stance in the run-up to independence in some way 'inevitable'".[43] It can be attributed just as much to calculation of a useful way forward for Africa in the prevailing situation as to love of France.

De Gaulle's Decolonisation and After

When Charles de Gaulle returned to power in May 1958 and a Constitution for the Fifth French Republic was adopted, the French Union was replaced by the French Community, in which the "overseas territories" were confirmed in self-government that was extensive but far from complete; the Community would be responsible for foreign affairs, defence, common economic and financial policy, currency and higher education.[44] Back in 1944, when the prominent Free French leader André Philip suggested that de Gaulle should go as far as autonomy for the French colonies, he had replied, « L' autonomie, Philip? Vous savez bien que tout cela finira par l'indépendance. »[45] Now, in 1958, de Gaulle offered the possibility for member states of the French Community to opt out, i.e. for independence, by voting « Non » in the constitutional referendum on 28 September 1958. The story of how Guinea under Ahmed Sekou Toure did just that has often been told.[46] The general's vindictive attitude, leading to ruthless action to wreck Guinea's economy as French rule ended, shows that he would have preferred the Community to continue. But he had said before the referendum that African countries entering the Community would soon leave it,[47] and in 1959–1960 the Mali Federation, formed by Senegal and French Soudan, was allowed to do so with French blessing; Cameroun became independent under a separate UN-influenced schedule on 1 January 1960, and the other French territories in Africa quickly followed.

De Gaulle seems to have realised that this was inevitable, and in retrospect it surely was. Less inevitable, perhaps, was the separate independence of each of the former colonies; the idea of maintaining and extending the power of the federal authorities of AOF and AEF, based in Dakar and Brazzaville under the Fourth Republic, was proposed by Senghor notably, but soon abandoned. Independence for the AOF and AEF federations united in two large states might have had some advantages, and France, which backed Houphouet-Boigny in opposing this idea, has been accused of "balkanising" those parts of Africa, leaving eleven states (not counting Guinea) independent on their own even though many were economically deprived and weak.[48] Whether the alternative could have worked is questionable, as political institutions and parties had been well developed at the level of each country; the Mali Federation quickly broke apart, with former French Soudan keeping the name Mali.

Since those events fifty years ago, the close ties maintained between France and its ex-colonies have been well known and often described. The present paper cannot recall details of this, but can briefly look at the question of whether this was and is exceptional for French countries. This involves, once again but with good reason, comparison with ex-British Africa in particular.

Certainly Francophone African elites and their successive governments, civilian and military, have retained very close ties to France. Most Francophone governments have continued to use the CFA (*Communauté Financière Africaine*) franc, tied at a fixed parity to the French franc until 2002 and since then to the euro. Economic ties have also included extensive French aid, very important for resource-poor countries such as Dahomey/ Benin. Most spectacularly, there have for many years been French military interventions, aimed at keeping friendly governments in power or in one case (in the Central African Republic in 1979) imposing a new one (to replace, it is true, the nightmare "Emperor" Bokassa).

Since the 1990s there have been changes;[49] the appalling sequel to years of French military intervention in Rwanda discredited the habit of uncritical support for violent regimes, and the intervention in Côte d'Ivoire in 2002 was not to keep the established government in power, while some interventions have been in cooperation with other Western countries. Francophone African countries seek aid, trade and investment everywhere, China now being a major source. At the popular level Francophone Africans migrating to the West (legally or otherwise) may prefer France for obvious reasons of convenience, but many now go to Britain and America, as the motivation is economic. Yet even now, Franco-African relations are special in a way for both sides. They involve some particular semi-secret ties between political, military and business leaders that are called *La Françafrique*. In that aspect and others, the Franco-African relationship is not one-sided; while some Africans bitterly resent French policies, others benefit by them and want them to continue. One-sided comments emphasising decisions in Paris are mistaken, as is the use of such words as "puppet" to describe African leaders close to France; President Houphouet-Boigny, for example, was a forceful character whose interventions in the civil wars in Nigeria (1968) and Liberia (1989) were his own initiatives.

What is unique to the French sphere? Not everything; the group photographs of heads of state attending the Summits of France and African States, held every second year, recall in a way the group photographs with the Queen at Commonwealth Heads of Government Meetings, though Africans are not in the majority there; the murky secret service and political police assistance to African regimes has a parallel involving Britain and Kenya. But between France and Francophone Africa there is, besides hard-headed calculation, a sentimental relationship, marked by a sort of jealous possessiveness on both the French and African sides. An example is the lasting French suspicion of "les Anglo-Saxons" (the USA and Britain) trying to lay hands on France's sphere of Africa (as on the French empire before).

Of course the French imprint on everyday life in Francophone Africa is very plain to see. Education curricula have been changed since independence, but schooling is still very much on French lines, with the secondary school classes numbered backwards and a *baccalauréat* at the end. There are paramilitary *gendarmes*, and ordinary police regularly armed, as in France. Notably, centralisation – a feature of French government from the Revolution onwards in France itself (until a partial decentralisation under Mitterrand in the 1980s), imposed throughout the French colonies – has been continued by ex-French African states, or even increased.[50] No ex-French country has had anything close to Nigeria's federal structure, or even to Ghana's limited regional autonomy.

These French-derived differences strike visitors to ex-French states, especially British and Anglophone African visitors. They caused quite a "culture shock" to people of ex-British West Cameroon when they joined ex-French Cameroun in 1961; the sense of difference due to the two different colonial traditions is still very present in Cameroon after half a century. But probably, for every French phenomenon seen in an ex-French African country, a British phenomenon can be seen in an ex-British one (judges' wigs in Nigeria, for example). The idea that Francophone Africans are specially imbued with the ex-colonial culture, culturally colonised to an unusual degree, is questionable.

And surely this consideration applies to the colonial past also? Probably much of what struck British commentators like Mumford and Perham seemed exotic and amazing to them because they were British. It was not really proof of France having a particular policy or aptitude for imposing its culture. Africans all over the continent sought for their own reasons the education made available (much less than they wanted) under colonial rule. The result – that sub-Saharan Africa is the only major part of the world where the official language and language of education is different from the people's mother tongues – has troubled some Africans, but it is irreversible. That use of the former colonial languages originally spread because of African needs as much as European decisions; it continues especially because few African countries have indigenous languages, known to the majority of a country's population, that could take their place. Francophone Africa is not unique in this respect.

Certainly there has been and still is plenty of sentimental attachment to France among Africans. But Francophilia is widespread around the world, and is quite consistent with criticism of, or even fury against French government policies or attitudes, as is found in African fiction in French, such as the works of Ousmane Sembène and Mongo Beti. In the colonial era critics of French rule still admired and liked much in France, and not only the French Revolution principles that they invoked against French policy (one Algerian fighting the French in the war of independence was heard saying how much he longed to see Paris again). Such Francophile feeling is perhaps not paralleled in African feelings towards other Western countries, but there is the universal fascination with America. Anyway such things are hard to measure, and perhaps, all things considered, Africans' relations with the former colonial power are not very distinctive in French-speaking Africa.

Concluding Remarks

All over Africa the imprint of the colonial era remains visible. In education and language use it is particularly marked and indeed increasing. The cultural imprint due to colonialism may appear particularly strong in Francophone countries, but that impression can be questioned. At the height of colonialism in the inter-war era, when colonial powers were most able to impose their policies on Africa, in French-ruled Africa those policies did not – contrary to some impressions – include cultural assimilation for more than a small minority of Africans. That minority of *évolués* was treated warily by French officials and kept in subordinate positions; only very few of them could acquire French citizenship, apart from the wholly exceptional case of the Four Communes of Senegal. Until the end of the Third Republic, too, there was no policy aiming at closer union of sub-Saharan colonies with France.

In short, France did not aim to create "black Frenchmen" except in very small numbers. As in British-ruled Africa, it was Africans who clamoured for Western education and wanted it to be equivalent to that offered in Europe, while the French rulers, like the British, came to widely favour "adapted" education. The end result was still very Western schooling, but even in the colonial era this was a product of African desires as much as, or more than, colonial imposition. In so far as there was "cultural assimilation", it was not imposed by French government policy, and it occurred in other parts of Africa also.

Yet after the Second World War there were remarkable developments in French Africa, of which there had been no inkling before the war, including elective representation of Africans in Territorial Assemblies and France's own National Assembly, those territories (the colonies) being now legally parts of France. Although the changes left French Africa still in a basically colonial situation, there were as many opportunities for Africans as in non-French colonies at the time, if not more. But despite proclamations of devotion to France and belief in the French Union, the unique Fourth French Republic arrangements turned out to be a preparation for independence, and some African leaders may have always seen them as such.

The close ties between France and ex-French African states since independence have not been quite so unique, but they are often seen as exceptional, and that was a fair impression until recently, though there have been changes. But there is also a good deal in common with other parts of Africa without experience of the French colonial impact, whose lasting effects should not be overstated.

Notes

1. Hargreaves, A. G. (1981). *The colonial experience in French fiction: A study of Pierre Loti, Ernest Psichari and Pierre Mille* (Chapters 5 and 6 on Mille). Basingstoke: Macmillan.
2. Biondi, J.-P., (1992) *Les anticolonialistes (1881–1962)*. Paris: Laffont, p. 169. On the Exhibition see Hodeir, C., & Pierre, M. (1991). *L'Exposition Coloniale.* Brussels: Complexe.
3. There was also *economic assimilation*, involving duty-free trade between France and some parts of the colonial empire by the Méline tariff of 1892. This "assimilation", quite distinct from the others, is not considered here.
4. And, of course, to extract wealth from Africa; but that has been proved to be just as easy without formal colonial rule.
5. Perham, M. (1933) France in the Cameroons, *The Times,* 17 and 18 May, reproduced in Perham, M. (1967). *Colonial sequence 1930 to 1949.* London: Methuen, pp. 68–76.
6. There was, for example, the work by Mumford, W. & Orde Browne, G. St. J. (1936). *Africans learn to be French.* London: Evans Bros.
7. Perham (1933) and see below on Lord Hailey.
8. Derrick, J. (1983). The "native clerk" in colonial West Africa, *African Affairs, 82*(326), pp. 61–74.
9. The detailed story of the different groups of *Originaires* and Diagne's triumph on their behalf is described in Johnson, G. W. (1971). *The emergence of black politics in Senegal: The struggle for power in the Four Communes, 1900–1930,* Stanford, CA: Stanford University Press, pp. 119–172; Genova, J. E. (2004). *Colonial ambivalence, cultural*

authenticity, and the limitations of mimicry in French-ruled West Africa, 1914–1956. New York: Peter Lang, pp. 18–28.

10. Betts, R. F., (1961) *Assimilation and association in French colonial theory, 1890–1914.* New York: Columbia University Press, p. 21.

11. Conklin, A. L. (1997). *A mission to civilize: The republican idea of empire in France and West Africa, 1895–1930.* Stanford, CA: Stanford University Press, pp. 102–103, 111–117, 188–190, 248–249.

12. Cohen, W. B. (1971). *Rulers of empire: The French colonial service in Africa*, Stanford, CA: Hoover Institution Press, pp. 117–118; Conklin (1997), pp. 193–210.

13. Cohen (1971), p. 116.

14. Dimier, V. (2002). Direct or Indirect Rule: Propaganda around a scientific controversy, Chapter 12 in T. Chafer and A. Sackur (Eds.). *Promoting the colonial idea: Propaganda and visions of empire in France.* Basingstoke: Palgrave Macmillan.

15. Gardinier, D. E. (1985). The French impact on education in Africa, 1817–1960. In G. W. Johnson (Ed.). *Double impact: France and Africa in the age of imperialism* (Chapter 18, pp. 333–344). Westport, CT: Greenwood Press.

16. Conklin (1997), p. 74.

17. Gardinier (1985), p. 338.

18. Sabatier, P. (1985). Did Africans really learn to be French? The Francophone elite of the École William Ponty. In G. W. Johnson (Ed.), *Double impact*, p. 185.

19. Coquéry-Vidrovitch, C. (1991). La colonisation française 1931–1939. In C.-R. Ageron (Ed.), *Histoire de la France Coloniale, III – Le Déclin, (1ᵉ partie)*. Paris: Armand Colin, pp. 124–125.

20. Genova (2004), pp. 113–115.

21. Vaillant, J. G. (1990). *Black, French, and African: A life of Léopold Sédar Senghor*. Cambridge, MA: Harvard University Press, pp. 147–165.

22. Much was said at that time, and later, about a great gulf between Western and African cultures; this was a theme of the *négritude* movement. The idea that this gulf was bound to make Western-educated Africans disoriented, or totally cut off from their family roots, or both, was widespread among colonialists (especially British ones) and shared by some Africans. This is a profound question of psychology; it cannot be discussed here in detail, but it can be suggested that many people, not only Africans, have always been well able to live easily in more than one culture.

23. Derrick, J. (2008). *Africa's "agitators": Militant anti-colonialism in Africa and the West, 1919–1939*. London: C. Hurst, pp. 230–237.

24. Cohen (1971), p. 116.

25. Genova (2004), pp. 179–190.

26. Randrianja, S. (2001). *Société et luttes anticoloniales à Madagascar (1896 à 1946)*. Paris: Karthala., especially Chapter 5; Domenichini, J.-P. (1969). Jean Ralaimongo (1884–1943), ou Madagascar au seuil du nationalisme, *Revue Française d'Histoire d'Outremer, LVI*(204), 3e trimestre, pp. 236–287.

27. Tiémoko Garan Kouyaté, a Soudanese (Malian) who was for years a leading left-wing anti-colonial activist in inter-war France, after softening his militancy was still bold enough to suggest in 1936, in the *Africa* magazine that he edited, a federation between France and self-governing African territories (Genova, 2004, 160–161). Henri Labouret, writing in the colonialist magazine *L'Afrique Française* in 1935, proposed gradual conferring

of full political and legal rights on Africans in their own countries (Cohen, 1971, p. 134).

28. Hailey, Lord (1957). *An African survey revised 1956.* London: Oxford University Press, p. 209.

29. Mortimer, E. (1969). *France and the Africans 1944–1960,* London: Faber and Faber, pp. 49–104.

30. Ageron, C.-R. (1991). De l'empire à la dislocation de l'Union Française (1939–1956). In C.-R. Ageron (Ed.), *Histoire de la France Coloniale, III – Le Déclin.* (2*e* partie). Paris: Armand Colin. 226.

32. See the full account in Mortimer, *France and the Africans.*

33. Ageron (1991), p. 199.

34. Ageron (1991), p. 203.

35. Ageron (1991), p. 226.

36. See Schmidt, E. (2007). *Cold War and decolonization in Guinea, 1946–1958.* Athens: Ohio University Press, Chapters 1–4.

37. Chafer, T. (2002b). *The end of empire in French West Africa: France's successful decolonization?* Oxford: Berg.

38. UNESCO. (1993). *Le rôle des mouvements d'étudiants africains dans l'évolution politique et sociale de l'Afrique de 1900 à 1975.* Paris: Editions UNESCO/L'Harmattan, pp. 101–27, 210–214, etc.

39. Chafer (2002b). *The end of empire,* pp. 94–98. Chafer suggests that French people had the same idea for a different reason, wanting to see Africans more completely Frenchified.

40. Chafer (2002b). *The end of empire,* pp. 76–77.

41. Deschamps, H. (1963). Et maintenant, Lord Lugard? *Africa, xxxiii*(4), pp. 291–306.

42. Chafer (2002b). *The end of empire,* p. 110.

43. Chafer, T. (2007). Education and political socialisation of a national-colonial political elite in French West Africa,

1936–47, *Journal of Imperial and Commonwealth History, XXXV*(3), pp. 437–458; 438.
44. Ageron (1991), pp. 405–406.
45. Ageron (1991), pp. 458.
46. See Schmidt (2007), pp. 144–168.
47. Ageron (1991), p. 461.
48. Mortimer (1969), Chapters 25–29; Chafer (2002b). *The end of empire*, 156–157, Chapters 6–7; Vaillant (1990), Chapter 11.
49. Chafer, T. (2002a). Franco-African relations: No longer so exceptional? *African Affairs, 101*(404), pp. 343–363.
50. Cohen (1971), p. 198.

References

Ageron, C.-R. (1991). De l'empire à la dislocation de l'Union Française (1939–1956). In C.-R. Ageron (Ed.), *Histoire de la France coloniale, III – Le déclin. (2ᵉ partie).* Paris: Armand Colin.

Betts, R. F., (1961) *Assimilation and association in French colonial theory, 1890–1914.* New York: Columbia University Press.

Biondi, J.-P., (1992) *Les anticolonialistes (1881–1962).* Paris: Laffont.

Chafer, T. (2002a). Franco-African relations: No longer so exceptional? *African Affairs, 101*(404), 343–363.

Chafer, T. (2002b). *The end of empire in French West Africa: France's successful decolonization?* Oxford: Berg.

Chafer, T. (2007). Education and political socialisation of a national-colonial political elite in French West Africa, 1936–47, *Journal of Imperial and Commonwealth History XXXV*(3), 437-458.

Chafer, T., & A. Sackur (Eds.). (2002). *Promoting the colonial idea: Propaganda and visions of empire in France.* Basingstoke: Palgrave Macmillan.

Cohen, W. B. (1971). *Rulers of empire: The French colonial service in Africa*. Stanford, CA: Hoover Institution Press.

Conklin, A. L. (1997). *A mission to civilize: The republican idea of empire in France and West Africa, 1895–1930*. Stanford, CA: Stanford University Press.

Coquéry-Vidrovitch, C. (1991). La colonisation française 1931–1939. *Histoire de la France coloniale, III – Le déclin*, (*1ᵉ partie*). Paris: Armand Colin.

Derrick, J. (1983). The "native clerk" in colonial West Africa, *African Affairs, 82*(326), January, 61–74.

Derrick, J. (2008). *Africa's "agitators": Militant anti-colonialism in Africa and the West, 1919–1939*. London: C. Hurst.

Deschamps, H. (1963). Et maintenant, Lord Lugard ? *Africa xxxiii*(4), 291–306.

Dimier, V. (2002). Direct or indirect rule: Propaganda around a scientific controversy. In T. Chafer & A. Sackur (Eds.), *Promoting the colonial idea: Propaganda and visions of empire in France* (Chapter 12). Basingstoke: Palgrave Macmillan.

Domenichini, J.-P. (1969). Jean Ralaimongo (1884–1943), ou Madagascar au seuil du nationalisme, *Revue Française d'Histoire d'Outremer, LVI*(204), 3ᵉ trimestre, 236–287.

Gardinier, D. E. (1985) The French impact on education in Africa, 1817–1960. In G. W. Johnson (Ed.). *Double impact: France and Africa in the age of imperialism* (Chapter 18, pp. 333–344). Westport, CT: Greenwood Press.

Genova, J. E. (2004). *Colonial ambivalence, cultural authenticity, and the limitations of mimicry in French-ruled West Africa, 1914–1956*. New York: Peter Lang.

Hailey, Lord (1957). *An African survey revised 1956* (p. 209). London: Oxford University Press.

Hargreaves, A. G. (1981). *The colonial experience in French fiction: A study of Pierre Loti, Ernest Psichari and Pierre Mille*. Basingstoke: Macmillan.

Hodeir, C., & Pierre, M. (1991). *L'Exposition coloniale*. Brussels: Complexe.

Johnson, G. W. (1971). *The emergence of black politics in Senegal: The struggle for power in the Four Communes, 1900–1930*. Stanford, CA: Stanford University Press.

Johnson, G. W. (Ed.). (1985). *Double impact: France and Africa in the age of imperialism*. Westport, CT: Greenwood Press.

Mortimer, E. (1969). *France and the Africans 1944–1960*, London: Faber and Faber.

Mumford, W. & Orde Browne, G. St. J. (1936). *Africans learn to be French*. London: Evans Bros.

Perham, M. (1933) France in the Cameroons, *The Times*, 17 and 18 May, reproduced in Perham, M. (1967). *Colonial sequence 1930 to 1949*. London: Methuen, pp. 68–76.

Perham, M. (1967). *Colonial sequence 1930 to 1949*. London: Methuen.

Randrianja, S. (2001). *Société et luttes anticoloniales à Madagascar (1896 à 1946)*. Paris: Karthala.

Sabatier, P. (1985). Did Africans really learn to be French? The Francophone elite of the École William Ponty. In G. W. Johnson (Ed.), *Double impact: France and Africa in the age of imperialism* (Chapter 9). Westport, CT: Greenwood Press.

Schmidt, E. (2007). *Cold War and decolonization in Guinea, 1946–1958*. Athens, OH: Ohio University Press.

UNESCO. (1993). *Le rôle des mouvements d'étudiants africains dans l'évolution politique et sociale de l'Afrique de 1900 à 1975*. Paris: Editions UNESCO/L'Harmattan.

Vaillant, J. G. (1990). *Black, French, and African: A life of Léopold Sédar Senghor*. Cambridge, MA: Harvard University Press.

CHAPTER 2

TROUBLE WITH THE NEIGHBOURS? CONTEMPORARY CONSTRUCTIONS AND COLONIAL LEGACIES IN RELATIONS BETWEEN SENEGAL AND THE GAMBIA

David Perfect and Martin Evans

The geographical situation of The Gambia, surrounded by Senegal, lends itself to a realist reading of contemporary relations between the two countries, focusing on competition over respective national interests and security along their long shared border. This, however, risks ignoring the important dimension of colonial history and its modern geopolitical repercussions in terms of how each country perceives and manages Senegambian space. The chapter therefore takes the long view of this relationship, exploring its colonial past and how it shapes the present, particularly in the context of ongoing conflict in Casamance – Senegal's southern limb, sandwiched between The Gambia and Guinea-Bissau.

Introduction

Even a brief glance at a map of the western extremity of West Africa reveals a potential geopolitical problem: The Gambia, the smallest state on the African continent, surrounded by the larger territory of Senegal which it partially divides. This peculiar cartography alone would support a realist reading of relations between the two countries, particularly in a sub-region afflicted by cross-border subterfuges of various kinds. It would indeed be easy to view historical and contemporary relations between the two countries through a lens of their respective national interests and security, reflected in competition for control of resources of all kinds (territory, natural products, trade and people) and played out along a disproportionately long border.

But such a reading, while it certainly has some validity, risks ignoring the important dimension of colonial history and what this means in the context of contemporary geopolitics. This history not only defined each country's borders, official languages and systems of production and trade. The different colonial histories of the two countries also brought different political cultures to each country and, over time, shaped the way in which each viewed its relations with the other, and the vision that each developed of how they should live together in the Senegambia, with its shared history and peoples.

The chapter begins by tracing the origins of the British colony of the Gambia and the French colony of Senegal, describing a process which culminated in the fixing of the borders between the two countries in 1889. It then explores the relationship between the two colonies up to Senegalese independence in 1960 and Gambian independence in 1965. This is followed by an analysis of the fluctuating relations from 1965 to 1994 between the two independent nations and their respective rulers: Léopold Senghor (1960–1981) and Abdou Diouf (1981–2000) in Senegal and Sir Dawda Jawara (1965–1994) in The Gambia. This period ended with Jawara's overthrow in a military coup led by Lieutenant Yahya Jammeh (1994–) who became the second Gambian President in 1996. The chapter examines Gambian/Senegalese relations under Jammeh, Diouf and Diouf's successor, Abdoulaye Wade (2000–2012) which have been largely shaped by the ongoing conflict in Casamance. The chapter concludes by considering the future of the relationship between The Gambia and Senegal.

Colonial Rivalries in Senegambia Before 1889

Both Senegal and The Gambia have long colonial histories. The first French settlement at the mouth of the River Senegal, Saint Louis, was established in 1659 (following an unsuccessful attempt to set up a base on the River Gambia in 1612) and remained the French headquarters in the area for the next two centuries. Further down the coast, the French captured the island of Gorée from the Dutch in 1677, before establishing a trading post (*comptoir*) on the north bank of the River Gambia at Albreda in 1681. Albreda was situated almost directly opposite James Island which the British had seized in 1661 from the Baltic Duchy of Courland. Its fort, James Fort, remained the centre of British trading activities until the late eighteenth century, first through the Royal African Company and subsequently through its successor body, the Company of Merchants Trading to Africa. During the later seventeenth and most of the eighteenth centuries, formal control over the Senegambia region fluctuated between Britain and France, often reflecting wider conflict between the European powers. James Island changed hands between Britain and France several times and the fort was twice blown up by the French, in 1695 and again in 1779. Meanwhile, the British gained control of Saint Louis and Gorée in 1758 during the Seven Years War and in 1765 they established the Province of Senegambia as a Crown colony. But after the French had recaptured Saint Louis and forced the surrender of James Island in 1779 during the American War of Independence, the British abandoned their colony and the Treaty of Versailles of 1783 returned the entire Senegambia region except James Island to France. The Company of Merchants Trading to Africa regained formal control over James Island but the fort was never rebuilt and the island remained uninhabited (Barry, 1998, pp. 46–77; Gailey, 1964, pp. 21–34; Gray, 1966, pp. 52–293; Hughes and Perfect, 2008, pp. 3, 40–41, 107–108, 192, 209–210).

In 1816, the British re-established a presence in the Gambia when Captain Alexander Grant purchased Banjul Island which he renamed St Mary's Island, from a local ruler. Grant had been instructed to establish a base on the River Gambia by the Governor of Sierra Leone, Sir Charles MacCarthy, as part of wider efforts to control the slave trade, but had rejected the old site of James Island as unsuitable. Grant founded the town of Bathurst (which was renamed Banjul in 1973). This was soon populated by British merchants who had moved from Gorée and their employees and servants, as well as by soldiers from the Royal African Corps. In 1821, the Company of Merchants Trading to Africa was abolished and the Gambia became a Crown colony under a Lieutenant-Governor subordinate to the Governor of Sierra Leone, with Bathurst as the nucleus of the new settlement (Gailey, 1964, pp. 36–37; Gray, 1966, pp. 294–323; Hughes and Perfect, 2006, pp. 55–56; Hughes and Perfect, 2008, pp. xxxiv–xxxv).

During most of the nineteenth century, the growth of the Gambia colony was slow. There was some very limited territorial acquisition, but, as late as 1881, the colony had an estimated total area of only 110 square kilometres and a recorded population of 14,150 (Hughes and Perfect, 2006, pp. 6–8). The British had made virtually no attempt to penetrate the interior of the Senegambia region or to take advantage of the ongoing conflict in many Senegambian kingdoms between their ruling classes (*Soninke*) and Muslim reformers (*Marabouts*). Local administrators who had wanted to adopt a more pro-active role had been prevented from doing so by the Colonial Office and on at least one occasion, a treaty signed with a local ruler was disowned.[1] In contrast, after a

French army officer, Louis Faidherbe, had been appointed Governor of Senegal in 1854, the French had sought to gain control over the whole Senegal valley through signing treaties with some local rulers and by launching military expeditions against others. This process continued for the next three decades (although there was a lull in the first half of the 1870s following France's defeat in the Franco-Prussian War of 1870 and the collapse of the Second Empire), with the pace of expansion accelerating during the 1880s (Barrows, 1976; Barry, 1998, pp. 145–242; Gailey, 1964, pp. 81–101; Gray, 1966, pp. 411–415; Quinn, 1972, pp. 143–187).

British and French attitudes towards their possessions in the Senegambia thus varied considerably. While the French were keen to expand their West African empire, the British were not only reluctant to do so, but from the 1860s actively sought to reduce their commitments as a way of saving money. In February 1866, in line with the recommendations of the Ord Commission, the Colonial Office introduced a new centralised administration, the West African Settlements, for its four West African colonies of Sierra Leone, the Gambia, the Gold Coast and Lagos. The latter three colonies lost their governors with (less expensive) administrators being appointed in their stead, their Executive Councils were abolished and their Legislative Councils downgraded, and each was placed under the overall jurisdiction of the Governor of Sierra Leone.[2]

Only a month later, in March 1866, the French formally proposed that the Gambia be exchanged for the three French settlements on the Ivory Coast – Grand Bassam, Assinie and Dabou – which they regarded as being of little value (Barrows, 1976, p. 112); they added Gabon to the offer in 1867. The British government welcomed the proposal, since the Gambia was increasingly seen as a drain on imperial resources, having frequently experienced budget deficits in recent years. Such deficits occurred in all but three years between 1849 and 1865 (including every year between 1859 and 1865) and a parliamentary grant was required between 1860 and 1871 to defray expenses (Hughes and Perfect, 2006, p. 35).

However, the British did not wish to inherit the former French settlements either, so in 1869, they put forward a counter offer, that the French should instead renounce their claims to the disputed Mellacourie region north of Sierra Leone (in modern Guinea-Conakry). This British offer was accepted in principle by the French in March 1870. But when rumours of an impending deal became public, they aroused strong opposition, particularly amongst the educated Liberated African community in Bathurst and the well-organised British merchants engaged in the Gambia trade (who mostly now resided in England). The merchants set up various memorials and the Liberated Africans organised three mass petitions between April and October 1870. Liberated Africans were concerned about the military system of government practised in Senegal; they also feared that their property rights would not be respected by the French and that they would not be allowed to practise their Protestant religion. The opposition was effective and negotiations between the two European governments broke down in July 1870.

The idea of exchange was revived by the French in April 1874, who this time proposed not only that the Ivory Coast should be given to Britain but also that the Mellacourie region should be recognised as part of the British sphere of influence. The British were slow to respond formally – the Secretary of State for the Colonies, Lord Carnarvon, still hoped for an even better offer – and eventually the negotiations broke down in March 1876. Once again a crucial reason for their failure was the effective opposition to exchange mounted by Liberated Africans and British merchants; the former organised three more petitions in 1875–1876. The possibility of exchange did not go away, with the British making further proposals in the 1880s and the French making their final overtures as late as 1911, but all these efforts came to nothing (Gailey, 1964, pp. 81–95; Gray, 1966, pp. 431–443; Hargreaves, 1963, pp. 125–195; Hargreaves, 1974, pp. 78–85, 223–245; Hughes and Perfect, 2006, pp. 67–73; Wyse, 1976).

Despite their best efforts to get rid of the Gambia, it thus remained in British hands as the "scramble for Africa" reached its climax in West Africa in the late 1880s. By the end of 1888, the French had established a presence in a number of places along the banks of the River Gambia, while the Gambian government was beginning to sign treaties with local rulers largely as a defensive measure against French expansion. At the Anglo-French Convention of 1889 which fixed the border between the two colonies, the British made no demands for territory in the Senegambia interior; all they sought was control over the River Gambia. This was achieved when the French eventually agreed that a narrow strip of land ten kilometres either side of the River as far as Yarbutenda, about 470 kilometres from the mouth of the River, should be British. The boundaries were fixed on the ground in the 1890s and have remained largely unchanged ever since except for a slight modification in the 1970s (Gailey, 1964, pp. 99–119; Gray, 1966, pp. 463–465; Hughes and Perfect, 2006, p. 6).

Meanwhile, in southern Senegambia, the French and Portuguese had reached a separate agreement in May 1886 to fix the borders between Portuguese Guinea (modern Guinea-Bissau) and Senegal, and between Portuguese Guinea and

French Guinea (Guinea-Conakry). Under the terms of the agreement, the French acquired the former Portuguese *comptoir* of Ziguinchor, some forty miles upstream of the mouth of the River Casamance, with Futa Jallon (in modern Guinea-Conakry) being recognised as a French protectorate. In return the Portuguese acquired the Rio Cassini valley (in the south of modern Guinea-Bissau), ceded from French Guinea, and fishing rights off Newfoundland (Barry, 1998, pp. 221–222; Marut, 2010, p. 56).[3] In Casamance beyond Ziguinchor, however, the influence of the French was more fragmented and tenuous, covering a patchwork of territories and protectorates that they had bought or conquered over time. It was not until around 1930 that the French achieved full control of Casamance as a unified space (Marut, 2010, p. 56). Still, with the exception of the River Gambia and its immediate hinterland, the French were, through agreement with the British and Portuguese, coming to control the whole Senegambia region.

Senegalese/Gambian Relations: 1889–1965

The fixing of the border proved of crucial importance in ensuring that the two separate colonies, one British and the other French, survived into the twentieth century. In line with the general pattern for most colonies in sub-Saharan Africa, both colonies had much greater trading links with their respective metropoles than with each other or with other African countries; at independence, for example, three-fifths of Gambian exports went to the United Kingdom which also supplied more than a third of its imports (Hughes and Perfect, 2006, p. 32). Moreover, educated Gambians were more likely to migrate to London and educated Senegalese to Paris than Gambians to Dakar or, in particular, Senegalese to Bathurst; for example, when President Senghor visited

Bathurst in 1964, it was apparently the first time he had done so since 1927 (Hughes and Perfect, 2006, p. 461, note 3). But there were key differences too in terms of educational systems, languages and political systems. Since 1872, the "citizens" of St Louis and Gorée had been permitted to elect a Deputy to the French National Assembly and in 1914, Blaise Diagne became the first African to win such an election (Idowu, 1968; Johnson, 1971, pp. 154–177). In contrast, it was not until 1947 that E. F. Small became the first African to be elected to the Gambia's Legislative Council which remained a purely local body (Hughes and Perfect, 2006, pp. 113–116).

For most of the period after 1889, there was extensive movement of individuals across what remained a very porous border. Senegalese "strange farmers" regularly travelled to the Gambia to help harvest the groundnut crop (Swindell, 1982), while other Senegalese travelled to Bathurst and other ports along the River Gambia to load groundnuts on to ocean-going ships during the trade season. Imported manufactured goods from Europe were "re-exported"/ smuggled from the Gambia to Senegal and agricultural produce was moved across the border in either direction in search of a better price, but there was virtually no official trade (Hughes and Perfect, 2006, pp. 22, 32–34). In addition, there was sometimes official cooperation between the Gambian and Senegalese governments, in the 1890s and early 1900s to combat unruly local warlords, and in the 1930s to deal with perceived "link subversives", as the British termed some of its radical critics.[4] There were also occasional official visits and agreements between the two colonial powers.[5]

Before and during the First World War and in the run-up to the Second, the Gambian colony acted as a refuge for those fleeing more zealous conscription regimes in French territory, and French heavy-handedness in Casamance at other times in the early decades of the twentieth century (Nugent, 2007, pp. 231–233). For a brief period during the Second World War, the relationship between the two colonial governments was very different. At the beginning of the war, the two had cooperated. But after France surrendered to Germany in June 1940, the High Commissioner of French (sub-Saharan) Africa based in Dakar, Pierre Boisson, supported the Vichy government. Senegal remained under Vichy control until 1943 and relations between the two colonial governments were tense, perhaps particularly after British forces had bombarded Dakar in September 1940.[6] There was no open conflict between the two colonies, a development that the colonial administration in the Gambia was very anxious to avoid, particularly after the Chiefs of Staff agreed in July 1940 "that the defence of Bathurst was too large a commitment for us to undertake against a determined attack". Indeed, Governor Thomas Southorn emphasised in a meeting of all British West African governors in April 1941 "that the peculiar geographical and strategical position of the Gambia makes it necessary for that Colony to maintain the friendliest possible relations with the Senegalese authorities".[7]

Nevertheless, cross-border subterfuges and economic warfare did take place. A small group of anti-Vichy Senegalese passed information from Senegal to the Gambia and a Free French Mission was established in Bathurst. The blockading of French West Africa by the Allies caused shortages of food and other commodities in Senegal which enhanced smuggling in both directions across the border with the Gambia. The British colonial administration there, as elsewhere in Britain's West African colonies, encouraged and regulated such trade, hoping thereby to undermine the Vichy regime economically and, again, used such networks for espionage. It allowed smugglers easy passage (while reacting harshly to those who smuggled goods into Senegal from the Gambia) and actively promoted this trade to those in Senegal through information about advantageous prices across the border (Blackburne, 1976, pp. 58–65; Crowder, 1968, pp. 487–489; Ginio, 2006, pp. 62–63, 146–147).[8]

Following the Second World War and until the 1950s, the British colonial government gave very little thought to the future of the Gambia. It was generally assumed that it would remain a colony forever or possibly unite with Sierra Leone to restore the administrative link that had operated between 1866 and 1888 when the Gambia had formed part of the West African Settlements (Hughes and Perfect, 2006, pp. 42–43).[9] But as the pace of political change quickened across West Africa, the British began to give serious consideration to the future of the Gambia with various solutions, including the "Channel Islands option" and the "Malta option" being considered and rejected (Hughes and Perfect, 2006, pp. 43–44; Senghor, 2008, pp. 74–77). At the same time, one day after Senegal had become a self-governing member of the French Community in 1958, its then Prime Minister, Mamadou Dia, made an official visit to Bathurst, clearly demonstrating Senegalese interest in the future of the Senegambia region, a preoccupation which increased after Senegal had achieved independence in August 1960 (Senghor, 2008, pp. 68–86).

Yet even in the early 1960s, it was assumed by the British Colonial Office and successive governors of the Gambia that, unlike its neighbour, the Gambia could never become independent and its future lay in political, social and economic union with Senegal. This was also the goal of Senegal's first President, Léopold Senghor, despite the earlier failure of the Mali Federation which had briefly united Senegal and the former French Soudan (modern Mali) in 1959–1960. Senghor hoped that the Gambia would be fully integrated into Senegal as its (then) eighth region. This was seen both as a means to achieve wider territorial unity in West Africa (despite the failure of the Mali Federation) and for domestic security reasons; particularly after 1962 when Senghor's former Prime Minister, Mamadou Dia, was ousted in a power struggle, Senghor was concerned that the Gambia might become a safe haven for Senegalese dissidents (Gellar, 1995, pp. 23–24; Hughes and Perfect, 2006, pp. 255–256; Senghor, 2008, p. 100; Senghor, 2013, pp. 240–241; Touray, 2000, pp. 30–32).

While recognising that there might be some economic advantages in closer ties with Senegal, most Gambians – including crucially the first Gambian Prime Minister, Dawda Jawara – opposed any kind of political union, while Senghor, chastened by the Mali Federation experience, adopted a cautious approach to the Gambia. Many Gambians were wary of too close a link with Senegal. English-speaking civil servants were afraid that they would lose out to French speakers if closer relations were established; lawyers and other professionals feared that their status and qualifications would be discounted; and political leaders who had enjoyed their first taste of power in recent years were reluctant to give this up (Hughes and Perfect, 2006, pp. 256–257; Senghor, 2008, pp. 85–86).[10]

In 1962, the British government announced for the first time that the Gambia might become independent (the assumption being still that this would be for a very short time only) and a United Nations mission in 1963–1964 outlined three options: total integration of the Gambia into an enlarged Senegal favoured by the Senegalese; a loose federation proposed by the Gambians; and a compromise "association" which would allow for a more leisurely progression towards closer union. But when negotiations between the Gambians and Senegalese in 1964 failed to achieve either the first or the second options, the third option of loose association was followed. Treaties covering foreign policy, security, defence and external representation were signed (and came into force when The Gambia moved to independence in February 1965), but there were no formal political links. Thus whereas Senegal had moved to independence as part of a planned process towards decolonisation, Gambian independence could be viewed almost as an accident and few external observers thought that the country would survive for long (Hughes and Perfect, 2006, pp. 254–259; Senghor, 2008, pp. 87–170; Touray, 2000, pp. 32–36; Welch, 1964, pp. 250–291).

Senegalese/Gambian Relations: 1965–1994
After Gambian independence in 1965, relations between the two independent nations fluctuated. They were generally fairly harmonious and following the signing of a Treaty of Association in April 1967, a number of joint institutions were established, notably the Senegalo-Gambian Inter-State Ministerial Committee which replaced an earlier, and largely ineffective, committee; and the Senegalo-Gambian Permanent Secretariat. Various trade and other agreements were signed, although few of these were ever ratified and the two sides differed over key policies to further economic integration, notably the long-running discussions over the best means to replace the notoriously unreliable ferry crossing at Farafenni, where the Transgambian Highway which links Dakar with Casamance crosses the River Gambia. However, at other times relations were distinctly frosty, particularly when border incidents flared up, notably in 1971 (when The Gambia actually complained to the United Nations about Senegalese aggression) and 1974 (Hughes and Perfect, 2006,

pp. 259–260; Jawara, 2009, pp. 302–306; Senghor, 2008, pp. 204–211; Senghor, 2013, pp. 229–234; Touray, 2000, pp. 36–43; 99–105).[11]

As noted above, a mutual defence pact had been signed in 1964 and came into force at Gambian independence. Subsequently, the Senegalese confirmed in 1967 that they would intervene in the event of internal Gambian disorder provided that specified Gambian ministers appealed for their assistance. It was this agreement that led Senghor (who was increasingly concerned about Libyan influence in the West African region) to send in Senegalese troops in October 1980 following the murder of the Deputy Commander of the para-military Field Force, E. J. Mahoney, by a disgruntled soldier (Hughes and Perfect, 2006, pp. 209, 260–261; Senghor, 2008, pp. 218–219; Touray, 2000, pp. 105–106).[12] Then in July 1981, Senghor's successor, Abdou Diouf, sent in an estimated 2,500 seaborne, airborne and land-borne forces to restore Jawara to power after he had been overthrown in a coup led by civilian radicals and discontented members of the Field Force; some Gambian ministers had escaped and were able to call on Senegal for renewed assistance under the mutual defence agreement. Diouf's decision to intervene reflected wider Senegalese concerns; Senegal had become increasingly worried in recent years about the emergence of Muslim fundamentalists, who were thought to be backed by Libya (with which Senegal had broken off diplomatic relations in July 1980) and to have recruited Gambian supporters (Hughes and Perfect, 2006, pp. 210–220; Jawara, 2009, pp. 308–317; Senghor, 2008, pp. 213–224).

The price for Senegalese intervention was the establishment of the Senegambia Confederation which came into being in February 1982. Much closer ties between the two countries were envisaged through the establishment of a confederal assembly, council of ministers and secretariat and the partial integration of the security forces of the two countries; foreign policy was to be coordinated. Diouf assumed the presidency of the Confederation, with Jawara as Vice-President. Although he put a brave face on it, both at the time and subsequently, it was apparent to many outside observers that Jawara had reluctantly entered into the Confederation and that his aim had been to get the best deal he could achieve, whereas the Senegalese clearly regarded the Confederation as a stepping stone to an eventual total union of the two countries (Hughes and Perfect, 2006, pp. 261–263; Jawara, 2009, pp. 342–346; Phillips, 1991; Senghor, 2008, pp. 224–231; Touray, 2000, pp. 107–112).

Although initially there was little overt Gambian (or Senegalese) opposition to the Confederation, primarily be-cause of the weakness of opposition parties in both countries, there was little enthusiasm for it either; and this quickly waned further in the face of growing tensions. The most damaging incident was in 1985 when the Senegalese High Commissioner in Banjul ordered Senegalese forces to quell disturbances at a football match in Banjul by force. This outraged the Gambian public who were thus reminded of their subordinate status in the Confederation. For its part, the Senegalese press became increasingly critical of what was seen as Gambian prevarication and evasion over the Confederation, particularly as Senegal was largely footing the bill for it (Hughes and Lewis, 1995; Hughes and Perfect, 2006, pp. 263–265; Senghor, 2008, pp. 253–263; Touray, 2000, pp. 112–115).

Eventually, in 1989, the Confederation broke down. This was after the Senegalese had lost patience with the Gambian government's refusal to support them when a border conflict erupted between Senegal and Mauritania (Parker, 1991), particularly as the Senegalese were simultaneously in dispute with Guinea-Bissau over the maritime border between the two countries. There was also resentment that The Gambia was providing a safe haven for Mauritanian refugees from the conflict. When Diouf began to pull Senegalese troops out of The Gambia after Jawara had raised a key Gambian concern – that the presidency of the Confederation should be rotated – it was clear that the Confederation was dead and it was formally dissolved in October 1989. Following its collapse, relations between the two countries deteriorated with the Senegalese imposing economic sanctions on The Gambia and, although a Treaty of Friendship and Co-operation was signed in 1991, they remained cool at the time of the 1994 coup that brought Yahya Jammeh, the current Gambian President, to power (Hughes, 1992; Hughes and Perfect, 2006, pp. 265–266; Jawara, 2009, pp. 354–357; Phillips, 1991; Senghor, 2008, pp. 236–239, 274–276; Senghor, 2013, pp. 242–243; Touray, 2000, pp. 115–116).

Senegalese/Gambian Relations: 1994–2012
The overthrow of Sir Dawda Jawara heralded the start of a new phase in Senegalese/Gambian relations. A critical factor in this has been the ongoing conflict in Casamance which in 1990 had moved into a fully militarised armed struggle between Senegalese forces and guerrillas of the separatist *Mouvement des forces démocratiques de la Casamance* or *MFDC* (Evans, 2004, p. 4). Jawara had been largely indifferent to Casamance: as a Mandinka from north of the river, he had no particular ties with the Casamance population.[13] Jammeh, by contrast, is a Jola, a member of the ethnic group from which the great majority of *MFDC* membership and support is derived. Jammeh's Gambian home village of Kanilai sits very close to the Casamance border and he epitomises the

74

transnational character of much of the Jola population straddling the border in northern Lower Casamance and neighbouring parts of The Gambia, particularly the Foni districts of Western Division.

As a result, many in both Senegal and The Gambia (particularly his domestic opponents) view Jammeh's position *vis-à-vis* Casamance with suspicion (Evans and Ray, 2013, pp. 266–267). Rumours abound that he has covertly supported particular *MFDC* factions through (among other means) supplying arms and tacitly allowing them to use Gambian territory as a rear base for military activities, particularly in northern Lower Casamance, and that he and his entourage also benefit from the guerrillas trafficking illegally cut Casamance timber, cannabis and other crops (Evans, 2003, p. 43). Some of Jammeh's public actions have certainly reinforced such a view, including his friendship with the late Brigadier-General Ansumane Mané, the former Chief-of-Staff in Guinea-Bissau but a Gambian Mandinka by birth (Evans and Ray, 2013, p. 268). Mané launched a coup against Bissau-Guinean President Nino Vieira in 1998 after the latter sacked him for alleged arms trafficking to the *MFDC*, precipitating a civil war in which Mané was supported by *MFDC* guerrilla factions based in areas of Guinea-Bissau bordering Casamance; in return, he provided them with light weapons.

But outside of certain actions, the picture regarding relations between Senegal and The Gambia in the Casamance conflict is more mixed than popular discourse on both sides of the border would suggest. In the wake of the civil war in Guinea-Bissau, The Gambia was actually seen as a safer pair of hands than Guinea-Bissau to help Senegal in Casamance (Foucher, 2003, p. 108). At the end of the 1990s, Banjul hosted and engaged in initiatives, notably *MFDC* meetings – held at Senegal's request – aimed at enabling the *Mouvement* to agree a united position for future negotiations with the Senegalese government. A high-profile conference of the *MFDC* was held in Banjul in June 1999 but failed to bring all factions together; key hardline guerrilla commander Salif Sadio was taken there by Ansumane Mané but did not take part in discussions (Evans, 2004, p. 13). The Diouf regime engaged positively with such moves: the December 1999 "Banjul Agreement" formally established the "Banjul Process", providing for monthly meetings between the Senegalese government and the *MFDC*. The first of these was held in January 2000, followed by the establishment of a ceasefire monitoring mission in Ziguinchor (capital of Lower Casamance) in February (Evans, 2000, p. 654). There is some debate about Diouf's motives in such cooperation: some argue that he rightly recognised Casamance as an issue requiring such a transnational approach; others see these belated actions as one more cynical attempt to shore up his regime by finally addressing a crisis that had haunted nearly all of his twenty-year presidency.

The election of Abdoulaye Wade to the Senegalese presidency in March 2000, however, brought a new approach (Evans, 2000, pp. 654–655). It soon became clear that Wade's relationship with The Gambia *vis-à-vis* Casamance was, along with his wider diplomatic approach to the conflict, ambivalent and contradictory. Wade generally sought to distance The Gambia diplomatically from the Casamance peace process although the grounds for this are questionable. One reason was probably Jammeh's continued friendship with Ansumane Mané although the latter was soon to be killed in another, failed coup attempt against President Kumba Yala in November 2000. With regard to the long-standing allegations of his links with and material support for *MFDC* guerrillas, Jammeh assured Wade, early in the latter's presidency, that

Gambian territory would not be used as a base for *MFDC* attacks. Soon after, however, Wade accused The Gambia of receiving arms from Libya to arm the *MFDC*, prompting Banjul briefly to suspend its Casamance mediation efforts, although in reality this made little difference to the failing Process.

Wade also took off the table the possibility of any form of autonomy for Casamance more vehemently and explicitly than Diouf, who was more versed in the politics of compromise and cooptation, had ever done. Early in his presidency, Wade famously condemned the suggestion, made by respected political commentator Babacar Justin Ndiaye in a televised debate with civil society leaders in late 2000, for being « *à la limite de la trahison* » – close to treason – for suggesting a special statute (i.e. some form of autonomy) for Casamance. While such arrangements have been rare and problematic in postcolonial African countries, even those with an Anglo-Saxon heritage that could lend itself more readily to such pragmatism (Tanzania is one clear example), this seemed to underscore from an early stage Wade's much more "French" view of Senegal as an inalienably unified national territory which The Gambia disrupted by its mere existence. It is unsurprising that, while a further *MFDC* meeting (again without hardliners) was hosted in Banjul in 2001, the Banjul Process as such was dropped by Wade, who asked The Gambia to cease its mediation efforts. This angered The Gambia and is still criticised by the *MFDC*.

This was part of a wider and explicit attempt by Wade to break from the practices of the *ancien régime* which he saw as counter-productive. The most important element of this policy was Wade's desire, again stated early in his presidency, that the Casamance conflict be treated as a domestic issue and without foreign "interference" (*Jeune Afrique*, 2000).

This represented the clearest rupture with the approach of his predecessor. Critics, including the *MFDC* itself, argue that Gambian political involvement was thereby closed off just at the moment when progress was being made through the Banjul Process which may have represented a good opportunity for peace. The political value of Gambian involvement in the Process may reasonably be contested but such an approach was, along Casamance's other border, clearly self-contradictory given Wade's material assistance to Guinea-Bissau in its efforts, from late 2000 onwards, to dislodge hardline *MFDC* guerrillas from its territory.

On the ground, Wade's position had mixed effects. Despite the shaky start in Senegalese/Gambian relations under his presidency, the first half of the 2000s saw growing cooperation between Senegal and The Gambia on security and refugee issues, side-stepping the more problematic politics of the Casamance question. This was evident in the context of periodic displacements of people from northern Lower Casamance into The Gambia, with cross-border efforts facilitating a voluntary return by refugees in some cases. Jammeh also finally accepted a long-standing desire of Senegal by signing an agreement in principle, in 2003, over the construction of a bridge over the River Gambia to replace the ferry at Farafenni (Foucher, 2003, p. 109). Since at least 1980, the Senegalese government had viewed the construction of the bridge as of critical importance to its Casamance policy.[14] It would greatly improve connections between Casamance and northern Senegal and thereby help physically integrate Senegalese national territory but, as noted below, it remains unbuilt in spite of donor funding being available.

These relative advances were not, however, built upon in the second half of the 2000s. The accord signed between elements of the *MFDC* and the Senegalese government in December 2004 reflected improvements in security in Casamance since Guinea-Bissau had – following the death of Mané – been able to take more direct action against hardline *MFDC* guerrillas on its territory, but the real significance of the accord as a political advance is debatable. It was arguably a public relations exercise to encourage further donor aid for negotiations and reconstruction in Casamance while masking structural problems in the peace process. Indeed, after initial talks in 2005 at Foundiougne in northern Senegal, nego-tiations (envisaged in the 2004 accord) between the Senegalese government and multiple *MFDC* elements stalled. The reasons for this include continued fragmentation (in part fomented by Wade himself) of the *MFDC* and Senegalese failure to view Casamance as a transnational problem. This was evident even in the choice of a domestic venue for peace talks which in itself discouraged *MFDC* hardliners – still fearful of Senegalese repression – from attending. It is noteworthy here that hardline *MFDC* guerrilla commander Salif Sadio, chased out of Guinea-Bissau, has in recent years based himself in The Gambia. The deepening stagnation in the Casamance peace process, reflected in upsurges in violence in 2009–2010, created an environment in which much Gambian/Senegalese cross-border cooperation even on operational issues regarding Casamance (including humanitarian action) was hamstrung.

In the resulting policy doldrums on both sides of the border, it became easy for continued suspicion of Gambian motives, reflected in abundant rumour and allegations but little hard evidence, to go unchecked. It is, however, worth interrogating possible motives on all sides for such continued ambiguity. As noted, it suited Wade to distance The Gambia from the Casamance dossier within his dubious logic of "domesticising" the conflict, and uncertainties over Jammeh's motives in Casamance provided a further justification (if Wade needed one) for this policy. It may have suited Jammeh himself to maintain this uncertainty and to leave others to suspect that he had more influence in Casamance than is the case, as a "bargaining chip" with Dakar (Foucher, 2007, p. 179). Perhaps paradoxically, it may also have been beneficial for the Gambian opposition, in its disarray, to find grounds on which to criticise Jammeh's foreign policy as well as his oppressive domestic actions.

Ways Forward in Senegalese/Gambian Relations

Another way to view Gambian/Senegalese relations regarding Casamance is to consider what has in reality been the very limited room for manoeuvre provided by both sides' respective policy positions. Wade's exclusion of The Gambia from formal mediation in the conflict closed off what the short-lived Banjul Process suggested could be a potentially valuable avenue in the search for peace. His failure to resolve the Casamance conflict while he tried to play the international mediator in disputes elsewhere was also an embarrassment to him, but his arrogance in viewing himself as a regional statesman perhaps prevented him from giving neighbouring countries a political role. To some extent his position was a self-fulfilling reprise of the sometime Senegalese view of The Gambia as a territorial "problem" and as politically uncooperative. Whatever the case, the latter part of the Wade presidency saw him increasingly bogged down in (northern Senegalese) domestic concerns amid (ultimately unsuccessful) attempts to get himself re-elected as President, and he did not prioritise Casamance beyond military responses to the volatile security situation.

Trouble with the Neighbours?

The election of Macky Sall as the new President of Senegal in March 2012 seems to have ushered in, again, a different approach but one more reminiscent of the late Diouf era. Even in his election campaign, Sall declared his intention to involve The Gambia (and Guinea-Bissau) in helping finally to resolve the Casamance conflict, and he started to pursue this soon after his inauguration. His first visit abroad as President, in April 2012, was to The Gambia, where he discussed bilateral relations in various domains. These included Casamance, although it remains to be seen what the outcome of such discussions may be, particularly in the troubled context of renewed and ongoing political crisis in Guinea-Bissau. In the meeting of the two presidents, Sall also raised the issue of the River Gambia bridge project. History again weighs heavily here, however: under Jawara, the project never moved forward; under Jammeh, an agreement has been signed with Senegal but the bridge has not been built and he does not appear particularly concerned to advance the project now (*Foroyaa*, 2012).

Jammeh has no immediate concerns about his own position either, given his own re-election as Gambian President by a large majority in November 2011 (Ceesay and Perfect, 2011; Perfect and Hughes, 2013, pp. 102–103; Saine and Ceesay, 2013, pp. 169–171). He may, however, remain beholden to certain domestic concerns in a context of strong cross-border ties among the Jola and pro-*MFDC* elements among this population in The Gambia. He needs to keep onside his predominantly Jola entourage (occupying a number of important government posts) and, perhaps more importantly, the constituency represented by the many Casamance Jola that are habitually registered as Gambian voters, particularly in the Fonis. This was highlighted in the 2001 presidential election when, although exact figures are clearly unknown and estimates are contested, the numbers involved were believed to have run into the thousands (Baker, 2002; Saine, 2009, pp. 45–46; Saine and Ceesay, 2013, pp. 163–164). After the last mass influx of Casamance refugees, in 2006, it was again rumoured that many were registered as voters and issued with voting cards for the presidential election that year (*Africa Research Bulletin*, 2006; Saine, 2009, p. 126). There were unsubstantiated rumours once again in 2011 that Senegalese (and Mauritanians) were transported into The Gambia by the security forces to be registered and thus to vote for Jammeh (Ceesay and Perfect, 2011; United Democratic Party/Gambia Moral Congress, 2011). A firmly pro-Senegal line on Casamance could backfire on Jammeh by alienating such constituencies. It would also, in the view of some Gambians, open the possibility of their country becoming, like Guinea-Bissau since late 2000, a vassal of Senegalese foreign policy in respect of Casamance, with expectations of military cooperation against *MFDC* guerrillas based in The Gambia. Memories of Senegalese interventions on Gambian territory in the 1980s and fears of renewed violation of Gambian sovereignty would clearly make this domestically unpalatable. The *MFDC*, meanwhile, continues to use the rather muddled late nineteenth-century settlement of borders and territories in the southern Sene-gambia, and the semi-autonomous (from Dakar) nature of French colonial rule in Casamance subsequently, as grist to the mill of their claim of *de jure* independence for Casamance. The *MFDC* has also lost faith in the stalled peace process, partly because of Wade's evident *divide et impera* policy towards its various factions but also, even now in the Macky era, in Senegalese involvement more generally and indeed in sub-regional or even regional mediation of any kind. Various

MFDC elements continue to call instead for some form of international intervention to restart negotiations.

Such an intervention would face the considerable challenge of having to break down the respective, entrenched policy positions of both countries, informed by their different histories. Both sides continue to play out roles set for them well over a century ago: Senegal as the serious, stable state, having to deal with troublesome and unstable neighbours (notwithstanding the embarrassment of Casamance), including the continent's smallest country as a thorn in its side; and The Gambia as the feisty, independent state, fiercely protecting its sovereignty while surrounded by French/ Senegalese territory. In the face of ongoing violence in Casamance, however, both should now recognise the need for more constructive management of their shared Senegambian space.

Notes
1. In April 1829, the Acting Lieutenant-Governor, William Hutton, signed a treaty with the King of Wuli which ceded the town of Fattatenda and 100 acres of land to the British (to facilitate trade), but the Colonial Office subsequently refused to approve the treaty. Curiously, however, for the next half century, both traders and the rulers of Wuli continued to believe the treaty was in force and acted accordingly. For a discussion, see Gray, 1966, pp. 341–342; [House of Commons], 1971, pp. 363–373. In 1862, Governor George D'Arcy proposed the establishment of a protectorate along both banks of the River Gambia to control the Marabouts and Soninke by force, but this was rejected by the Colonial Office; see Quinn, 1972, p. 135. During an exploration of the upper River area in 1881, Administrator Valesius Gouldsbury

made a number of treaties with local rulers, but these were not followed up; see Gailey, 1964, p. 101; Hughes and Perfect, 2008, p. 89.

2. In 1874, the arrangements were revised with the Gambia remaining under Sierra Leonean jurisdiction and Lagos being placed under the Gold Coast. See Gray, 1966, pp. 431–433, 459–460; Hughes and Perfect, 2006, pp. 41, 65–66.

3. Quinn, 1972, pp. 145–146, notes that by 1850, the French had established a *comptoir* at Carabane near the mouth of the River Casamance and another trading centre at Sédhiou in the interior. See also Gray, 1966, p. 414 (who calls the town Seju). Sédhiou subsequently became, for a relatively short period (1894–1909) "the capital" of Casamance, although Ziguinchor subsequently regained its role as such until the administrative division of Casamance region in 1984.

4. The British and French cooperated to destroy the power of two prominent Gambian warlords, Fode Sillah and Fode Kaba, for example; the 1901 expedition which resulted in Kaba's death was conducted by both powers working together. See Gray, 1966, pp. 468–472; Hughes and Perfect, 2008, pp. 126–127; Quinn, 1972, pp. 187–191. The Gambian government was also delighted when E. F. Small, whom it termed a "link subversive" at this time, was formally expelled from Senegal (in absentia); Small's Senegalese agent, Babucarr Secka, was actually expelled. See Hughes and Perfect, 2008, pp. 98–99.

5. For example, in 1928, Governor John Middleton made an official visit to Dakar, during which he presented the Governor-General of French West Africa, Jules Carde, with the honour of Knight Commander of the British Empire that Carde had been awarded by George V.

Middleton was invited to visit French Soudan by Carde in early 1929, but by then he had left the colony and it does not appear that his successor, Edward Denham, took up the offer. For details, see Colonial Office (CO) file, 87/227/6 at the National Archives, Kew. One agreement between the colonies concerned the provision of wireless services in 1934; see CO 87/239/2 for details.

6. Gambian history during the Second World War remains an under-researched area, but see Blackburne, 1976, pp. 56–68 for an account by the Colonial Secretary of the time.

7. CO 323/187/32, Dill to Lloyd, 20 October 1940; CO 554/129/10, minutes of West African Governor Conference, 7–10 April 1941.

8. In 1942, Barra Turay, the Seyfu (chief) of Lower Saloum, was removed from his post by Governor H. R. R. Blood. Turay had facilitated the escape of two Africans from Senegal who had "endeavoured to interfere with the movement of cattle from the Senegal to the Gambia" and had "actively participated in smuggling cotton goods from the Gambia into the Senegal". See CO 968/67/38, Blood to Cranborne, 26 August 1942. The Secretary of State for the Colonies, Viscount Cranborne, approved the governor's actions; see Cranborne to Blood, 20 October 1942, in the same file. Two Gambians were reportedly executed in Dakar (presumably for espionage) in November 1941, although in one instance at least, the press report seems to have been inaccurate; see Foreign Office (FO) file, 371/28599, National Archives, Kew.

9. Kent, 1990, p. 78 states that in 1939, the Dufferin Committee recommended consideration of the creation of a federation between the Gambia and Sierra Leone.

But the Colonial Office appears to have discounted the suggestion.

10. In his autobiography, Jawara briefly outlines his views; see Jawara, 2009, pp. 299–301.

11. The Gambians favoured replacing the ferry at Farafenni with a barrage, the Senegalese preferred a bridge.

12. The Gambian government claimed officially that the Senegalese had only sent troops as part of regular joint exercises, but this version of events was regarded with scepticism by the British High Commissioner in Banjul. See Foreign and Commonwealth Office (FCO) file, 65/2281, National Archives, Kew, Smith to Macrae, 8 November 1980.

13. It is instructive that Jawara mentions the Casamance only a few times in *Kairaba* and the *MFDC* only once. His approach to Casamance, at least in the early years after Gambian independence, appears to have been to support the Senegalese government's position; see, for example, FO 1106/2, Crombie to Spreckley, 9 August 1967; Spreckley to Crombie, 25 August 1967. J. N. T. Spreckley, who was based in the British embassy in Dakar, suggested that the main value of the 1967 defence agreement to the Senegalese was to shore up their position in the Casamance.

14. FCO 65/2393, Squire to Johnson, 13 March 1980, discusses Senegalese-Gambian relations essentially from a Senegalese perspective (C. W. Squire was the British ambassador to Senegal at the time).

References

Africa Research Bulletin: Political, Social and Cultural Series. (2006). The Gambia: No idle boast, 43(10), November, 16820C–16821B.

Baker, B. (2002). Political sensitivities in Gambian refugee policy, *Journal of Humanitarian Assistance*, posted online June 2002 at http://sites.tufts.edu/jha/

Barrows, L. C. (1976) Faidherbe and Senegal: A critical discussion, *African Studies Review*, *19*(1), 95–117.

Barry, B. (1998). *Senegambia and the Atlantic slave trade*. Cambridge: Cambridge University Press.

Blackburne, Sir K. W. (1976). *Lasting legacy: A story of British colonialism*. London: Johnson.

Ceesay, E., & Perfect, D. (2011). The Gambia's Presidential Election, 2011, *African Arguments Online,* available at: http://africanarguments.org/

Crowder, M. (1968). *West Africa under colonial rule*. London: Hutchinson.

Evans, M. (2000). Briefing: Senegal: Wade and the Casamance dossier, *African Affairs*, *99*(397), 649–658.

Evans, M. (2003). Ni paix ni guerre: The political economy of low-level conflict in the Casamance. In S. Collinson (Ed.), *Power, livelihoods and conflict: Case studies in political economy analysis for humanitarian action* (pp. 37–52). Humanitarian Policy Group Report, 13. London: Overseas Development Institute.

Evans, M. (2004). *Senegal : Mouvement des forces démocratiques de la Casamance (MFDC)*, Africa Programme Armed Non-State Actors Project Briefing Paper, 2. London: Chatham House.

Evans, M., & Ray, C. (2013). Uncertain ground: The Gambia and the Casamance conflict. In A. Saine, E. Ceesay & E. Sall (Eds.), *State and society in The Gambia since independence: 1965–2012* (pp. 247–287). Trenton, NJ: Africa World Press.

Foroyaa (2012). West Africa: Senegal–Gambia relations: Casamance and the bridge/dissidents and open borders,

Foroyaa newspaper online, 19 April, retrieved from: http://www.foroyaa.gm/

Foucher, V. (2003). Pas d'alternance en Casamance? Le nouveau pouvoir sénégalais face à la revendication séparatiste casamançaise, *Politique Africaine, 91*, 101–119.

Foucher, V. (2007). Senegal: The resilient weakness of Casamançais separatists. In M. Bøås & K. C. Dunn (Eds.), *African guerrillas: Raging against the machine* (pp. 171–197) Boulder, CO: Lynne Rienner.

Gailey, H. A. (1964). *A history of the Gambia*. London: Routledge & Kegan Paul.

Gellar, S. (1995). *Senegal: An African nation between Islam and the West*. Boulder, CO: Westview Press.

Ginio, R. (2006). *French colonialism unmasked: The Vichy years in French West Africa*. Lincoln, NE: University of Nebraska Press.

Gray, Sir J. M. (1966). *A history of the Gambia*, (2nd ed.). London: Frank Cass.

Hargreaves, J. D. (1963). *Prelude to the partition of West Africa*. London: Macmillan.

Hargreaves, J. D. (1974). *West Africa partitioned: The loaded pause, 1885–1889*. London: Macmillan.

[House of Commons] (1971). *British Parliamentary Papers Colonies Africa 56*. Shannon: Irish University Press.

Hughes, A. (1992). The collapse of the Senegambian Confederation, *Journal of Commonwealth and Comparative Politics, 30*(2), 200–222.

Hughes, A., & Lewis, J. (1995). Beyond Francophonie? The Senegambia Confederation in retrospect. In A. Kirk-Greene & D. Bach (Eds.), *State and society in Francophone Africa since independence* (pp. 228–243). Basingstoke: Macmillan.

Hughes, A., & Perfect, D. (2006). *A political history of The Gambia*. Rochester, NY: University of Rochester Press.

Hughes, A., & Perfect, D. (2008). *Historical Dictionary of The Gambia* (4th ed.). Lanham, MD: Scarecrow Press.

Idowu, H. O. (1968). The establishment of elective institutions in Senegal, 1869–1880, *Journal of African History, 9*(2), 261–277.

Jawara, D. K. (2009). *Kairaba*. Haywards Heath: D.K. Jawara.

Jeune Afrique. (2000). Wade: « Je n'ai pas changé, mais … », *Jeune Afrique/L'Intelligent*, 23–29 mai.

Johnson, G. W. (1971). *The emergence of black politics in Senegal: The struggle for power in the Four Communes, 1900–1930*. Stanford, CA: Stanford University Press.

Kent, J. (1990). Regionalism or territorial autonomy? The case of British West African development, 1939–49, *Journal of Imperial and Commonwealth History, 18*(1), 61–80.

Marut, J.-C. (2010). *Le conflit de Casamance: ce que disent les armes*. Paris: Karthala.

Nugent, P. (2007). Cyclical history in the Gambia/Casamance borderlands: Refuge, settlement and Islam from *c*.1880 to the present, *Journal of African History, 47*(2), 221–243.

Parker, R. (1991). The Senegal-Mauritania Conflict of 1989: A fragile equilibrium, *Journal of Modern African Studies, 29*(1), 155–171.

Perfect, D., & Hughes, A. (2013). Gambian electoral politics: 1960–2012. In A. Saine, E. Ceesay & E. Sall (Eds.), *State and society in The Gambia since independence: 1965–2012* (pp. 79–111). Trenton, NJ: Africa World Press.

Phillips, L. C. (1991). The Senegambia Confederation. In C. L. Delgado & S. Jammeh (Eds.), *The political economy of Senegal under structural adjustment* (pp. 175–193). Westport, CT: Praeger.

Quinn, C. A. (1972). *Mandingo kingdoms of the Senegambia.* Evanston, IL: Northwestern University Press.

Saine, A. (2009). *The paradox of third-wave democratization in Africa: The Gambia under AFPRC-APRC Rule, 1994–2008.* Lanham, MD: Lexington Books.

Saine, A., & Ceesay, E. (2013). Post-coup politics and authoritarianism in The Gambia: 1994–2012. In A. Saine, E. Ceesay & E. Sall (Eds.), *State and society in The Gambia since independence: 1965–2012* (pp. 151–184). Trenton, NJ: Africa World Press.

Senghor, J. C. (2008). *The politics of Senegambian integration, 1958–1994.* Bern: Peter Lang.

Senghor, J. C. (2013). The 'Senegambia' experience: Twelve pointers for regional integration in Africa. In A. Saine, E. Ceesay & E. Sall (Eds.), *State and society in The Gambia since independence: 1965–2012* (pp. 215–245). Trenton, NJ: Africa World Press.

Swindell, K. (1982). *The strange farmers of The Gambia: A study in the redistribution of African population.* Norwich: Geo Books.

Touray, O. A. (2000). *The Gambia and the world: A history of the foreign policy of Africa's smallest state, 1965–1995.* Hamburg: Institute of African Affairs.

United Democratic Party/Gambia Moral Congress (2011). Final Report of the UDP–GMC Alliance on the Presidential Election held on 24 November, available at: http://www.maafanta.com/UDPGMCFinalReport Elections2011.html

Welch, C. E. Jr. (1964). *Dream of unity: Pan Africanism and political unification in West Africa.* Ithaca, NY: Cornell University Press.

Wyse, A. J. G. (1976) The Gambia in Anglo-French relations, 1905–12, *Journal of Imperial and Commonwealth History*, 4(2), 164–175.

PART 2
GEO-POLITICAL CONFLICTS IN AFRICA
AND THE INDIAN OCEAN

CHAPTER 3

HISTORIOGRAPHIES, NATIONALISMS AND CONFLICT IN CASAMANCE, SENEGAL

Martin Evans[1]

"History will prove us right."[2]
(Interview with member of *MFDC* political wing,
Ziguinchor, 26 April 2011)

War commonly sees politicised readings of history by each side to justify its position and mobilise support. In the ongoing civil conflict in Casamance, Senegal, the separatist claims of the *Mouvement des forces démocratiques de la Casamance* (*MFDC*) and the Senegalese government's defence of territorial integrity stem from different colonial historiographies; academics thus get embroiled in such disputes, however unwittingly. Local historical under-standings, meanwhile, get submerged, even though some Casamançais view the contemporary situation through histories of violence particular to their area. The chapter explores how nationalist (Senegalese and Casamançais) and local historio-graphies are deployed and contested in the conflict.

Introduction

Violent conflicts typically involve the deployment not just of combatants and armaments but also of history. Even in peacetime, selective histories or certain readings of them are used, implicitly or explicitly, to justify a certain political position, to help forge a common identity, or to mobilise people around a political project. In the heated rhetoric and execution of armed violence by states or non-state actors, such historiographies – understood here as particular narratives about the past derived from particular sources and their interpretation – may become all the more important. The use of history in the construction of nationalism, specifically, is analysed by Benedict Anderson in his classic work *Imagined Communities*. Anderson notes that nationalist narratives involve not only a shared imaginary of the nation rooted in a common view of its past (however distorted this is, compared with reality) but also require a degree of collective amnesia. He quotes the nineteenth-century French historian Ernest Renan on this point: "Indeed the essence of a nation is that all individuals should have lots of things in common, and also that they should all have forgotten lots of things"[3] (Anderson, 1991, p. 6). Points of historical fact that do not fit the needs of the contemporary nationalist project are forgotten, ignored or actively suppressed.

But local, rather than national, histories also matter to people caught up in such conflict. These histories may either sit within the grander narrative of nationalist struggle, or may apparently be separate from them. The latter case requires some qualification, however: though seemingly irrelevant to the conflict in question, local folk memory and understandings of history may become distorted in quite complex ways within the fraught spaces of current political violence, creating perceived linkages with the present and hence possible reinforcement of certain responses (Nugent, 2007, pp. 223–224). Any notion of and reasons for historical patterns somehow repeating themselves, in modern African wars or elsewhere, is deeply contentious (Ellis, 2001, p. 56; Nugent, 2007, p. 223) and this debate is not explored here. Rather, the concern is that history as understood on the ground, today, may have resonances and repercussions that should be considered in any critical analysis of conflict. This is all the more important in the face of the facile labels of atavism, tribalism, anarchy and greed that plague popular accounts of violence in sub-Saharan Africa.

With these points in mind, the chapter shows how historiographies and nationalisms play out in the context of ongoing violence in Casamance – the southern limb of Senegal, sandwiched between The Gambia and Guinea-Bissau. This has the invidious distinction of being the scene of West Africa's longest-running civil conflict, concentrated in Lower Casamance with its ethnic Jola (Diola in French orthography) majority.[4] The contemporary violence origina-ted in Casamançais discontent with the Senegalese administration in the 1970s and early 1980s (Evans, 2004, p. 1). This discontent was mobilised in protest marches in 1982 and 1983 in Ziguinchor, capital of the then unified Casa-mance region. At these marches, the *Mouvement des forces democratiques de la Casamance* (*MFDC*) demanded inde-pendence for Casamance from Senegal. Although the marches were largely peaceful in intent, they prompted an increasingly oppressive and violent reaction from the Senegalese authorities. There were over 100 arrests following the first march in 1982. At the second march in 1983, Senegalese forces fired on protestors with live rounds, killing between 50 and 200 people, then pursued, arrested and harassed many other marchers and their associates. These actions drove the *MFDC* underground and, faced with ongoing government oppression and seeing no political solution, it procured firearms and launched an insurgency against Senegalese forces in Casamance in 1990. The deployment of the Senegalese army in response led to full-scale militarisation of the conflict. The consequences have included an estimated 3,000–5,000 combat-related deaths; human rights abuses by both sides; and displacement of more than 60,000 people, the majority as internally displaced persons, others as refugees in The Gambia or Guinea-Bissau. The latter country, particularly, has also hosted rear bases for the *maquis*, the armed wing of the *MFDC*. The conflict has brought severe economic problems to many Casamançais as important economic sectors (agriculture, fishing and tourism) have been damaged by the conflict, sometimes deliberately targeted, while foreign aid and investment have been withdrawn.

While political changes at international level since late 2000 had, until recent years, led to improvements in security in Casamance, progress in resolving the conflict as such has proved elusive. The most recent accord between elements of the *MFDC* and the Senegalese government was signed in December 2004, although peace talks arising from this stalled the following year (Evans and Perfect, this volume). Only piecemeal contacts between the government, in the person of then President Abdoulaye Wade or his various emissaries, and self-appointed interlocutors for particular *MFDC* factions continued. Some aid workers in Casamance therefore refer to the accord as no more than another ceasefire, following others in the 1990s, and it has evidently failed even in those terms. Sporadic violence continues at time of writing. Macky Sall, elected as President in March 2012, has launched new initiatives in the peace process but their success or otherwise remains to be seen.

The grounds on which the *MFDC* demands independence for Casamance are of central concern to the argument of the chapter. These grounds include poor governance from Dakar, purported deliberate under-development of Casamance, and its cultural differences from the rest of Senegal. But most importantly, the *MFDC* and associated separatist thinkers have adopted a profoundly historical approach to their demand, particularly through the much-disputed claim that Casamance had full political autonomy during colonial times. The *MFDC* has also more or less consistently framed its struggle as a nationalist one, presenting itself and its secessionist project as representing all peoples in the ethnically diverse space of Casamance. The realities of such claims, both in their historiographic base and their current manifestations, are problematic. The purpose here, then, is not to discuss the actual roots of Casamance separatism itself – this has been ably done by other authors (Marut, 2010; Foucher, 2002, Barbier-Wiesser, 1994; Roche, 1985) – but how particular historiographies are used to justify or challenge that political position.

The chapter is based on field research conducted by the author since 2000, and on a range of secondary sources. It starts by considering the ways in which the politics of the conflict have become historicised over the past three decades or so, and the consequences for politicians and commentators (including academics and journalists) drawn into these dynamics in various ways. The chapter then considers a case, from an area of Middle Casamance bordering Guinea-Bissau, in which local understandings apparently diverge from the narratives of the main actors on both sides of the conflict. This reveals how the histories and indeed daily concerns of local people may be neglected and marginalised by more dominant, if contested, discourses.

The Deployment of History in the Casamance Conflict

A historical register has been evident in much of the *MFDC*'s nationalist rhetoric from the beginning (Marut, 2010, pp. 33–34). A separatist tract entitled *La voix de la Casamance* is typical. As presented in an academic journal (Darbon, 1985), it comprises around seven pages of historical (pre-independence) argument before a shorter section (five pages) on contemporary grievances, even then with some reference to colonial history. Such a pattern has reproduced itself in other *MFDC* outputs, as shown later. One personage – the late Catholic priest Abbé (Father) Augustin Diamacoune Senghor, who became the long-time symbolic leader of the *MFDC* up until his death in 2007 – was crucial in producing and inspiring such historically inflected discourse. Abbé Diamacoune (as he was popularly known) became prominent in advocating Casamance independence from 1980 onwards. He was arrested after the first separatist march in Ziguinchor in 1982 and spent five years in prison. Arrested again in 1990, he then spent much of the rest of his life under Senegalese official guard and surveillance in the Catholic compound in Ziguinchor, although he received visiting politicians and researchers (the author included) and was allowed to attend peace talks in the city and elsewhere. Those who met him or read his works were commonly struck by his encyclopaedic knowledge of Casamance history. Questions to him, even on very contemporary matters (including the violence of the conflict), were usually answered with a historical anecdote. Politically, however, he seemed naïve and various observers felt that he and his name were manipulated by more unscrupulous operators within the *MFDC*, particularly in his later years.

It is worth considering, too, how historical discourse has been transmitted within the *MFDC*, particularly from thinkers like Abbé to the rank-and-file of the *maquis*. In the early 1980s, before and after the outbreak of the rebellion, senior activists held "awareness meetings" where they explained the grounds for claiming independence, especially those rooted in the *MFDC*'s colonial historiography. One *maquisard* interviewed explained how "[t]hey made us understand that we weren't the same [as the rest of Senegal] because we had our autonomy" (Evans, 2004, p. 7). Accounts of such meetings have been heard in discussions with other *MFDC* members, and by other researchers (Foucher, 2007, pp. 174–176). There has, then, been an "oral tradition" through which such discourse has spread, although the various tracts and polemics produced by separatists have undoubtedly been influential, too. For example, in one MFDC refuge – a quarter of São Domingos in Guinea-Bissau where members of the *maquis* live and work with their families when not on operations – the author has witnessed Abbé Diamacoune's *Casamance, Land of Denial* (discussed later) being read and quoted by *maquisards*, some fourteen years after its production. The written word remains important.

The relationship and at times iterations between academic research and separatist discourse are also worth exploring. From the outset, the long-standing adherence to and respect for schooling and scholarship among the Jola should be noted (Foucher, 2002, pp. 380–393). Abbé Diamacoune's reputation as a "historian" was, as Marut (2010, p. 33) perceptively notes, based largely on his memory for dates, a legacy of older-style education by rote-learning. More generally, Diamacoune's and the *MFDC*'s "scholar-ship" was based not on original research but mainly derived from histories, particularly of the colonial period, written by French and other academics, with whom he was sometimes in dialogue; indeed he is acknowledged in some of their works. While such academics have been rigorous and impartial in their research, a certain iteration in tone is still sometimes evident between the way their work is presented and the language of the rebellion. Titles such as *Under-standing Casamance: A Chronicle of Contrasting Integration*[5] (Barbier-Wiesser, 1994) and *History of Casamance: Conquest and Resistance, 1850–1920*[6] (Roche, 1985) speak, however subtly, to a view of the region as "apart" and downtrodden but at the same time feisty in the face of its troubled fate. In turn, a historicised notion of "resistance" is frequently reproduced in separatist discourse: for example, newsletters produced by *MFDC* activists in the diaspora see Casamance as enduring centuries of struggle against Portuguese, French and now Senegalese colonisers (*MFDC*, 1994, pp. 3, 8; *MFDC*, 1999, p. 6). Furthermore, points made by French academics are sometimes quoted in discussion by separatists in arguing their case, even when they come from researchers whose work clearly does not support them (notably geographer Jean-Claude Marut). Such selectivity of evidence and interpretation is seen even in rather better examples of separatist thinking, such as the recent book *Casamance: Essay on the Tumultuous Destiny of a Region*[7] – a title echoing the tone noted above – by a Casamançais (Diatta), returned to later.

In the Senegalese political sphere, the rhetoric on both sides escalated once the rebellion had become a full-blown insurgency in 1990 and government forces were deployed in response. The government of then President Abdou Diouf produced a document the following year, effectively a counter-polemic to the *MFDC*'s claims, called *The Facts in Casamance: The Law Versus Violence*[8] (République du Sénégal, 1991). While primarily an appeal to pluralism, national unity and the rule of law, as well as a vigorous condemnation of *MFDC* "terrorism" (République du Sénégal, 1991, p. 18), this document is notable for how few historical references it contains. Indeed, it appears to seek to break rather than establish such connections. It only refers to the colonial period in pointing out the gap in time, politics and methods between the original *MFDC* – a regionalist political party, formed in 1947 but subsequently absorbed into the *Bloc démocratique sénégalais* of Léopold Sédar Senghor, later the first President of independent Senegal – and the current, separatist *MFDC*, which took its name (République du Sénégal, 1991, p. 19; this lack of connection with the original *MFDC* and other regionalist projects of the colonial period is affirmed at length by Marut, 2010, pp. 69–76). It reproduces, as an annex, one of the first separatist tracts (République du Sénégal, 1991, pp. 33–35), which is predictably rich in references to colonial history, but makes no comment on these historical claims. Overall, then, *The Facts in Casamance* stays largely on contemporary political and legal ground.

The Senegalese government was, however, soon to move publicly on to historiographic terrain in what remains the most important war of words in the Casamance conflict, with consequences to this day. The historical debate outlined above was being explored by Senegalese nationalists (intellectuals and politicians) who, seeing its potential value in discrediting the separatist project, encouraged Abbé Diamacoune to pursue the matter with the French (Foucher, 2011, p. 95). In 1993, following previous letters that he had written to successive French governments, Abbé Diamacoune wrote again to the then President of France, François Mitterrand, requesting arbitration between Senegal and Casamance (which Diamacoune viewed as separate entities). The French Ambassador to Senegal replied on Mitterand's behalf, agreeing not to arbitration but to engaging an "independent expert" to conduct "a historical study" on the hotly disputed issue of the status of Casamance under French colonial rule (Diatta, 2008, p. 192). A key issue was whether Casamance was administered separately once it started to fall under formal French control in 1886 as part of the settlements reached around the Berlin Conference (see Perfect and Evans, this volume, for a full account of that process). This is critical to the separatists' claim: Casamance only ended up as part of independent Senegal, they contend, through administrative sleight-of-hand by the French, which effectively replaced one colonial power in the region (France) with another (Senegal). A French archivist was chosen to produce this study:[9] Jacques Charpy, who had been keeper of the French West Africa collection in the Senegalese National Archives. Charpy's study found no evidence for the *MFDC*'s claim, nor have subsequent attempts by other French scholars (Marut, 2010). All that they have found, disputably, is a certain degree of *de facto* administrative separation and sometimes ambiguously worded official views of Casamance's status, perhaps inevitable given a territory (Senegal) effectively split in two by the British colony of the Gambia.

The separatists, enraged by the lack of support for their cause in Charpy's study, continue to seize on such ambiguities in the facts and in language used by the colonisers. Even Charpy's work was entitled, unhelpfully in retrospect, *Casamance and Senegal at the Time of French Colonisation;*[10] the "and" alone has been grist to the separatist mill. In 1995, Abbé Diamacoune produced a point-by-point refutation of Charpy's document, called – yet again in provocative language – *Casamance, Land of Denial: Reply to Mr Jacques Charpy.*[11] Some of these points were reproduced in another letter from Diamacoune to another French President (Jacques Chirac)[12] in 2000 (*MFDC*, 2000). The letter comprises nearly nine pages of historical argument underlining, in its interpretation, the right of the Casamance claim to independence. It then requests that the French government should, in essence, recognise Casamance independence and take responsibility for ending Senegalese "aggression" and "recolonisation" (*MFDC*, 2000, p. 9). While other parts of this letter may reasonably be regarded as pedantry (it includes fine-grained readings of what were probably no more than unthinking comments made by colonial administrators), it points again to a constant search for ambiguity in Casamance's historical status into which the separatists seek to insert their own claims. This unrelenting thirst for historical evidence has also been apparent in various interviews that the author has conducted with separatists over the years.

In this context and despite Senegal's strong democratic tradition, the efforts of President Wade, who succeeded Diouf in March 2000, in trying to master the conflict at times focused on historical scholarship. This was done within a broader attempt to control, contain and suppress information about Casamance and events there (Evans, 2002). Wade's sensitivities were made clear at an early stage when, in the run-up to new peace talks in late 2000, he had two journalists of the independent Dakar daily newspaper *Le Populaire* held for several days for publishing a three-part commentary on the origins and history of the Casamance conflict (*Le Populaire*, 12, 13 et 14 décembre 2000). The piece was based purely on published work and information from Senegal's National Archives, and not perceptibly partisan or polemical. Subsequently, in 2009, Wade banned for a while the import into Senegal of the book, mentioned above, by Casamançais teacher and journalist Oumar Diatta, published in France and again largely derivative. While clearly separatist in his argument and reflecting the particular historiographic tradition of Abbé Diamacoune, Diatta is as scathing about the *MFDC* as he is about the Senegalese government's conduct in Casamance. Jean-Claude Marut's book *The Conflict in Casamance: What the Arms Say*[13] was, perhaps even more strangely given its dryly critical tone towards separatist discourse, also banned in Senegal by Wade in October 2010 despite vigorous denunciations of this action by human rights groups (Seneweb).

Such repressive measures aside, a more critical look is needed at the *MFDC*'s search for historical legitimacy. Following Anderson's logic, what is being forgotten in this search is that colonialism was never a precise science. This was perhaps particularly true in West Africa, within the logic of Indirect Rule and where white settlement and presence were small; and even more so in the case of a peripheral, border area such as Casamance, away from the centres of power in northern Senegal. The messy administrative arrangements and ill-defined borders of colonialism have haunted many African countries since independence. It is surprising that, among historians (real and *manqué*), anyone should think otherwise; a definitive, historical answer to the "Casamance question" will probably never be found because it seems very unlikely that it could exist.

The *MFDC*'s discourse may have been unhelpful even for its own cause. Its claims echo those made by groups elsewhere in Africa, notably those of Anglophone separatists in western Cameroon, who are similarly exercised by the constitutional arrangements around the transition from colonial rule to independence (Konings and Nyamnjoh, 2003). The extent to which historical arguments have, and continue to be, taken in Casamance is extreme, however. Such an approach in the *MFDC*'s rhetoric has tended to overwhelm discussion of the contemporary political issues that are (or would be) relevant to the majority of the Casamance population, whose youthful demographic means that most have been born since the start of the rebellion, let alone since independence in 1960.[14] This has arguably allowed successive Senegalese governments more strength in determining the terms of debate and action in Casamance. Wade, particularly, had some success in reducing the international profile of the conflict (Evans, 2002) and operated what many perceived as a divide-and-rule policy towards the *MFDC*, using development goods as a means to try to buy off separatist elements and conflating reconstruction with sustainable peace (Evans and Ray, 2013). While this badly backfired in the context of a moribund (from 2005 until 2012) peace process, fomenting more violence at times and particularly in northern Lower Casamance, Wade succeeded in keeping any meaningful political arguments off the table. Stuck in its historiographic obsessions, meanwhile, the *MFDC* has often only been able to make itself heard through further attacks on military targets and armed robberies of civilians.

The *MFDC* has anyway failed, since the beginning of the rebellion, to articulate coherently a viable political project (Evans, 2004, p. 13; Hughes, 2004, p. 860). Comparisons may again be drawn with other insurgencies in West Africa that, while seeking some historiographic underpinning to their actions, still advocated a political programme of sorts. The Revolutionary United Front's *Footpaths to Democracy: Towards a New Sierra Leone*, inspired in turn by the late Colonel Gaddafi's *Green Book* (Richards, 1996, pp. 52–55) is one example. It is telling that no such equivalent exists for the *MFDC*. Instead, the separatists' political canon consists largely of the historically argued tracts and polemics identified. The legacy of Abbé Diamacoune remains strong even since his death, from natural causes at the age of seventy-eight, in early 2007. Somewhat ironically given his misplaced belief that France was the final recourse and could right historical wrongs, he passed away, his demands unfulfilled, in a French military hospital in Paris. His influence is still evident in the separatists' historiographic arguments and, under Wade, it was mirrored in the

Senegalese government's increasingly heavy-handed attempts to control what it regarded as dangerous scholarship on the region. Yet despite the hold that separatist historical discourse still holds over those professing a whole-Casamance nationalism, it is clear that other Casamançais have quite different narratives about the conflict, to which the chapter now turns.

Forgotten narratives
To understand further what is being forgotten by the separatists, it is first necessary to highlight what is still actively remembered. From 1963 to 1974, then Portuguese Guinea, immediately south of Casamance, fought its ultimately successful "Liberation War" against Portuguese colonial rule. Then President Senghor of Senegal refused to allow the *PAIGC* (*Partido Africano da Independência da Guiné e Cabo Verde*, the party of liberation) to have military rear bases in Casamance but did, after a time, allow non-military bases there, including a hospital in Ziguinchor (Chabal, 1983, pp. 84, 119). In reality, however, the porous border meant that Guinean combatants could cross into Casamance. The Portuguese in turn did not respect Senegal's attempts to distance itself from the Liberation War, famously bombing Sédhiou (the principal town of Middle Casamance) and other parts of Casamance on occasion. Beside broader sympathies in Guinea-Bissau for the Casamance rebellion, which have allowed the *MFDC* to establish rear bases and get material support there, the *MFDC* has itself at times invoked historical claims of reciprocity across the border. Casamance supported Guinea-Bissau in achieving independence, it argues, so Guinea-Bissau should now support Casamance in its own struggle against Senegalese colonialism.

In late 2000, however, in the wake of political changes within Guinea-Bissau, the country's formal political and military position with respect to the *MFDC* changed. An early manifestation of this was an attack on hardline *maquis* elements by Bissau-Guinean forces, in conjunction with *maquis* moderates and with Senegalese material support, from late December 2000 into early January 2001 (Evans, 2004, p. 5). The attack included the seizure of weaponry formerly given to the hard-liners by other elements of the Bissau-Guinean military in reward for *maquis* support for a successful coup staged against then President Nino Vieira in 1998–1999, in which forces from Senegal and Guinea-Conakry came in to try to bolster Vieira's position. The civil war in Guinea-Bissau thus became in part a proxy war for the Casamance conflict, with the *MFDC* and Senegalese forces fighting each other on the streets of Bissau.

In response to the attack on his positions in 2000–2001, hardline *maquis* commander Salif Sadio wrote to the President of the Bissau-Guinean Parliament in January 2001 "to make Guinea-Bissau face up to its responsibilities".[15] As well as the formal, corrective tone of the letter (from, it should be noted, a guerrilla leader acting outside national and international law[16] writing to the institution of a sovereign state), the letter is intriguing in its recourse to historical reciprocity:

> God knows well that CASAMANCE has counted its dead to save Guinea-Bissau during the Liberation War against the Portuguese colonisers and during the attempted recolonisation of Guinea-Bissau by the intervening armies of Senegal and Guinea-Conakry. It's very important to remind the brotherly people of

Guinea-Bissau of that (*MFDC*, 2001; emphasis in original).[17]

Not everyone in Casamance would see the matter in terms of betrayed brotherly unity, however. Casamance is a large (comprising one-seventh of the land area of Senegal) and diverse space. Only a few tens of kilometres upstream from Ziguinchor, in Lower Casamance – the epicentre of the rebellion – lies the Balantacounda, an area of Middle Casamance between the south bank of the Casamance River and the Guinea-Bissau border. The Balantacounda has sometimes been significantly affected by the Casamance conflict, notably in *MFDC* attacks including an infamous massacre of civilians at a dance in Djibanar in 1997 (Evans, 2004, pp. 9–10), and it has suffered significant internal displacement as a result.[18] At the same time, though, the area has remained relatively marginal in the politics of the conflict and indeed has not benefited to nearly the same extent from influxes of donor aid for "post-conflict" return and reconstruction as parts of Lower Casamance. Indeed, this has been part of the instrumentalisation of administrative space by the Senegalese government during the conflict: in 1984, the Diouf government divided Casamance region into Ziguinchor region to the west (Lower Casamance) and the much larger Kolda region to the east (Middle and Upper Casamance). This is still widely viewed as an attempt to isolate discursively the Casamance rebellion as a Lower Casamance (and more specifically, as shown below, ethnic Jola) problem; and to help forestall claims to a whole-Casamance nationalism by taking the name of the region off the administrative map. Greater recognition of Middle Casamance only came recently when, in 2008, it became a region (Sédhiou) in its own right and the Balantacounda effectively became a department (Goudomp) within it.

In contrast with the displacement situation in Lower Casamance (Evans, 2007), villagers interviewed in the Balantacounda situate their experiences of the violence of the Casamance conflict *proprement dit* in a deeper history of insecurity, dating back to the Liberation War in neighbouring Guinea-Bissau, particularly during the late 1960s when the War was at its height. It was at that time, they say, that cross-border cattle raids really began, when guerrillas of the *PAIGC* and other elements fighting in Guinea-Bissau came in search of cattle. This may have been driven in part by genuine need caused by the deliberate Portuguese strategy of undermining food production, including the destruction of agricultural infrastructure, in *PAIGC*-held areas (Galli and Jones, 1987, p. 111). Whatever the case, the cattle raids caused fear and displacement among people in the Balantacounda. The Senegalese government was forced to act and, local people recall, deployed troops in the area to repel such raiders. Cattle-raiding has continued at times since then, undertaken by the *MFDC* and other elements acting along the border, often opportunists operating under the cover of the conflict. The Balantacounda therefore remains visibly depleted of cattle compared with claims of vast herds in the past, the result – as local people see it – of a history of intermittent cattle-raiding and other violence spanning four decades or so, from the Liberation War to the present.

Clearly, people in the Balantacounda are not alone among Casamançais, particularly those living in the border zone, in regarding the *MFDC* as a threat and in resenting the support that the *maquis* has sometimes received in Guinea-Bissau (Evans, 2009). What is particularly telling here, however, is the way in which the standard narrative of the

MFDC vis-à-vis the Liberation War – of Casamance and Guinea-Bissau united in their respective historical struggles against colonial oppression – is turned on its head in the folk memory of ordinary people. The *MFDC* talks of Casamance suffering at the hands of the Portuguese, while forgetting or ignoring what people on the ground remember: their suffering at the hands of the *PAIGC*, against whom the Senegalese army had to protect them.

Research elsewhere in Casamance has similarly pointed to the importance of local histories in informing understandings of the rebellion. Working in part of the Gambian border area, Nugent (2007, p. 221) argues that historical experiences of violence among some ethnic sub-groups (including Jola groups), dating back to the nineteenth century, leave them largely uninterested in the Casamance nationalist project; like people in the Balantacounda, most would prefer to be left out of the whole affair. A similar situation is found among the majority of the Jola of Oussouye, who again do not support the rebellion and indeed are similarly alienated from the Senegalese state (Tomàs, 2005). The *MFDC* has not respected such stands, however, and has at times inflicted reprisals on Casamance villages, Jola and otherwise, for not supporting the separatist cause; the Djibanar massacre is a case in point.

In sum, local history may be quite different from that constructed by the separatists, which in turn rests, again, on a particular historiography – in the case of Guinea-Bissau, one that seeks to justify claims on a cross-border historical reciprocity. The *MFDC* is actively forgetting what does not neatly fit into its historical narrative and the political claims that this underpins. The final aspect of this dynamic, now considered, is the ethnic dimension of Casamance nationalism.

"The Part for the Whole"?[19] Ethnic Versus Nationalist Historiographies

Marut perceptively points out that one key problematic in analysing the Casamance conflict is the conflation of the part (Lower Casamance, with its Jola majority) with the whole (Casamance as a diverse, multi-ethnic space) in the discourse of various parties. While the rebellion cannot be simplified into an "ethnic conflict", and certainly not what President Diouf famously dismissed as "a Jola affair"[20] (de Jong, 1998, np), from an early stage the *MFDC*'s predominantly Jola concerns have been evident to observers (Darbon, 1985). The *MFDC* has always struggled to reconcile its strongly Jola roots and evident Jola predominance among its membership with its claim to represent all Casamançais (Lambert, 1998), even if a few members of other ethnic groups are involved.

Discussion of the role of historiographies in the conflict can also be viewed through this lens. The outlook of Abbé Diamacoune, and of some other separatists that the author has interviewed, was particularly Jola, and his polemic *Casamance, Land of Denial* is framed around a Jola historio-graphy and Jola society. This is in spite of the lack of much sense of Jola identity (let alone nationhood) existing until well into the twentieth century (Foucher, 2002, pp. 402–404; Hughes, 2004, pp. 858–859); the Jola remain a heterogeneous grouping. Among the problems that this creates is the lack of rapport between the Casamance (Jola) separatist project and the majority of the Casamance population that are not Jola, or indeed the greater part of the territory (Middle and Upper Casamance) where other groups predominate. It is un-surprising that these groups, with different relationships with the political economy of the Senegalese state and with different sets of transnational loyalties – particularly the other two main ethnicities present, the Mandinka and the

Peulh (Fulani) – have not bought into the rebellion, nor have some Jola sub-groups, as noted. Grassroots understandings such as those seen in the Balantacounda among mixed Mandinka, Peulh, Balanta and other communities, and in the Gambia border area among Mandinka and some Jola sub-groups (Nugent, 2007, p. 243) or in Oussouye, again among the Jola there (Tomàs, 2005, p. 414), are further manifestations of such diversity and difference. The complexity of the picture is further illustrated by the appropriation of a historical figure, a Jola spiritual leader of the 1940s – Aline Sitoe Diatta – as an anti-colonial resistance heroine by both Senegalese and Casamance nationalists (Toliver-Diallo, 2005, p. 339).

Like most groups with a radical political project, the *MFDC* fails to realise that self-determination means allowing people their own histories. The stated dislike among separatists of the new Sédhiou region (interviews, Ziguinchor: separatist thinker, 5 July 2009; members of *MFDC* political wing, 31 July 2009) may stem, in part, from their view of it as further "Balkanisation" of Casamance following its original division in 1984. But a subtext to this objection may also be that the new Sédhiou region could move the centre of Casamance gravity away from Ziguinchor region and the Jola heartlands of the rebellion, bringing forth different historiographies of Casamance from those promulgated by the *MFDC*. Indeed, it is the stated hope of one of the political architects of the new region (interview, Ziguinchor, 18 July 2010) that a revitalised Middle Casamance will act as a new pole of political and cultural activity and help glue the wider region together, not as part of a separatist project but within a more integrated Senegalese nation-state. He also points towards Sédhiou town's former, if short-lived, saliency in Casamance, of which it was briefly the colonial "capital" from 1894 to 1909. The harsh reality for the *MFDC* may be that what it claims to represent – a whole-Casamance, multi-ethnic project – is actually what it would most fear, since most of the population possess neither the historio-graphic understandings of, nor interest in, independence.

Conclusion

The chapter shows complex relationships between history, memory and territory that are, as Anderson observes, common in the construction and contestation of nationalism. It is worth adding that for all their ethnic and local inflections, the cases cited here still revolve, at least ostensibly and to some extent, around nationalisms: whether in the spurious construction of shared histories; claims to reciprocity of support for national independence; or in the local defence of national territory. In a continent where nation-building is identified as a central problematic in post-colonial history, and borders as arbitrary impositions cutting across social realities, nations still matter and the borders between them, however porous, are still invoked as defensive spaces. But deeper analysis of such discourse here supports more familiar, long-standing problematics in African Studies: the complex articulations between ethnic and national identities; and the marginalisation of the majority, par-ticularly in rural areas. In this case, it is instead largely the historical claims of the *MFDC* (censorship notwithstanding) and rebuttals of it that get aired nationally and, occasionally, at international level; not the histories of ordinary, rural people. It is difficult to see how both sides can now extricate themselves from the impasse in the political present that is partly the result of three decades of unhelpful historiographic arguments.

Notes
1. The author thanks the many Casamançais who helped during the fieldwork on which some of the chapter is based, notably Oumar Badiane, his research assistant, and various members of the *MFDC* political wing and *maquis* who have given generously of their time, thoughts and official documents over the years. Research in Middle Casamance and on the administrative changes there was made possible by a British Academy Small Research Grant, which is gratefully acknowledged. Thanks also go to Vincent Foucher, David Perfect and an anonymous reviewer for reading earlier drafts of the chapter and making many useful comments.
2. « *L'histoire nous donnera raison.* »
3. « *Or l'essence d'une nation est que tous les individus aient beaucoup de choses en commun, et aussi que tous aient oublié beaucoup de choses.* »
4. The most recent official figures available record Jola as comprising some 60% of the population of Ziguinchor region, i.e. Lower Casamance (République du Sénégal, 2005, p. 8). This is the only one of the three regions of Casamance in which the Jola reach a double-figure percentage.
5. *Comprendre la Casamance : chronique d'une intégration contrastée.*
6. *Histoire de la Casamance : conquête et résistance : 1850–1920.*
7. *La Casamance : essai sur le destin tumultueux d'une région.*
8. *Les faits en Casamance : le droit contre la violence.*
9. The French « *témoignage* » – evidence or testimony – is generally used by the *MFDC* when discussing this study. The legal tone of terms like arbitration and evidence sits within the separatists' view that the incorporation of Casamance into Senegal at independence was unlawful.

10. *Casamance et Sénégal au temps de la colonisation française.*
11. *La Casamance, pays de refus : réponse à Monsieur Jacques Charpy.*
12. The letter was copied to the French Prime Minister and Presidents of the National Assembly and Senate, as well as the Secretary General of the UN, the President of the UN Security Council, the Secretary General of the Organisation of African Unity (by then formally the African Union (AU)), and the Secretary General of Amnesty International. To the author's knowledge, from interviews the following year with members of the *MFDC* editorial committee (*comité de rédaction*) who helped to draft the letter, none of the recipients ever replied.
13. *Le conflit en Casamance : ce que disent les armes.*
14. For example, in common with trends across much of sub-Saharan Africa, some 47% of the population of Ziguinchor region is less than fifteen years old (République du Sénégal, 2005, p. 6).
15. « … *pour mettre la Guinée-Bissau devant ses responsabilités*».
16. Among other points it may be noted here that, as a member of the African Union – one of whose objectives is to "defend the sovereignty, territorial integrity and independence of its Member States" (African Union, 2000, p. 5) – Guinea-Bissau is quite correct to remove armed non-state actors seeking secession in a region of a neighbouring state.
17. « *Dieu sait bien que, la CASAMANCE a compté ses morts pour sauver la Guinée-Bissau pendant la guerre de libération contre les colons portugais et, pendant la tentative de recolonisation de la Guinée-Bissau, par les armées du Sénégal*

et de Guinée Conakry interposées. C'est très important de le rappeler au Peuple Frère de Guinée-Bissau. »

18. Figures indicate that some 30% of the total displacement caused by the Casamance conflict – perhaps about 18,000 people – has happened in Middle Casamance, and the great majority of that must have been in the Balantacounda and neighbouring areas along the Guinea-Bissau border (Evans, 2007).

19. *« … la partie pour le tout »* (Marut, 2010, p. 62).

20. *« une affaire diola ».*

References

African Union. (2000). *Constitutive Act of the African Union adopted by the Thirty-Sixth Ordinary Session of the Assembly of Heads of State and Government*, 11 July, Lomé, Togo.

Anderson, B. (1991). *Imagined communities*, revised ed. London: Verso.

Barbier-Wiesser, F.-G. (1994). *Comprendre la Casamance : chronique d'une intégration contrastée*. Paris: Karthala.

Chabal, P. (1983). *Amílcar Cabral: Revolutionary leadership and people's war*. Cambridge: Cambridge University Press.

Darbon, D. (1985). « La voix de la Casamance » … une parole diola, *Politique Africaine, 18*, 125–138.

de Jong, F. (1998). *The Casamance Conflict in Senegal*. The Hague: Netherlands Institute for International Relations.

Diatta, O. (2008). *La Casamance : essai sur le destin tumultueux d'une région*. Paris: L'Harmattan.

Ellis, S. (2001). Les guerres en Afrique de l'Ouest : le poids de l'histoire, *Afrique contemporaine, 198*, 51–56.

Evans, M. (2002). The Casamance Conflict: Out of sight, out of mind?, *Humanitarian Exchange 20*, 5–7.

Evans, M. (2004). *Senegal: Mouvement des forces démocratiques de la Casamance (MFDC)*. Africa Programme Armed Non-

State Actors Project Briefing Paper, 2. London: Chatham House.

Evans, M. (2007). "The suffering is too great": Urban internally displaced persons in the Casamance Conflict, Senegal, *Journal of Refugee Studies*, 20(1), 60–85.

Evans, M. (2009). Flexibility in return, reconstruction and livelihoods in displaced villages in Casamance, Senegal, *GeoJournal*, 74(6), 507–524.

Evans, M., & Ray, C. (2013). Uncertain ground: The Gambia and the Casamance conflict. In A. Saine, E. Ceesay & E. Sall (Eds.), *State and society in The Gambia since independence 1965–2012* (pp. 247–287). Trenton, NJ: Africa World Press.

Foucher, V. (2002). Les « évolués », la migration, l'école : pour une nouvelle interprétation de la naissance du nationalisme casamançais. In M.-C. Diop (Ed.), *Le Sénégal contemporain* (pp. 375–424). Paris: Karthala.

Foucher, V. (2007). Senegal: The resilient weakness of Casamançais separatists. In M. Bøås & K. C. Dunn (Eds.), *African guerrillas: Raging against the machine* (pp. 171–197) Boulder, CO: Lynne Rienner.

Foucher, V. (2011). On the matter (and materiality) of the nation: Interpreting Casamance's unresolved separatist struggle, *Studies in Ethnicity and Nationalism*, 11(1), 82–103.

Galli, R. E., & Jones, J. (1987). *Guinea-Bissau: Politics, economics and society*. London: Frances Pinter.

Hughes, A. (2004). Decolonizing Africa: Colonial boundaries and the crisis of the (non) nation state, *Diplomacy and Statecraft*, 15(4), 833–866.

Konings, P., & Nyamnjoh, F. B. (2003). *Negotiating an Anglophone identity: A study of the politics of recognition and representation in Cameroon*. Leiden: Brill.

Lambert, M. C. (1998). Violence and the war of words: Ethnicity *v.* nationalism in the Casamance, *Africa*, *68*(4), 585–602.

Le Populaire. (2000). Commentaires, 12, 13 et 14 Décembre.

Marut, J.-C. (2010) *Le conflit de Casamance : ce que disent les armes*. Paris: Karthala.

MFDC. (1994). *La voix de la Casamance*.

MFDC. (1999). *Casamance Kunda : La voie de la liberté*, novembre-décembre.

MFDC. (2000). Letter from the Secretary-General to His Excellency the President of the French Republic, 15 November.

MFDC. (2001). Letter from Salif Sadio to the President of the Republic of Guinea-Bissau, 3 January.

Nugent, P. (2007). Cyclical history in the Gambia/Casamance borderlands: Refuge, settlement and Islam from *c.*1880 to the present, *Journal of African History*, *47*(2), 221–243.

République du Sénégal. (1991). *Les faits en Casamance : le droit contre la violence*. Dakar: République du Sénégal.

République du Sénégal. (2005). *Situation économique et sociale régionale*. Ziguinchor: Service Régionale de la Statistique et de la Démographie de Ziguinchor.

Richards, P. (1996). *Fighting for the rain forest: War, youth and resources in Sierra Leone*. Oxford: James Currey in association with International African Institute.

Roche, C. (1985). *Histoire de la Casamance : conquête et résistance : 1850–1920*. Paris: Karthala.

Seneweb. (2010). Interdiction d'un livre sur la Casamance : la Raddho et Amnesty international dénoncent, *Senewebnews*, 14 October, http://www. seneweb.com/ news/Societe/ interdiction-d-un-livre-sur-la-casamance-la-raddho-et-amnesty-international-d-noncent_n_36292 .html.

Toliver-Diallo, W. J. (2005). "The woman who was more than a man": Making Aline Sitoe Diatta into a national heroine in Senegal, *Canadian Journal of African Studies*, 39(2), 338–360.

Tomàs, J. (2005). « La parole de paix n'a jamais tort. » La paix et la tradition dans le Royaume d'Oussouye (Casamance, Sénégal), *Canadian Journal of African Studies*, 39(2), 414–441.

CHAPTER 4

TIES THAT BIND AND TIES THAT DON'T: FRANCE'S ROLE IN THE COMOROS ARCHIPELAGO

Simon Massey

Although football is the most popular sport on the Comoros archipelago, the national team known as the Coelacanths, has enjoyed only limited success since its creation in 1979. This goes some way towards explaining the reaction of Comorian football supporters to France's victory in the 1998 World Cup final when, at the final whistle, thousands spilled on to the streets to proclaim "we won ... we won". The co-option of a "foreign" football team betrays the ambiguous and equivocal relationship between the populations of the Comoros islands and the former colonial power. Most conversations with Comorians touch upon the migration issue – the fact that the majority are unable to obtain a visa to visit relatives and friends or conduct business on one of the four islands of the archipelago since that island is a *de facto* part of the French Republic and France is notoriously mean in approving applications from Comorians to travel to its shores. Yet, many from the archipelago are still content to locate themselves psychologically within a wider *Francophonie*, escaping the parochialism of their small, isolated islands, retaining a certain reverence for French culture, the French language and, indeed, French football.

The Comoros archipelago lies about 300 kilometres off the northern coast of Mozambique and 350 kilometres north-west of Madagascar. It consists of four main volcanic islands: Ngazidja, more usually known by its French name Grande Comore, Nzwani (Anjouan), Mwali (Mohéli) and Maoré (Mayotte). The first three of these islands constitute the independent Union of the Comoros, whilst the last, Maoré

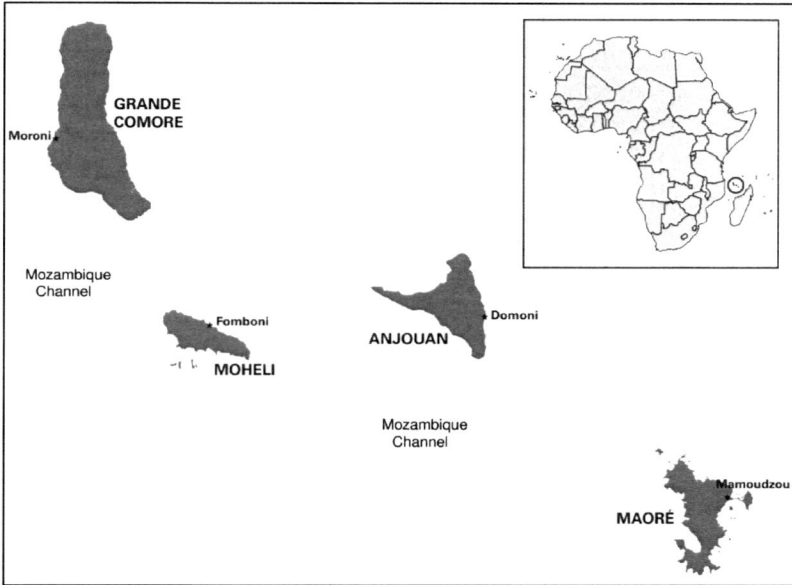

Fig. 2. Map of the Comoros islands.

has since 2011 been a full and intrinsic part of France. Located between the African mainland and Madagascar, the islands were valued for their strategic location by Arab and Portuguese merchants prior to Maoré being ceded to France in 1841, several decades before the three other islands acquired or accepted protectorate status. Comoros was established as a unified French colony in 1912. Although independence was achieved in 1975, the country has since struggled to realise political and economic viability. Though the current population of all four islands is about 966,000, up to 200,000 live abroad, with between 85,000 and 150,000 in metropolitan France (United Nations, 2011). Indeed, it is the remittances of this diaspora that provide the means for economic survival for the islanders today with the archipelago rated among the leading locations in the world in terms of remittances per capita (da la Cruz et al., 2004).

This chapter will investigate the relationship between France and the Comoros archipelago and the unequal impact of that relationship on the populations of the four islands. The role that French colonial culture played and continues to play in mitigating the absence of a cohesive Comorian nationalism is examined, alongside the neocolonial role France has played in stoking an already virulent rivalry between the islands. Finally, the separate and incongruent trajectories of the independent Union of the Comoros and French Maoré will be scrutinised to account for the deep social alienation that characterises life on Maoré.

A Comorian Nation?
The islands' original settlers probably arrived from Melano-Polynesia in the sixth century. Later settlement from Arabia, Europe, east Africa, Indonesia, Madagascar and Persia has contributed to a complex ethnic mix. Ngazidja and Maoré are separated by 150 miles of ocean, a geographical reality that has militated against strong cultural bonds between the peoples of the four islands. A unified nation in the eyes of the United Nations General Assembly, it is moot whether many Comorians recognise a distinct national identity.

There are, however, shared socio-cultural practices that have been maintained through inter-island migration, inter-marriage and shared kinship. Linguistically, Shikomoro is one of three national languages alongside French and Arabic. Each island has its own dialect, but the variants are mutually comprehensible. Yet, despite its official status as a language of the nation, the absence of an accepted orthography, as well as the use of both Latin and Arabic scripts and the pro-liferation of French as the language of instruction has, in the opinion of some, hobbled the development of Shikomoro as a *lingua franca*, undermining the language's capacity to foster a national identity (Ottenheimer, 2001).

In terms of religion, almost all Comorians adhere to the Shafi'i Sunni faith and religion provides an overarching sense of belonging, with influential Comorian clerics revered throughout the archipelago and beyond. Yet, though faith is a point of unity, Iain Walker argues that it exists as an expression of wider Islam rather than as a formalised, specific Comorian construct (Walker, 2007, p. 587). Other socio-cultural practices that could be held to inculcate a sense of identity between the islands include cooking, male and female dress, women's application of *msinzano* sandalwood paste, music and dancing. Yet, whilst the *aada* or *shungu* "grand marriage" ceremonies exist across the islands, the importance of these ceremonies in according social status varies considerably from island to island.

Walker argues that such socio-cultural homogeneity as exists does not coalesce beyond the sum of its parts into a formal "nation". Rather, he argues that there is an inhibition that has developed organically against formalised homo-geneity which accounts for the Comorian "enthusiasm for things French". In his view, the lack of a subjective sense of nationhood "explains the often exaggerated differences be-tween the islands ... these differences are exaggerated in a denial of the socio-cultural unity that would imply, or so it is feared, a homogenised space and the domination of one island over the others" (Walker, 2007, p. 600). It appears that the island nature of Comoros allows both proximity and distance; a sense of kinship and yet a determination to assert separation.

Chronic Political Instability

This national ambivalence has been reflected in a fraught and unstable political environment since independence. The country has experienced between nineteen and twenty-five successful or attempted coups, four of which (1975, 1978, 1989 and 1995) were organised by the notorious French mercenary Col. Bob Denard. The construction of a functioning state apparatus failed after the fall of the revolutionary socialist Ali Soilihi in 1978. Under Soilihi, and using brutal authoritarian methods, an attempt was made to "Comorianise" the state and foster a sense of national identity. Public meetings were conducted in Shikomoro and the civic registry was symbolically burnt. Having come to power with the help of Denard, his radicalism condemned him and he was ousted by the mercenary to be replaced by the puppet Ahmed Abdallah, who set about "de-Comorianising" the state, replacing the Comorian governance structures that Soilihi had established, such as the regional *mudiriya* administrative offices, with French structures such as *communes* and *préfectures* (Walker, 2007, p. 596). Abdallah also resurrected the French practice in the Comoros of Indirect Rule, restoring the state's relationship with customary elders. Under Abdallah and his successors Taki and Azali, access to the state became seen as a "privilege of status" (Walker, 2007, p. 597). Patronage crystallised and state resources were channelled from state funds via the customary elite to clients at village level. In Walker's words, "as state assets were appropriated by the elite and state symbols were commoditised, any formal sense of national identity came to be seen as impossible" (Walker, 2007, p. 597).

The key locus of instability, however, lay outside the Comorian political elite. The interventions by Denard, both a few weeks after the independence of the Union in 1975 to overthrow Abdallah and to return him to power 1978 but as a puppet president, ensured that Comoros at this time was compliant to the interests of France. When in 1989, Abdallah attempted to reassert authority, he was assassinated by Denard. It is widely accepted, although officially denied, that Denard's interventions in Comoros were sponsored by successive French governments (Renou, 2006). Whilst intrinsically peripheral to France's interests, Comoros did prove a useful conduit for the sale of French technology to *apartheid* South Africa. Yet, despite its marginality, the impulse to control remained. For Pierre Caminade, a member of *Survie*, an organisation that is highly critical of French African policy, France has sought to "sabotage" the three islands of the Union whilst "protecting" its interests in Maoré (Caminade, 2004).

Inter-Island Conflict
French rule on Maoré as an alternative political model to the Union sustained a persistent tension between the islands, prolonging instability and engendering secessionism. When resources are scarce in a small island state, inter-island disputes over the sharing of those resources are inevitable. In particular, the people of Nzwani have long felt marginalised by the Union government in Moroni, at once the Union capital and capital of the island of Ngazidja. The revised constitution of 1982 concentrated power at the centre and made the island governors nominees of the Union president. Moreover, revenue from Nzwani was managed by the Union government, even though Nzwani regarded itself as the island with the strongest economy. The grievances against the Union government were only exacerbated by the actions from 1996 of the corrupt and authoritarian Mohammed Taki.

His constitutional amendments further reinforced the primacy of the presidency; and the corruption he permitted so undermined the national economy that the salaries of public sector workers were ten months in arrears. The protests and general strike against the situation were brutally put down by Union government forces. The seeds of secessionism had been sown.

In August 1997, 7,000 protestors in Mutsumudu, the capital of Nzwani, tore down the Comorian flag and raised the French tricolour and the colours of the last independent sultan of Nzwani. They formally declared independence, set up their own government, the *Etat d'Anjouan*, and at the same time called for the island's "reattachment" to France (Alwahti, 2003; Cornwell, 1998). Two days later the scene was repeated in Fomboni, the capital of the island of Mwali, with separatists erecting barricades and raising the tricolour over the Palais du Justice.

To settle the dispute, the Organisation of African Unity (OAU) helped to negotiate the Antananarivo Agreement granting partial autonomy to the islands and a rotating presidency for the renamed federal Union of the Comoros. Union presidents would serve terms of four years: Ngazidja would provide the first Union president, followed by Nzwani and then Mwali. Yet though the agreement, was accepted by Ngazidja and Mwali, it was resisted by Nzwani. Its refusal sparked rioting in Moroni, and after three days of fighting, President Abbas Djoussouf was ousted by army commander Colonel Azali Assoumane, who declared himself president.

Meanwhile on Nzwani, the separatists won an election to the island assembly, albeit on a turnout of just 15%. As the new administration refused to move from its separatist position, the OAU began preparations for a military intervention. Subsequent negotiation produced the Fomboni Accord in 2000. It explicitly recognised that neither independence nor a renewed relationship with France were options. Instead it established a *communauté comorienne* with accepted borders and confirmed the previously agreed federal structure. Despite continued unrest, elections were conducted in April 2002 and on a turnout of 25%, Azali was elected Union president.

The constitutional changes did not address the almost intractable problem of meeting both the need for inter-island co-operation to ensure viability, and the need to recognise island differences and ensure freedom from domination by any other island. Symptomatic of the unresolved issues was the continued political unrest in Nzwani. The island's president, Mohamed Bacar, who received his *gendarme* training in France, maintained a harsh and personal rule and his re-election as island president in 2002 was only as a result of a flawed process. Though he remained uncooperative with the Union over the sharing of revenues between the islands, assembly and presidential elections nationwide continued without incident. The national and island assembly elections of 2004 resulted in parties opposed to President Azali dominating all three island assemblies and the National Assembly. For its part, the Union presidential elections of 2006 saw Nzwani–born Ahmed Abdallah Sambi elected to replace the retiring Azali. However, it was the island presidential elections of the following year that brought further trouble. The Union government intervened to postpone them in Nzwani, accusing the authorities there of serious irregularities and intimidation. Union President Sambi nominated an interim president of Nzwani to serve until elections could be held. Bacar, however, refused both to stand down as required by the Constitution or to cancel the elections. And even though the Union government sent armed forces to prevent him, Bacar's *gendarmerie* easily expelled them. He proceeded with the election and declared a landslide victory for himself.

The Union government responded by declaring the elections null and void, whilst the AU imposed a naval blockade and targeted sanctions on the political leadership of the Bacar regime. Unable to effectively enforce the sanctions, however, the AU agreed to requests from the Union government to prepare an intervention force. Despite South African opposition, four AU countries – Libya, Sudan, Senegal and Tanzania – promised troops and military support (Ghorbal, 2008). On 25 September 2008, AU and Comorian forces landed on Nzwani. The capital, Mutsumudu, was captured with only minimal resistance. Bacar fled to Maoré, where he was taken into custody alongside 23 supporters. Arrests were made on Nzwani of up to 100 persons suspected of committing criminal offences and human rights abuses, with 30 of the most serious cases being taken to Moroni.

Migrants from Nzwani living in Maoré rioted, furious at France having played what was widely believed to have been a double game, officially supporting the Union position whilst tacitly supporting Bacar's idiosyncratic, but pro-French, rule. According to the Comorian army commander on Nzwani, French forces were involved in covert activities prior to the intervention. He was sceptical about the official explanation that a French helicopter that crashed on 19 March 2008 was a police aircraft carrying immigration agents, assuming that the personnel involved were in fact "special forces". Likewise, he understood that the French navy intercepted, and rescued, Bacar mid-way between Nzwani and Maoré rather than Bacar making landfall.

Comorian government requests for Bacar's extradition were turned down by the French courts on the grounds that he faced a real risk of persecution in Comoros. A Comorian request that he should face charges at the International Criminal Court was also rejected by France. On 19 July 2008, Bacar was deported from Réunion to Cotonou in Benin where he has been granted conditional leave to stay. The unrest on Maoré was finally quelled by the deployment of 100 extra *gendarmes* from Réunion, a measure that the French authorities would be forced to repeat in subsequent years.

In the wake of the Nzwani rebellion, new constitutional arrangements to diminish the power of the island presidents, who would be renamed governors, and streamline island governance were passed by referendum. The referendum also approved an extension of Sambi's term in office, although fears that he intended to orchestrate a constitutional coup were proved false when he handed power to his elected successor, and ally, Ikililou Dhoinine, the first president from Mwali. If the peaceful transfer of power has prompted optimism in some quarters, the quality of life for most Comorians remains precarious and opportunities for betterment scant. In these circumstances the dream of reattachment to France will be difficult to extinguish completely, whilst the lure to migrate to the one island that remains French will remain strong.

A Country Divided

An independence campaign throughout the 1950s led to France granting internal autonomy to the four islands in 1961. France also shifted the administration of the islands from Maoré to Moroni, arguably to facilitate the eventual split of the islands into the independent Union of the Comoros and French-controlled Maoré. In 1974, France agreed to a referendum that produced a significant majority for independence. However, whilst the combined total of the votes from Ngazidja, Nzwani and Mwali was 96% for independence, on Maoré, which had been under French rule for longer than the other islands, 64% of those that participated in the poll voted against independence. When the leader of the independence movement, Ahmed Abdallah, declared unilateral independence on 6 July 1975, the French accepted the independence of the three islands, but reneged on the stated rules of the referendum to accept the decision of the archipelago's electorate as a whole, and opted to retain control of Maoré as a *collectivité territoriale*. In 2001, Maoré was recategorised as a *collectivité départementale* and in 2003 as a French overseas *collectivité*. Following a referendum in 2009, on 31 March 2011 the island became a full overseas department and region of France. The decision to encourage the people of Maoré, the Mahorais, to remain part of overseas France was based on France's enduring priorities in its dealings with its former colonies and overseas territories: status, strategic necessity and an abiding impulse to preserve its cultural legacy.

Political division and the subsequent unequal economic development, however, created tensions that persist. The UN General Assembly Resolution 31/4 (1976) condemned the presence of France on Maoré and called upon the international community to defend the sovereignty and territorial integrity of the Comorian state. There has been near unanimous support in the General Assembly and within Africa, most recently at the 2011 African Union Summit in Equatorial Guinea, for recognising Maoré as part of Comorian territory. In international law, therefore, Maoré is under French occupation. Understandably, Comorians cannot accept that travel without a visa to an island where many have relatives is "clandestine migration" or that the export of vegetables or fish to a potentially lucrative market is banned by European Union health and hygiene regulations. The disparate language of a press release from the Franco-Comorian High-Level Working Group reporting on the migration issue in 2007 is instructive. For the Union the key issue is the "circulation" of Comorian citizens between the four islands. For France, it is the curtailment of "clandestine" migration into French territory.

In 1995, the visa regime for inter-island circulation was tightened still further by France. The "Balladur-Pasqua visa", named after the French prime minister and interior minister at the time, makes it very difficult for ordinary Comorians to obtain travel documents to legally enter Maoré/France. Nevertheless, there are somewhere between 45,000 and 60,000 irregular migrants on Maoré. Indeed, these migrants are by far the most productive section of the population. Many arrive on small boats called *kwassa kwassa* named after the swaying Congolese dance rhythm that they mimic during the precarious crossing from Nzwani. Each year about 100 drown in the attempt, despite the French having increased patrols and built a radar station to detect *kwassa kwassa* entering its territorial waters (France only documents drownings that occur within its territory). France has also increased the repatriation of irregular migrants, deporting 24,000 illegal migrants in 2010 alone. This accounts for more than half of all deportations from France. The French government charters aircraft from commercial airlines to repatriate migrants to Nzwani. Officials from the Nzwani government recounted the story of a Mahorais from the countryside, arrested in the capital of Maoré, Mamoudzou, and summarily deported to Nzwani where he was forced to sleep rough and rely on handouts until he could persuade

French diplomats on the island that he had been deported in error. The conditions at Maoré's detention centre at Pamadzi have provoked an outcry, it is grossly overcrowded and its inmates are almost all irregular migrants, some of whom have passed through the system four or five times having been smuggled back to the island following deportation.

The chief pull-factor is economic. In 2008, the Comorian GDP per head was measured at €560 per capita, whilst in 2009, on Maoré GDP per head was €6,570 (*INSEE*, 2011). This disparity is not, however, reflected in a standard of living amongst local Mahorais and irregular migrants uniformly a great deal higher than on the islands of the Union. Income distribution is uneven with local Mahorais earning very much less than ethnic French residents. The many irregular migrants on Maoré receive no welfare provision whilst welfare provision for legal, but unemployed or sick, Mahorais will remain considerably less than in metropolitan France for a twenty-year transition period. Most significantly, the cost of living is very high. Much of the extra money that Mahorais receive in comparison with their Union counterparts is absorbed by the high price of basic commodities. That said, the islanders do have access to a range of social benefits analogous to those available in mainland France, including high quality healthcare and free education. Although, since 2005, access to free healthcare for "foreigners" has officially been restricted, a study completed in 2007 by a team of French doctors concluded that there was little difference in terms frequency of healthcare attendance between both the local and migrant communities (Florence et al., 2010). As a result of the pressure on social services, hospitals and schools are under severe strain. In the maternity wing of the main hospital, the second largest in any French department, 77% of the patients are non-residents. Yet, the results of the study by the French doctors indicate that as a pull-factor, access to healthcare is a relatively low priority with only 8.8% of migrants citing it as the main reason for emigrating as against 49.4% who cited economic opportunities (Florence et al., 2010).

Nonetheless, the number of babies being born to irregular migrants on Maoré has generated a heated political debate in France, with racial associations, with some calling for a suspension of the *jus soli*, birthright citizenship, on Maoré. France's Constitution allows French citizenship, albeit with conditions, to those born on French territory, including Maoré prior to its accession to full departmental status. A child born on Maoré is French from birth, but only if born after 2 August 1975 with a parent born in Maoré or another French territory, or born in the former French colonies before independence. Otherwise, the child would have to apply for citizenship through residence and only after the age of thirteen. Any amendment to the *jus soli* is contentious, since it would reverse the tradition that citizenship in France is through territorial birthright and not through blood; nor is it obvious that the Constitution can be applied partially to some parts of France and not to others. It is also questionable whether this measure would stem the flow of migration since that is, in large part, impelled by immediate economic factors rather than a long-term desire to become French, or indeed effectively "European" through France's membership of the Schengen Area.

A Part of the Indian Ocean that is Forever France?
French policy towards Comoros, and notably France's continued presence on Maoré, prolongs a baleful influence on the archipelago's political security and economic development. Why did France resolve to retain control of Maoré and

ultimately to allow the island to become a department and region of the Republic? The stated reason was to respect the wishes of the Mahorais as expressed in the 1974 referendum and even more forcefully expressed in a further referendum in 1976 in which 99.4% of those who participated chose to live under French authority.

The hardening of support between these two votes was an expression of the pragmatic acceptance by the local population of the clear economic advantages to remaining a part of France, a point hammered home by the French government who ran a propaganda campaign emphasising the poverty and growing authoritarianism on the other three islands. A literal reading of the result of the 1974 referendum would conclude that two-thirds of those eligible to vote on Maoré had a greater affinity to France than the putative Union. The third of the electorate that opposed independence not only included the minority of Mahorais who embraced Comorian identity, but also those from other islands living on Maoré. Thus, the French government argued that there was a high proportion of true Mahorais who felt themselves to be French, and cited its responsibility to uphold this majority's right to self-determination. There was also a significant proportion of the population with direct family connections, through birth or marriage to metropolitan France and a greater insertion of French-owned commercial enterprises on Maoré than the other islands. However, for France, there was scant economic justification for encouraging Mayotte to remain tied. Maoré is not rich, producing little beyond ylang-ylang perfume essence and vanilla.

Beyond neocolonial continuity and responsibility, and the marginal economic interests, and given the timing of the referendum at the height of the Cold War, there was a perceived strategic imperative for France to retain a sovereign base in the Mozambique Channel. At the time, the French navy was proposing the construction of a deep water harbour on Maoré. This was never built. However, France has since constructed a satellite listening station which came into service in 2000.

A final explanation for the decision to remain tied to France is the role played by young Mahorais in the French army, reportedly sent back to their home villages to "persuade", sometimes forcibly, their fellow villagers to vote "no" in the referendum (Fouillet, 2007).

In effect, the decision to keep Maoré became irrevocable when in September 2008, the French government announced that it would hold a single-alternative referendum to offer the Mahorais electorate, although not the electorate of the Republic in its entirety, the opportunity to vote for full integration with France as a *département d'outre-mer* (DOM). A nationalist pressure group based in Moroni, the *Comité Maoré*, described the referendum as "state terrorism" (*Comité Maorais*, 2012). As with past referenda, the outcome was not in question. With a turnout of just over 60%, 95% of those that participated chose to become France's 101st department. The only real opposition came from a section of the Islamic clergy who objected to the secularisation of the legal system, required by France's strict doctrinal *laïcité*, when the island became a full department. Since its full incorporation into the Republic, Maoré's Islamic "cadi courts", based on Koranic law and local custom, have been abolished and replaced by the French legal system. Likewise, traditional laws governing social relations have been required to conform to French standards with women granted equal inheritance rights, the legal age for marriage raised from fifteen to eighteen, and the

Islamic practice of polygamy banned, although existing multiple marriages have been recognised.

Whilst access to twenty-first century healthcare and education, and particularly the opportunity to earn a living wage, are clearly ineluctable enticements for individuals from the Union islands (and for a sizeable population of irregular migrants from Madagascar), life on Maoré is not without significant tensions and traumas. A dispassionate visitor soon becomes aware of an informal segregation operating on the island with the ghettoised ethnic French population largely living separate lives from the majority Mahorais. For their part, many local Mahorais distance themselves physically and socially from the communities of irregular migrants, often condemned to live in corrugated metal shanties on the outskirts of the capital Mamoudzou or on the smaller island of Petit Terre. Whilst kinship and friendship bonds between the Mahorais and those from other islands exist, there is equally an antipathy towards irregular migrants manifest in collaboration between sections of civil society and the authorities and regular denunciations of *sans-papiers*. This despite a deep-seated cultural aversion to manual labour amongst the Mahorais that would see the local economy – agricultural labour, construction, transport – collapse without migrant labour.

The conspicuous tension between these communities partially explains why the tourism sector has remained stagnant. Despite the blue skies and clear waters, tourists cannot escape the pervasive climate of resentment. The island is blighted by almost permanent demonstrations and strikes, and in October 2011 was paralysed by a general strike that led to the closure of all shops on Maoré, barricades on the main roads and violent clashes between youths and *gendarmes* that led to deaths and serious injuries. Once more, the government was forced to deploy three battalions of *gendarmes* from Réunion, and even mainland France, to contain the violence. The trigger for this escalation in tension was a sudden steep rise in the price of basic commodities, notably the frozen chicken legs that form the staple protein in the local diet. These *mabawas*, in keeping with all imported food, were already much more expensive on Maoré than on Réunion and twice the price of metropolitan France. The targets of the protestors were many and varied including an apathetic government in Paris; the patrician French Prefect of Maoré; the three wholesalers accused of running a commodities cartel and, of course, the *gendarmes*. The minister for overseas territories, Marie-Luce Penchard, paid a very brief visit that served to underline how far removed are events in Maoré from the mainstream of French political, economic and media life. After forty-four days, the trade unions, the consumers association and an *ad hoc* pressure group, the *Collectif des citoyens perdus*, accepted an accord that temporarily reset the price of a basket of basic commodities including beef, gas and sand.

Ill-feeling, however, continues to run high. Sporadic strikes, spontaneous demonstrations and the creation of a, previously absent, youth gang culture appear to have exported the stresses of the *banlieues* of metropolitan cities to the Indian Ocean. In order to dissipate the unrest, the government of Nicolas Sarkozy resorted to a tactic already used in other overseas departments, extending the *Revenu de solidarité active* (RSA), a personal allowance that guarantees a minimum income, to win over the protestors. The escalation of political unrest reflects a pattern of protest in French overseas departments following similar disputes in France's Caribbean departments of Guiana, Martinique and Guadeloupe. Yet, as in Maoré, despite a perception of second-class citizenship, the electorates of these DOM, when faced with the choice of loosening their ties to France, ultimately vote for the economic security of continued inclusion, albeit in gradually diminishing numbers.

Faced with the politics of *fait accompli*, the reaction of the Union government has been essentially pragmatic. Despite using his speech to the UN General Assembly in September 2008 to denounce France's continued occupation of Maoré, Sambi was accused by the pro-independence *Comité Maoré* of underestimating the importance of the referendum (*Malango Actualité*, 25 janvier 2009). Dhoinine, Sambi's chosen successor as president of the Union, has seemingly adopted a still more realistic stance. In his first speech to the General Assembly, he merely commented that he was "convinced that the solution lies in tripartite negotiations between France, the Comoros islands and the Mahorais" (*Indian Ocean Newsletter*, 2011). That one island out of four remains *de facto* if not *de jure* under foreign rule, as well as a constantly tempting destination for would-be migrants, is intrinsically destabilising for the Union government.

However, relations with France are multi-dimensional and remain key to Comorian foreign and economic policies. The Comorian franc is guaranteed by the French Treasury making Comoros a *de facto* member of the CFA Franc Zone. France also provides considerable development assistance to the Union, even though this amounts to only a tenth of funding provided to Maoré. In 2006, France agreed to give €88m over five years to help Comoros to reach the UN Millennium Development Goals. French technical assistance to the Union has also increased since 2007. Next to the Netherlands, France is the Union's principal destination for exports and the principal country of origin for imports. If for the sake of fiscal necessity and diplomatic propriety, relations between the two countries are superficially cordial, there are also clear signs of strain. Sambi's presidency was marked by a willingness to look beyond the former colonial power for trading and diplomatic partnerships. In response to this apparent snub of its former colonial master, the then French Secretary of State for cooperation, Brigitte Giradin stated that "the interests of France are not the preserve of the Comoros". In response, Sambi declared that "France is a friendly country, not a fraternal one ... she defends her interests, we'll defend ours". In practical terms this has meant looking elsewhere for foreign investment. The contract with the French firm Comaco to operate the Union's ports and harbours was not renewed, but awarded to Al Marwan and Gulftainer, companies based in the United Arab Emirates. Likewise, the contract to administer the country's oil supplies, formerly managed by the French multinational Total, was also not renewed. The contract was given to the nationalised *Société Comorienne des Hydrocarbures*, amid signs that the Union government was looking to Iran to secure supplies of diesel and petrol. To date, however supplies remain sporadic and the lack of fuel frequently cripples economic life on the Union islands.

Yet, France remains the Union's closest economic partner, and the enduring relationship between the two countries was further emphasised by the seemingly unlikely negotiation of a defence pact in September 2010. Ostensibly, predicated on assuring a joint response to rising piracy, the pact is a concrete testament to a current, if temporary, realism. A parliamentary report questions its utility given that there has been almost no pirate activity as far south as the Comoros and France's existing capacity to respond to the threat from its bases in Réunion and Maoré (Muselier, 2011, p. 11). However, it is this last factor that really serves French interests with France needing continued engagement with the Union to stem the flow of migrants to its newest department. For the Union government, the pact evidences a tacit recognition that the Maoré dispute can act as a lever to ensure continued inflows from France be they monetary or in kind.

Conclusion
The political situation in the Comoros archipelago is intractable. The financial cost of retaining Maoré as a part of France is hefty, if not ruinously so. However, having chosen to retain control of the island and having offered and granted the Mahorais full departmental status, it would be now almost inconceivable to reverse this policy. Likewise, despite lingering aspirations for reattachment to France in Nzwani and Mwali, the government in Moroni would be unlikely unequivocally to drop its claim, regularly supported by the UN and AU, to Maoré as intrinsic to its territorial integrity.

Since 1995, when the Balladur-Pasqua visa was introduced, the strip of water between Nzwani and Maoré has represented a moat between the developing and the developed worlds. Yet, the inflexibility of the visa process masks the complicated reality that the current position of Maoré in relation to the Union satisfies none of the protagonists. For the Union there remains the disjointing of the archipelago, illegal in international law, and for its people the almost insurmountable obstacle of the visa, dividing families and restricting trade. For the Mahorais, there is an unstated second-class status, part of and yet removed from France, mistrustful of their fellow ethnic Comorians and French compatriots alike. The previous French government acted in the knowledge that, for the most part, policy options are constrained by decisions taken in the past. Under

Sarkozy, the office of the president was content to allow opportunistic interlocutors, invariably with personal financial motives, to shape African policy with the relevant ministries without presidential intervention. So *Françafrique* persisted, but the top-down micro-management typical of Sarkozy's predecessors was largely absent. French commercial interests outweighed the sentimental arguments of cultural imperialism and colonial responsibility. Likewise, Sarkozy was unconvinced about the supposed strategic advantage of retaining control over Maoré. The new defence pact with the Union suggests that even with a four-island Comoros, France could negotiate a continued military presence in the archipelago, possibly including the construction of a base on Nzwani which has the advantage of an existing deep water harbour. Yet, even under the pragmatic, sceptical Sarkozy, France continued to shoulder the political, social and financial costs: reproach from the General Assembly; the unending pressure of policing persistent irregular migration; and the price in welfare payments of keeping the Maoré project afloat and mitigating the antagonism of the Mahorais.

Sarkozy proved to be a one-term president. His successor François Hollande, was the only candidate in the 2012 presidential election to visit Maoré. Claiming that, unlike Sarkozy, he would not be drawn into making promises he could not keep, Hollande nonetheless evoked a raft of reforms in the public sector. As for irregular migration, he would continue to defend Maoré's borders, complete the construction of a second detention centre and ensure that non-EU citizens would be prohibited from voting in local elections. Seeking a solution, Hollande indicated that increased economic assistance to the Union should check the numbers willing to attempt the crossing. In short, a policy whereby a yet more prosperous Maoré would cease to be a draw for, possibly, slightly better off Comorian youth. Whether as a result of apathy on the part of the black electorate or entrenched gratitude for departmentalisation, on a low turnout, Sarkozy made up twenty percentage points from the 2007 election to just win the second round of the 2012 presidential poll on Maoré. In the six months after Hollande's visit, Maoré and the Comoros disappeared, to nobody's surprise, from the columns of the national press. The disparity between the importance of France to the Comoros and the Comoros to France looks set to continue. Thirty-seven years after independence, the former colonial power continues to play a decisive role in the Comoros archipelago, accused of neocolonial intervention in the affairs of its former colony, yet with some justice citing the Mahorais' repeated exercise of their right to self-determination to retain their ties to France.

References

Alwahti, A. (2003). Prevention of secessionist movements in a micro-state: The international mediation in the Comoros Islands, *International Affairs, 13*(1), 65–83.

Caminade, P. (2004). La France et l'Union des Comores : saboter et protéger, *Multitudes*, 3(17), 119–122.

Comité Maorais. (2012). Déclaration du Comité Maorais: A bas le visa Balladur, 29 Mai. Available at: http://mouroua.centerblog.net/21-declaration-du-comite-maore

Cornwell, R. (1998). Anjouan: A spat in the Indian Ocean, *African Security Review, 7*(3), 57–58.

da Cruz, V., Fengler, W., & Schwartzman, A. (2004). *Remittances to Comoros*. Washington, DC: World Bank. Available at: http://www. worldbank.org/afr/wps/wp75.pdf

Florence, S., Lebas, J., Parizot, I., et al. (2010). Migration, health and access to care in Mayotte Island in 2007: lessons learned from a representative survey, *Revue d'épidémiologie et de santé publique*, *58*(4) 237–244.

Fouillet, Agnès (Director) (2007). *Comores: un aller simple pour Maoré*, Les Films Bonnette et Minette.

Ghorbal, S. (2008). Sambi sur le pied de guerre, *Jeune Afrique*, no 2457, février.

Indian Ocean Newsletter (2011), 1317, 1 October.

Institut national de la statistique et des études économique (2011). Produit intérieur brut à Mayotte en 2009, *Mayotte Infos*, 55, novembre. Available at: http://www.insee.fr/fr/insee_regions/mayotte/themes/infos/infos5 5/infos55.pdf

Malango Actualité (2009), 25 janvier.

Muselier, R. (2011). Rapport fait au nom de la Commission des Affaires étrangères sur le projet de loi, no. 3598, autorisant l'approbation de l'accord entre le Gouvernement de la République française et le Gouvernement de l'Union des Comores instituant un partenariat de défense, Rapport de l'Assemblée Nationale, no. 3979, 16 novembre.

Ottenheimer, H. (2001). Spelling Shinzwani: Dictionary construction and orthographic choice in the Comoro Islands, *Written Language and Literacy*, 4(1), 15–24.

Renou, X. (2006). *La privatisation de la violence.* Paris: Agone.

United Nations. (2011). *World population prospects: The 2010 revision*, New York: United Nations. Available at: http://esa.un.org/ unpd/wpp/ Documentation /pdf/ WPP2010_Volume-I_ Comprehensive-Tables.pdf.

Walker, I. (2007). What came first, the nation or the state? Political process in the Comoro Islands, *Africa*, *77*(4), 582–605.

PART 3

REDEFINING THE POSTCOLONIAL
IN SOCIAL AND EDUCATION POLICY

CHAPTER 5

SHIFTING CENTRES AND STATIC PERIPHERIES: GEOGRAPHIES OF POWER IN FRANCOPHONE AFRICAN DEVELOPMENT POLITICS

Claire H. Griffiths

Social policy and particularly the gender dimensions of this policy field have not been extensively explored in Francophone African research during the postcolonial era, in significant contrast to scholarship focusing on the former British African colonies. Only since the turn of this century has the need to generate a conceptual and linguistic vocabulary in which to frame and critique gender policy in the developing areas of the Francophone world been widely recognised. This chapter contributes to that endeavour by exploring the journey social policy has taken as it crossed the historical divide between colonial French West Africa and postcolonial Francophone Africa in the area of policy known initially as « *femmes et développement* » and more latterly as « *genre et développement* ». The discussion here seeks to throw light not simply on this one area of policy making but on the wider political dynamics that shape social policy-making in the Francophone African postcolony.

Considering the title of this volume, the politics of gender and development may not seem the most promising field in which to explore a historiographical "divide" in Francophone Africa. However, where postcolonial development intersects with gender politics we find ourselves in the arena *par excellence* in which to observe the exercise of political power in the postcolonial state.

The reasons for this are both historical and structural. Far from being a relative newcomer to the policy-making field, the origins of contemporary gender and development politics actually stretch far back into the colonial period. The aim of this chapter is to illustrate how contemporary gender and development politics are still, even today in twenty-first century West Africa, to a large degree a response to policies initiated in the colonial era and as such are an example of a far-reaching dynamic that has been driving "development" in the sub-region, and particularly its social dimension, for almost 100 years.

A further reason for focusing on the gender and development field in a collection such as this one is its capacity to illuminate how the political power that lies behind policy-making works in two key areas of the polity, on the one hand in the formal political infrastructure of the state and on the other in civil society. The last section of the chapter will look at the degree to which the strict separation that operates in the centralised state between the formal and the informal polity is contributing to the failure of policy-making in this field.

The discussion starts in a historical mode exploring the evolution of gender and development politics on both sides of the chronological divide separating colonial French Africa from postcolonial Francophone Africa. The aim is to show who is included and who is excluded in gender and development politics, and highlight how policy-making is monopolised by structures that exclude the largest possible number of policy stakeholders. In effect these stakeholders are excluded from virtually all political activity conducted within the formal political arena in just the same ways they were excluded from the workings of the formal polity in the colonial era (in gender and development politics, as it is defined in Francophone Africa, these are almost invariably women). This section of the stakeholder population is, in effect, silenced by its exteriority to the formal state apparatus and its inability to participate in fashioning discourses of development (the term *discourse* here includes ways of conceiving of development policy as well as formulating and articulating development policy).

The method employed to deconstruct the politics of gender and development in the postcolony uses research tools drawn from political science, notably a structural "top-down" analysis of the formal polity alongside a critical sociological approach that looks at the issue from a "bottom-up" perspective, in other words from the point of policy impact in the target population.

This multidisciplinary approach shines a light on political inclusivity and exclusivity making it a particularly illuminating field in which to describe the exercise of political power as it crossed the historical divide and continued into the postcolony.

Gender and Development: Crossing the Historical Divide

Throughout the history of the Francophone African post-colony, gender and development politics have occupied an important place on the agenda of successive governments. At independence, the incoming postcolonial elite in Senegal presented the discriminatory gender politics of the outgoing French colonial regime as a manifestation of some of the deepest ethical and social scars of colonial occupation. The visible legacy of colonial gender policy was presented in terms of the decadence and alienation of European colonial society.[1] The incoming political elite trumpeted not only this legacy of deprivation but also its intention to correct it. The new government, of independent Senegal, under the leadership of Léopold Sédar Senghor, referenced the colony explicitly as it laid out the foundations of its postcolonial gender and development policy. At that time, in the early 1960s, the policy operated under the slogan *revaloriser la femme*, the implication being that Senghor's government would restore to women the place they occupied in society prior to the arrival of the French. In this sense, the state at independence made the female population a repository of its postcolonial political identity, and a marker of the ethical distance that separated it from its colonial predecessor.

How that policy developed during the first twenty years of independence reveals not only how the postcolonial elite saw gender in relation to development, it also reveals a great deal about the gender politics of those who ran the postcolony during this period. We need to ask what was a woman's "rightful place" in the postcolony as reflected in this effort towards her *revalorisation*? Did legislation lead the female population out of the marginal position it occupied under colonisation? And finally did this process signify a step change in the quality of women's lives on either side of the historical divide that separates "colonial" French West Africa from "postcolonial" Francophone Africa?

The incoming postcolonial elite certainly had a wealth of evidence on which to build a case against the French colonial authorities. Women had been subject to differentiated treatment throughout the French colonial occupation of West Africa. The exclusion of women from the political arena during this period was, to all intents and purposes, comprehensive. As Senegalese sociologist Fatou Sow has argued:

> During the colonial period political institutions were completely closed to women. This represented a step backwards compared with their position in pre-colonial society ... In the immediate aftermath of Independence, the State launched a national development plan ... for the

advancement of women … that would mark a clear break with colonial practice"(Sow, Diouf and Le Moine, 1993, pp. 10–14).[2]

However, this configuration of the colonial/postcolonial divide offered by the incoming elite raises a number of questions. If we take the case of Senegal, the underlying assumption was that gender oppression in Francophone Africa was a phenomenon imported to the sub-region from Europe through French occupation. The assertion that this was a wholly exogenous cultural legacy needs closer inspection and will be explored in the next section of this chapter which looks at the historical evidence of gender politics in the region before the French arrived, and considers the degree to which the coloniser can be deemed to have reconfigured gender politics during the colonial era.

The focus of the discussion then turns to exposing the postcolonial African elite's engagement with gender politics. Looking at both the process of policy-making and the outcomes of this engagement, the analysis highlights who was allowed access to the policy-making arena and in what ways access to and participation in policy-making is reflected in policy outcomes. The key question here is whether gender policy in the postcolonial era is an illustration of the way in which the postcolonial (male)[3] elite "recolonised" the political centre in the post-independence era, and in so doing drew on a realignment of exogenous (foreign but no longer strictly speaking "colonial") political forces.

The conclusion will return to the question implicit in the title of this chapter. The notion of shifting centres refers to the transfers of power that have taken place at the centre of the policy-making system while the static peripheries refer to the unchanging areas of exclusion from the political process populated by those who continue to have little or no influence over the policy-making process nor any control over its outcomes.

Gender Politics in the Colony: A Prelude

Historical accounts of pre-colonial gender politics in Francophone Africa tend to fall into one of two camps. The first is a traditional approach we encounter in myriad British and French histories of former African colonies, exemplified by the quotation below, where it is argued that African women were, by and large, thoroughly subjugated to male domination in pre-colonial African society: "Girls were educated to submit to male authority. They were taught from a very young age not to speak in public and never to address a man first before he had spoken to them and never to look him in the eye (this would have been considered insolent)" (Coquéry-Vidrovitch, 1994, p. 99).[4]

This representation of African gender politics in the pre-colonial era has not gone unchallenged. An alternative tradition has evolved building on research undertaken by French scholars working in West Africa in the late colonial period. An example is French anthropologist Denise Paulme who responded to what she saw as the dominant but erroneous view circulating in French Africa in the 1930s and 1940s that African women had always lived – in pre-colonial as well as in colonial times – wholly under the authority of men. In her seminal work on the subject published in French in 1960 and then translated for publication in English as *Women of Tropical Africa* in 1963, she argued that the representation of African women as a subjugated race was wrong: "This is a fondly entertained masculine ideal that does not tally with the realities of everyday life" (Paulme, 1963, p. 5).

Referencing a number of societies in West Africa then living under colonial rule, Paulme argued that French colonisation had in fact had a devastating impact on the socio-economic position of women throughout the West African sub-region under imperial occupation. The erosion in the economic status of women had had a cumulative effect and led to a multiple loss of status throughout the course of the colonial era in almost all aspects of women's lives, social, economic, political and cultural.

Picking up this theme of cumulative disadvantage experienced by African women following the introduction of the colonial economic and legal system in the French African empires, particularly in the first decade of the twentieth century, scholars working in Africa in the 1950s and 1960s provided further evidence in support of this hypothesis.

After working for a time among the Baule of Côte d'Ivoire, Mona Etienne argued that attempts to map African gender relations on to European social structures were not only fraught with conceptual difficulties but also likely to lead to erroneous conclusions (Etienne, 1983, pp. 303–313). Indeed she would go as far as to refute what she considered the commonly held view of African women in French Africa as portrayed in European scholarship: "the absence of relations of domination-subordination between husband and wife was one aspect of the generalised absence of such relations in Baule society" (Etienne, 1983, p. 305).

Annie M. D. Lebeuf, a French political scientist working in Central Africa in the 1950s theorised the changes in the relative statuses of male and female in the African societies as resulting from their contact with French culture:

> By habit of thought deeply rooted in the Western mind, women are relegated to the sphere of domestic tasks and

private life, and men alone are considered equal to the task of shouldering the burden of public affairs. This anti-feminist attitude, which has prevented political equality between the sexes from being established in our country [France] until quite recently (and even so the equality is more *de jure* than *de facto*[5]) should not allow us to prejudice the manner in which activities are shared between men and women in other cultures, more particularly, so far as we are concerned, in those of Africa. And we are entitled to ask ourselves if it is not an attitude of this kind that is at the bottom of many erroneous ideas about the very real authority exercised by women in African political systems; and whether it has not contributed, to a certain extent, to the initiation of policies which deprive women of responsibilities that used to be theirs (Lebeuf, 1963, p. 93).

The tendency among European scholars, male and female to construct a history of African social relations from an entirely European perspective has been amply critiqued in both French and African scholarship. The latter is exemplified most famously by the work of Cheikh Anta Diop who began revising the European historical archive of Africa in the mid-century. But also the more traditional oral historical methods of scholars such as Amadou Hampâté Bâ have contributed an effective critique of "westernised" histories by positing alternative notions of what constitutes a valid historical source and by employing different modes of recording and disseminating historical material, as in the case of Bâ who recorded the oral histories of the Peul people of West Africa while in the employ of the French colonial authorities.[6] A recent study of the slave trade in the Bight of Biafra by Ugo Nwokeji provides evidence of how an absence of knowledge and understanding of gender has led to misapprehensions in Western scholarship of Africa.

Such new and rigorous historical enquiry at the very least throws up a challenge to persistent generalising claims of the uniformly subjugated status of African women in the pre-colonial era, and evidence suggests that in some West African societies women exercised considerably more political influence than their European counterparts at the time. So, while we can conclude that there is a growing body of evidence testifying that women did have a share of political power in pre-colonial Africa, can we likewise conclude that this power was totally destroyed by the coloniser?

The Impact of French Gender Politics on African Society and Economies

The simple answer to this question is that the impact of the coloniser on the lives of West African women can scarcely be overestimated. Various starting points to the effective exercise of French influence prior to the formalisation of the colonial state suggest themselves. The impact of the French Atlantic slave trade on gender politics, both for men and women, was explicit and comprehensive throughout the process of capture in Africa and indenture in the plantation colonies. The differential value attached to the reproductive and productive roles of female and male slaves at the point of sale both on departure and later on arrival in the Caribbean, redefined relations between individuals in the enslaved environments.

The rapid expansion of the French slave trade from the early 1600s through to the creation of the largest slave colony in the world in Saint Domingue (Haiti) in the mid-eighteenth century, through to the legal abolition of slavery in the French colonies from 1848, ensured that the scale of this sociological disruption on both sides of the Atlantic was enormous. The influence of gender in the context of slavery is as yet an under-researched area, however what is clear from research to date is that after the 1848 legislation gender segregation and differentiation imposed by Europeans in the context of slave labour in the plantation colonies of the New World operated differently from the gender segregation and differentiation witnessed in the context of slavery, forced labour and then wage labour under European control in the African colonies. For example gender was not the key factor in the division of labour in agricultural work in the slave plantation; both men and women worked in the cane fields and in rum production in the island colonies of the French Caribbean.

A similar absence of gender as the key factor in the organisation of field labour has been identified in the West African slave plantation, particularly during the development of the groundnut industry in the last quarter of the nineteenth century (Bashir Salau, 2011). In contrast to this, legal abolition of slavery did have a differential impact on non-enslaved men and women on the mainland, coinciding as it did with a significant growth in public works and manual work in the French African colonies. After 1848, the loss of a "legal" slave labour force in French West Africa preceded the introduction of alternative forms of forced labour such as *la corvée* for road building and civil engineering works in French Africa, all of which drew particularly heavily on the male population at the height of the French imperial mission (B. Fall, 2002).

These developments foreshadow the segregation that will characterise the colonial economy on the African mainland from the late nineteenth century. While it would be true to say that the highly gendered nature of French society at home was reflected in European colonial society in Africa from the earliest settlements of the mid-seventeenth century and throughout the expansion of French presence in the sub-region, it was not until the long nineteenth century reached its end that these relations will reveal themselves in their most far-reaching and discriminatory form.

During the period of imperialist rule that followed the Berlin Act of 1885, the differential status of the colonial male and female was gradually formalised across the French West African region culminating in the introduction of the French legal code in in the first decade of the twentieth century. As Senegalese political scientist Rokhaya Fall argues, this reduced African women to a position akin that that of French women by reclassifying them as: "minors, the status accorded to wives in the French Civil Code" (R. Fall, 1994, p. 17).

The legal position of women was further undermined by the *régime foncier colonial*. The land registration system that came into force in French West Africa from 1905 to 1906 required privately owned land to be registered by the head of the household, « *[l]eur acquisition se fait sur la base de règles inspirées du code civil français ou du droit public* » (Dialla, 2003, p. 8). Under the French Civil Code the "head of a household" was a man. By neglecting to recognise women as heads of households, colonial law disenfranchised African women from lands hitherto held under *le régime foncier coutumier* (traditional land registration) and *le droit coutumier* (traditional law) where family inheritance might historically have passed down the female line, as in a matrilineage. The existence of matrilineal social systems was not unknown to the coloniser although early encounters with it had led to misinterpretations: in some cases they were presented as inversions of the European social order of patriarchy and described as "matriarchies" rather than "matrilineages"[7].

Colonial administrators and legislators acted as if they were operating in a French context and conceived the need to protect traditional and ancestral rights to property within the land registration laws exclusively in relation to the rights of the African male landowner, only defaulting to a female landowner in the case of the absence of any male claimants from the household or family group.

The political and legal disenfranchisement summarised above was followed in the decade before and after the First World War by a series of economic plans for the region that intensified the economic marginalisation and impoverishment of women. When the French arrived in West Africa they encountered societies where, with very few exceptions, women worked as full economic members of the society as a matter of course. Only those of very noble birth, the very young, the old, and the temporarily and permanently incapacitated would be excused from making a sustained and key contribution to the welfare and subsistence of the group. In societies based on growth as well as subsistence, women would also have been involved in the expansion of the group. There are many examples of women serving in the ranks and occasionally at the head of armies in West Africa, the sixteenth-century ruler known as Amina of the Zaria being one of the more famous examples of the warrior queens. A more recent example from the period of French rule would be Sarraounia Mangou, queen and prophet from the region of Lougou in colonial Niger, who led a spectacular resistance to the oncoming French army and eventually perished at its hands. However, as Elara Bertho has illustrated in relation to Queen Sarraounia's resistance to the armed "pacification" of Niger by the French in 1899, it remains a monumental task to reconstruct a comprehensive and accurate picture of resistance leadership by women in this and earlier eras.[8] The histories as they were told then and now remain highly gendered and in many cases the participation of female warriors still lies lost to view in a historical hinterland of mythology and oral history.

In smaller communities, most non-noble women and men were subsistence farmers. In larger societies and empires the range of female roles was wider but again did not follow the binary formula so prevalent in the European socio-economic structures. One example of the difference between European and African economies in early modern Africa are the Hausa city-states which operated a socially complex economic system based around trade. This system depended to just as large a degree upon female traders as male traders.

Just as the arrival of colonial powers in the coastal zones of the region undermined the economic and political stability of African imperial powers, the start of the more territorially invasive European imperial missions in the post-1885 era had an increasingly direct impact sociologically on the African populations of the region. The acquisition of territory in the hinterlands upset the local agricultural economy of West Africa and this affected all parts of these rural societies. Evidence suggests that the destruction of agricultural economies of the West Africa region had a different and significantly more detrimental impact on the female work-force.

With the introduction of import–export trade, the disruption of subsistence farming was profound in those areas where plantations were developed for intensive cultivation, such as the infamous Niger Office.[9] Lands tradi-tionally designated for the cultivation of subsistence crops (and primarily cultivated by women in these areas) were taken over for the production of cotton, rice and other cash crops destined for France, Europe and other overseas markets. As a consequence, subsistence farming became increasingly marginalised and through this process women were doubly disadvantaged in comparison with men. Women lost on two fronts in that their most fertile lands were requisitioned by the colonial economy, and as a consequence they suffered a decline in the quality and quantity of indigenous produce.

Simultaneously as the colonial economy grew, local farming communities lost a crucial section of their workforce. The development of the mining industry in West Africa in the early twentieth century accelerated the exodus of male labour from subsistence agriculture. Mining also led to the loss of arable land. While the best farming lands had been taken over for intensive cash crop production, land around the new mining installations was taken by the mining companies to produce high carbohydrate crops to feed the miners. As these industries progressed, and more arable land was absorbed into the modern economy, subsistence farmers were pushed further and further out into the poorer lands.

As the traditional female labour force witnessed ever greater numbers of their male counterparts disappearing into the export farming economy and the industrial mining sector, the first European World War accelerated the departure of rural manpower from West Africa. Some 200,000 *Tirailleurs Sénégalais* (as all conscripts and volunteers from the French West African colonies were called) served in the Great War. Over 30,000 of them would not live to return home (Michel, 2003).

While political upheaval in Europe and economic exploitation in West Africa changed the gender of production at every level, male status assumed an unprecedented significance in the hierarchy of production. Where labour may have been differentiated to a greater or lesser extent in the pre-colonial economies, the introduction of European wage labour facilitated an intensification of segregation and discrimination that was then consolidated by the colonial education system introduced across the French African empires in the inter-war period.

Elementary education had begun as a segregated system for the education of colonial boys in the "four communes" of West Africa: Saint-Louis, Gorée, Dakar and Rufisque. Then in the 1820s, the Mother Superior of a teaching order, the Sisters of St Joseph de Cluny, visited the colony of Senegal with the intention of founding a teaching mission in Africa (Barthel, 1985, p. 140). Her plan was encouraged by Jean Roget, the Governor-General of the time, who had been expressing some concerns about what he perceived as the absence of appropriate role models for young colonial girls. It would not be fanciful to assume that Jean Roget's preoccupation was influenced by the lifestyles of a group of businesswomen in the Communes known as *Signares*. The *Signares* were famous for their sexual freedom and their dislike of European marital regimes. Their lifestyle was viewed with disapproval among traditional Catholic colonial women whose segregated and cloistered existence gave them minimal influence over the *Signares*. The Sisters of St Joseph were encouraged to come and set up schools for girls without delay and within a year the first Catholic girls' school was opened on Gorée island, at the epicentre of the *Signare* community. In the course of the nineteenth century the *Signares* became increasingly colonised, donning the fashions and manners of the European female population and ultimately losing their power and their businesses as they were integrated into French society.

For its part, the girls' education system remained very limited in scope, enrolling only a handful of girls every year

159

up to the 1850s. At this point educational reforms under the Second Empire changed the nature of elementary education for both girls and boys in France and the colonies. While educational opportunities for all children expanded in France from the mid-nineteenth century, in the colonies girls' education became increasingly less academic and more akin to a practical skills-based training for domestic service. This curriculum proved much more popular with both Muslim and Catholic local families and increasing numbers of African girls were enrolled in schools. When they had graduated from these schools, increasing numbers entered the workforce as domestic servants.[10] Later in the century and into the twentieth century, this female workforce diversified as job opportunities multiplied for office and factory cleaners and unskilled support workers in industrial, commercial and agricultural sectors.

Educational opportunities expanded in French West Africa in the inter-war period and boys' education continued to develop separately from girls' education. As the number of places in French schools multiplied, Georges Hardy, serving as Inspector General of Education for French West Africa, sought to reassure Muslim families that the expansion of educational opportunities for girls was not to be feared, on the contrary it was designed to reinforce existing gender differentiation and traditions: "our official education ... respects the doctrines of Islam and in no sense aims ... to emancipate women or modify the fundamental bases of the Muslim family" (Barthel, 1985, p. 144).

In conclusion, the impact of colonisation on the legal, political economic and educational status of women as distinct from men was comprehensive. The claims made by the incoming African political elite that European colonisation had in fact effected the most systematic disempowerment of women in the history of the continent appear therefore to have been grounded in fact.

Was Gender and Development Policy Decolonised in the Post-Independence Era?

Whether the incoming postcolonial regime went on to achieve real and lasting change in the deeply differentiated and divided societies they inherited at independence is the question explored in this final section.

It is at this point in the discussion that the distinction between the activities of the formal polity and those of the informal polity is particularly salient. If we take first of all a traditional political science approach with its focus on the formal structures of the polity as the means through which social need is identified and appropriate responses are formulated, we will conclude that the postcolonial Franco-phone African state has actively engaged with the issue of gender discrimination both in terms of developing a political infrastructure to formulate and implement change and in terms of policy-making aimed at bringing about that change in society. In this "top-down" view of the workings of the political system, we can see a picture emerging of a macro-level national policy-orientated response to the colonial legacy of female exclusion and disempowerment. Senegal provides a particularly fruitful example of this approach in action, simply because it is here, in the historical heartland of Francophone African educational culture, that gender policy in the postcolonial era has been researched, documented and analysed more closely and systematically than in other former colonies of French Africa. Indeed in some of these erstwhile colonies gender is still not established as a research category. Such has been the resistance to gender theorising in former French empire generally that even in relatively forward-looking Senegal, the social science departments of its leading university institutes resisted establishing gender research programmes and centres until the end of the first decade of the twenty-first century when the first gender studies department opened at the flagship social science institute, *IFAN* (*Institut fondamental d'Afrique noire*) and a "women's studies" department was opened at the country's oldest university, UCAD, in Dakar.[11]

While the incoming Senegalese government was clearly not alone in espousing a rhetoric in favour of the "advancement" of women in Francophone West Africa, Sekou Touré for one had been very active in Guinea in promoting women's participation in the liberation movement which brought him to power in the late 1950s (Schmidt, 2005), Senegal distinguished itself in the consistency and effort it put into promoting and advertising pro-women policies in the first three decades of post-independence era. The careful documentation of this policy area over several decades allows us to go some way towards evaluating the extent to which the marginalisation and exclusion of women was not only addressed but actually countered by the policies of the incoming elites.

Not surprisingly under the premiership of Léopold Sédar Senghor the philosophy underlying the *revaloriser la femme* policy of the 1960s drew heavily from the tenets of *négritude*, the literary movement that Senegal's first president had championed alongside the Guyanese poet Léon-Gontran Damas and the Martinican poet and politician, Aimé Césaire, since they were all students together in Paris in the 1930s. Now at the helm of the postcolonial State, Senghor brought the same construction of female identity that infused *Femme noire*, his famous hymn to traditional African womanhood, to his policy of reinstating African women to their rightful "traditionally African" position in society. As a great placard bearing extracts of the speeches of the former president in the *Musée de la femme* on Gorée island reminds us, Senghor would declaim that an African woman has no need for European style of "women's lib" because African women had been liberated for centuries.

Undoubtedly Senghor's efforts helped put gender discrimination on to the political agenda of the postcolonial Francophone African state. It served both as a vehicle for his own gender philosophy and, as suggested in the introduction, as a marker of the ethical superiority of the postcolonial regime in contrast to its predecessor. The formulation and implementation of actions to improve women's position were put in the hands of government and party agencies. These reported to a ministerial unit for women's affairs in the Social Affairs Ministry which ultimately became a Ministry of Women Affairs. All were tasked with the role of improving « *la condition feminine* » in Senegal. And such was the pattern of gender and development politics in the three decades that followed independence throughout Francophone Africa.

The presidential rhetoric, the creation of an infrastructure and the formulation of policy objectives did not however translate into much by way of tangible improvements in « *la condition feminine* » when measured in terms of better education, higher living standards and more participation in the economic and political life of the nation. This stagnation was well known nationally and regionally but only came to the attention of the wider international development community in the early 1990s when information on this aspect of development started being published and disseminated globally, initially in annual reports and later in the UN's online databases. In the early 1990s, these reports were providing devastating statistics purporting to reveal a general lack of progress towards agreed development targets for women. What was particularly noticeable was the degree to which Francophone African countries were failing to make progress. By the mid-decade it appeared to be the least successful region in the world for meeting social targets for women and girls.

At the same time, the new rules governing French funding for development projects was coming into effect following the 1990 Franco-African summit held at La Baule at which the then President François Mitterrand had called for a "democratisation" of the former colonies (by which he meant the introduction of parliamentary institutions along the model of France) and closer attention to *bonne gouvernance*. His institutional approach to "democratisation" required the establishment of a number of formal state structures, including a Ministry for Women's Affairs where one was not already in existence. As a consequence, Senegal set up its first Ministry for Women's Affairs in 1991. The title of this institution, *Ministère de la Femme de l'Enfant et de la Famille* tells us something of the political philosophy underlying this initiative. The language used here can be seen to marginalise as clearly as it defines the role of women in society. Within what is essentially a corporatist political philosophy, the population is conceived in terms of groups or classes, that, depending upon their gender and position in the economy, serve certain functions in society.

While ministerial structures charged with reversing historic disadvantages experienced by women living in West Africa continued to multiply, the policies generated by this Eurocentric institutionally based response provide another insight into the political factors driving this area of postcolonial policy-making and brings us to the central question explored in this volume: can we identify a clear historical divide between politics and policies of the colonial and postcolonial eras in Francophone Africa?

In a sense we can in that while France has maintained and in some cases recently escalated its military and diplomatic activities in its former colonies, it has all but disappeared from the social policy-making arena. This is not to say that it is not present on the ground, but its presence as a driving force at national and regional level has diminished greatly and this role – such as it was in the colonial era, when it was at best sporadic and generally of very limited scope[12] – has been taken over by other external agents among which are the international NGOs and UN agencies. While the sheer scope of activity is incomparable between pre- and post-independence eras, where the historic divide is much less visible is in the outcomes of policy efforts in this area. Indeed the outcomes of gender and development policy in the postcolonial era have been so varied as to include innumerable cases where ill-conceived policies have exacerbated gender discrimination and impoverished women. In his analysis of gender in HIV/AIDS policy in Francophone Africa, Vinh Kim Nguyen describes how international aid to a women's support group in Côte d'Ivoire effected a deterioration in the welfare of the members of AWA (Abidjan Women against AIDS). This study provides a contemporary example of how policy makers formulate development policies outside the local cultural context and parachute the policy response into an exogenous environment in much the same way their colonial forebears did. In other words policy made in ignorance of the economic, social, political and cultural environment in which it will be implemented can have unexpected and sometimes devastating results. In the case of AWA the donor community had brought together HIV-positive women in urban Côte d'Ivoire in a programme grafted from the self-help movement that emerged in American cities in the early years of the AIDS epidemic in the US. Back in the 1980s, when there was no effective treatment for the disease, the rationale behind the self-help groups had been primarily to campaign for research and drug trials and to develop care and support for the terminally ill. In the case of African cities over a decade later, the context was quite different. The discovery of an effective treatment for AIDS in the mid-1990s meant the disease was no longer fatal for those with access to treatment. It was this reality that undermined any hope of self-help and solidarity in the AWA group set up in the late 1990s in Abidjan at a point when some women were receiving effective treatment for their condition and some were not.

> In the context of the desperate poverty in which AWA's women lived, the dynamic within AWA was not one of self-help and solidarity but rather of competition over resources ... All the women in the group struggled to get by in everyday life but the stark evidence of injustice stared them in the face every time they met (Nguyen, 2010, pp. 82–83).

In the first year two women in the AWA group died of AIDS. In a situation of life and death competition for medical treatment, and where the difference between those who were receiving treatment and those who were dying from the disease was visible to the eye every time the group met it broke down "consumed ... by an argument over how resources were to be allocated within the group" (Nguyen, 2010, p. 82).

The approach to public policy-making in the international donor community in late twentieth century and twenty-first century Francophone Africa exemplified by the example above is compared by Nguyen with public policy formulation in colonial French West Africa. He takes the example of the first state-owned housing corporation which started building homes for Africans in colonial Abidjan in 1951. The building programme involved three types of housing:

> [C]heaper collective housing for labourers, built with rooms around a common courtyard, kitchens, and toilets; smaller apartments for the intermediary class of "boys" – as domestic servants were condescendingly called – and chauffeurs, which could accommodate a small family; and more spacious apartments for African white-collar workers. The design of the housing and the price were determined by an all-settler commission of the *Société* on the basis of European assumptions of how "Africans" lived (Nguyen, 2010, pp. 127–128).

The policy failed at a number of levels. The higher paid African workers had social obligations to the family which meant they would need to occupy larger communal housing units which in any case had been priced way beyond the reach of the labourers. In the event only the last of these three socio-economic categories benefited, whereas the housing policy had been set up in response to concerns over the growing numbers of urban poor in colonial Abidjan.

Following independence, efforts were made in 1961 to revise the housing policy. Here again the legacy of colonial social stratification along the lines of gender and occupation came into play as the research commissioned to revise the housing policy was based on colonial census data which even then failed to capture the sociological and economic realities of the African urban landscape in the aftermath of colonial rule.

Problems associated with using exogenous technologies of knowledge production, established in the colonial era and beyond, have beset social and public policy-making in the Francophone African space throughout the last fifty years. These "technologies" favour a statistical approach to capturing social data from which numerical values are drawn to define "progress". This is demonstrated in the HIV/AIDS policy case in particular and in gender and development policy generally. Women's empowerment and advancement in the postcolonial era is calculated in relation to a limited and closely defined range of arithmetically measurable "development indicators".

These indicators evaluate empowerment through the number of women in parliament and advancement in terms of access to a personal income and above all, access to formal education. Undoubtedly independence has brought more opportunities for girls to enter the formal education system in French West Africa, but the positive impact of this on the relative political status of men and women has not been clearly established. Alphonsine Bouya among others has argued that throughout Francophone and Anglophone West Africa, the objectives that dictated the content of schooling for girls in the colonial period, namely to prepare girls for marriage and motherhood, have been largely retained in African education systems in the postcolonial period (Bouya, 1994, p. 14). Although clearly going against the grain of international development policy, the view is not uncommon in the region; as Thérèse Assié-Lumumba has argued, education in the Francophone African region is "a social institution whose main function is to transmit technical skill, values and norms, it is in essence conservative" (Assié-Lumumba, 2001, p. 98).

In this sense the conservative education system described by Georges Hardy, when he was serving as Inspector General of education in French West Africa, has not changed in some fundamental aspects. And notwithstanding the tone and ambition of the political rhetoric surrounding *la revalorisation de la femme* in the post-independence years, Francophone African countries have throughout this period consistently underperformed in the area of human development, most significantly in relation to reducing gender inequalities. When this deficit became a matter of global public knowledge and concern in the early 1990s, it was the American-led international donor community that stepped up its involvement in gender and development activity in the region, not always with the intended results.

By the end of the twentieth century, Francophone African gender and development politics were being shaped by the UN development institutions, the World Bank, with support from a few Francophone bilateral aid missions, notably Canada and Belgium and a raft of usually Anglophone international NGOs. Even the vast majority of the 104 local non-governmental gender and development organisations operating in Senegal in the year 2000[13] were following the policy lead of the UN and affiliated institutions in the region, not least because any attempt to gain financial and institutional support would be predicated upon being seen to operate within this overarching development discourse and within the accepted parameters of gender and development policy.

In essence, by this point the Francophone West African gender and development policy-making agenda was under the control of exogenous and largely Anglophone influences.

It has only been in the past decade, at the beginning of the twenty-first century, that a Francophone voice has emerged in the international and development community. The French Canadian aid community launched a counter-offensive in the form of a parallel international alliance of Francophone gender and development agencies in the year 2000 with a global Francophone development conference for women. What then became apparent and is particularly relevant to this discussion is that far from providing an alternative discourse in which to re-evaluate gender and development politics in the first decade of the twenty-first century, the alliance adopted the same conceptual and structural model of gender and development politics devised by the Anglophone international development community. Its initial action points were linguistic goals – to establish a Francophone vocabulary in which to articulate the same concepts and development models as those articulated by the Anglophone gender and development community.

The example of the Anglophone avatar and the later Francophone translation confirms what was proposed earlier in this discussion – that social policy-making in the former French colonies of West Africa has altered in only two relatively insignificant respects. The language in which policy is conceived and formulated has changed as the centre of development policy-making shifted from the European capitals to the Bretton Woods institutions located in the United States. In the social policy-making field, France left a vacuum and the international community stepped in. It has begun to reconquer its linguistic terrain in recent years but conceptual control over what constitutes advancement, empowerment and modernity for women and men in Francophone West Africa remains in the hands of the paymasters of social development. So long as the former colonies of French Africa remain the world's most poverty stricken and under-developed nations, the "centre" of social policy-making, once located in Paris and now located in a more diffuse but nevertheless Western geopolitical space remains at a point that is both culturally and geographically remote from its implementation.

In conclusion, the evidence reveals that far from living up to the expectations of the women who fought alongside men for independence in the 1950s, postcolonial African states have not succeeded in putting right the socio-economic disadvantages the female population inherited from colonisation. Not only this, but by failing to reverse the discrimination and marginalisation experienced by African women under colonisation, the political elite offered up a terrain where exogenous political power could once again take root.

Notes

1. On average across Francophone West Africa less than 10% of school places were occupied by girls in the two decades before independence.
2. Author's translation: "In the colonial period political institutions were completely closed to women. This represented a step backwards compared with their position in pre-colonial society. ... In the immediate aftermath of independence, the State launched a national development plan for the whole of Senegalese society. This included a commitment to developing policies for the advancement of women that would mark a break with colonial practice."
3. That this was in fact made up almost exclusively of men – and still is in most Francophone West African states – is not the most significant characteristic in analysing

gender politics. The presence of women in elite political and economic positions does not of itself indicate a different or oppositional perspective on gender politics. Indeed historically, women recruited by male elites to their own ranks very rarely manifest an oppositional stance to the prevailing gender politics.

4. Author's translation.

5. Lebeuf is referring here to the recent reform in France allowing women to vote in national elections and expressing the view that it takes more than the extension of the franchise to dismantle the architecture of inequality in which French women live.

6. Bâ's ironically titled memoir *Oui, mon commandant* ! describes his period of employment as a clerk in the French colonial service up to his entry into the *Institut francais de l'Afrique noire (IFAN)* on the eve of the Second World War.

7. Both Denise Paulme and Annie Lebeuf provide examples of this misapprehension born of an education that did not admit variations to the gender hierarchy that prevailed in Europe.

8. I am grateful to Arnold Hughes for pointing me towards this example of a recent addition to the historiography of French West Africa.

9. The Niger Office, established in the French Soudan in January 1932, was an agricultural project centred on cotton and rice production inspired by an earlier British initiative in colonial cotton production in the Sudan.

10. For a fascinating and detailed account of female education in West Africa, by the eve of the Second World War, see the eighteen field reports of Denise Savineau, education adviser during the *Front populaire* government in French West Africa who conducted an enquiry into

female education and the family. These are published online at www.francophoneafrica.org and accessible in their original form in the National Archives in Senegal.
11. During discussions with social scientists from these institutions it emerged that previous attempts at establishing research units in the 1990s had met with opposition within these institutions.
12. For further discussion on this see Griffiths, *Globalizing the postcolony* (2010).
13. These organisations were studied during a twelve-week period of fieldwork in Senegal in January to April 2000.

References

Assié-Lumumba, N. T. & CEPARRED. (2001). Gender, access to learning and production of knowledge in Africa. In AAWORD, *Visions of gender theories and social development in Africa: Harnessing knowledge for social justice and equality*. Dakar: AAWORD.

Bâ, A. H. (1994). *Oui mon commandant ! : mémoires II*. Arles: Actes sud.

Barthel, D. (1985). Women's educational experience under colonialism: Towards a diachronic model, *Signs, 11*(1), 137–154.

Bashir Salau, M. (2011). *The West African slave plantation: A case study*. Basingstoke: Palgrave Macmillan.

Bertho, E. (2011). Sarraounia, une reine africaine entre histoire et mythe littéraire (Niger, 1899–2010), *Genre et Histoire, 8*. Available at: http:// genrehistoire. revues. org/1218

Bouya, A. (1994). Education des filles : Quelles perspectives pour l'Afrique subsaharienne au XXIème siècle, *Afrique et Développement, 19*(4), 11–34.

CONGAD. (2000). *Répertoire des organisations non gouvernementales membres du Conseil des organisations non gouvernementales d'appui au développement.* Dakar: CID/CONGAD.

Coquéry-Vidrovitch, C. (1994). *Les Africaines : Histoire des femmes d'Afrique noire du XIXe siècle au XXe siècle.* Paris: Editions Desjonquères.

Dialla, B. E. (2003). *La question foncière sur les périmètres hydro-agricoles du Burkina-Faso.* Available at: http://www.capes.bf/ IMG/pdf/Question-fonciere.pdf

Diop, C.A. (1960). *L'Afrique noire pré-coloniale : Étude comparée des systèmes politiques et sociaux de l'Europe et de l'Afrique noire, de l'antiquité à la formation des états modernes.* Paris: Présence Africaine.

Etienne, M. (1983). Gender relations and conjugality among the Baule. In C. Oppong (Ed.), *Female and male in West Africa.* London: George, Allen and Unwin.

Fall, B. (2002). *Social history of French West Africa.* Amsterdam and India: SEPHIS/CSSSF.

Fall, R. (1994). *Femmes et pouvoir dans les sociétés Nord-Sénégambiennes.* Dakar: CODESRIA.

Griffiths, C. H. (2010). *Globalizing the postcolony: Contesting discourses of gender and development in francophone Africa.* Lanham, MD: Lexington Books.

Lebeuf, A. M. D. (1963). The role of women in the political organisation of African societies. In D. Paulme (Ed.), *Women of tropical Africa.* London: Routledge & Kegan Paul.

Michel, M. (2003). *Les Africains et la Grande Guerre : l'appel à l'Afrique, 1914–1918.* Paris: Karthala.

Nguyen, V. K. (2010). *The republic of therapy: Tirage and sovereignty in West Africa's time of AIDS.* Durham and London: Duke University Press.

Paulme, D. (Ed.) (1963). *Women of tropical Africa.* London: Routledge & Kegan Paul.

Schmidt, E. (2005). *Mobilizing the masses: Gender, ethnicity, and class in the Nationalist Movement in Guinea, 1939–1958.* New York: Heinemann.

Sow, F., Diouf, M., & le Moine, G. (1993). *Femmes sénégalaises à l'horizon 2015.* Dakar: Ministère de la Femme/The Population Council.

Ugo Nwokeji, G. (2011). *The slave trade and culture in the Bight of Biafra.* Cambridge: Cambridge University Press.

CHAPTER 6

RELOCATING THE TRADITIONAL IN THE SENEGALESE CLASSROOM

Brenda Garvey

The twenty-first century has seen an advocacy for oral literatures and national and regional languages in Francophone West Africa that suggests a reaffirmation of traditional practices and a rejection of the language and culture of the coloniser. This article uses the educational programme of the *Case des Tout-Petits* to illustrate the potential challenges faced in trying to relocate the traditional.

While debates around *literature-monde* and *littérature francophone* are being played out in European academic circles, a double shift away from both written literature and the French language is becoming increasingly apparent in West Africa through a re-evaluation of oral literature and the promotion of national and local languages. The two go hand in hand. As traditional tales are given more prominence in cultural and academic spheres, so too do the languages in which these tales are told move centre stage. For some, this return to pre-colonial narratives and local languages marks a restitution of traditional values, seen as having been eroded by Western influences, for others, the promotion of individual national languages heralds a new type of dominance that threatens the very existence of local languages and the stories and traditions bound up in them.[1] The first decade of the twenty-first century has seen a relocation of the traditional in Senegalese society, which can be read as a response to the failure of fifty years of Francophone fidelity, and a reassertion of literary and linguistic forms that were repressed during colonial times. This article will use the example of an educational initiative introduced in Senegal in 2000, the *Case des Tout-Petits*,[2] to discuss the potential successes and conflicts inherent in relocating the traditional in contemporary society.

At independence in 1960, Senegal, along with most West African Francophone countries, opted to maintain French as the language of education, continuing the system imposed by the coloniser.[3] However, West African countries are not truly Francophone; while French may have remained the official language, the number of French speakers is limited to a minority and, generally, to an elite. In Senegal, it is estimated that between 10 and 15% of people speak and/or understand French, while the vast majority of people speak one or more of the thirty-five regional languages, six of which, those that represent the greatest percentage of the population (Wolof, Pulaar, Serer, Diola, Soninke, Mandinka), are officially recognised.[4] Language, in Senegal, is closely linked to ethnic group and, while people may speak more than one language, they usually identify themselves according to the ethnic group with which their mother tongue is associated. The largest ethnic groups, therefore, have the largest numbers of speakers of their related language and in Senegal, this means that Wolof and Pulaar are spoken more widely than the other languages. As Chumbow and Bobda point out, "Little effort would have been needed at independence to make Wolof the official or co-official language (with French) in Senegal, Bambara in Mali, and Sango in Central African Republic" (Chumbow and Bobda, 2000, p. 44). However, the choice of French made sense for several reasons: it allowed for the continuation of a functioning educational system with trained instructors and, albeit Eurocentric, teaching materials; it was an international language which could benefit the future of the country; it was a single, potentially unifying language in a multilingual country and region. Historically heavy but nationally neutral, the use of French side-stepped the problems raised by promoting a single national language in countries that were ethnically and linguistically diverse.

Despite suppositions to the contrary, the use of French has not threatened local or regional languages and, as Senegal moves further from its colonial past, a repositioning of regional languages is becoming apparent, particularly in the field of education. Increased awareness of the importance of vernacular language in early years education, coupled with a promotion of literacy and creativity in languages other than French, has led to a relocation of local languages in an education system that was, until recently, rigidly French. UNESCO's touchstone 1953 publication on *The Use of Vernacular Languages in Education*, recognised the cultural importance of language and its role in identity formation:

> Every child is born into a cultural environment; the language is both a part of, and an expression of, that environment. Thus the acquiring of this language (his "mother tongue") is a part of the process by which a child absorbs the cultural environment; it can, then, be said that this language plays an important part in moulding the child's early concepts. He will, therefore, find it difficult to grasp any new concept that is so alien to his cultural environment that it cannot readily find expression in his mother tongue (UNESCO, 1953, p. 49).

The report differentiates between the impact of second languages from similar or vastly different cultures and warns that a child faced with the task of learning a second language from a very different culture, "at an age when his powers of self-expression, even in his mother tongue, are but incompletely developed, may possibly never achieve adequate self-expression" (UNESCO, 1953, p. 49). The expert opinion gathered in this and subsequent UNESCO reports suggests that the use of mother tongue as the language of instruction in early years as a stepping stone to education in the second language, benefits linguistic competencies in the first language, the acquisition of the second language and leads to enhanced academic achievement (UNESCO, 2003, p. 14–15). A closer look at early years educational provision in Senegal will allow us to explore the challenges around first and second language instruction and the relocation of traditional cultural practices in the classroom.

The *Case des Tout-Petits*[5]

The first of UNESCO's six "Dakar goals", agreed at the World Education Forum in the Senegalese capital in 2000, is the expansion of early childhood care and education, especially for the most vulnerable and disadvantaged children. It was at this international forum that the newly elected President Abdoulaye Wade, presented his concept for the *Case des Tout-Petits* to provide nursery-level education which had, thus far, been largely missing from the Senegalese school system. During colonial times, a scattering of pre-schools had been set up by Catholic missionaries but these were confessional and received very few children. In the early days of independence several more nursery schools were established but only in urban areas and catering to the elite. These public schools had to compete with the more popular *daaras* or Koranic schools which instructed children in Arabic. The first government policy for pre-school education began in 1971 but, by the end of the century, there were still fewer than 100 pre-schools in the country, accessed by only 2.7% of the population.[6] With the *Case des Tout-Petits*, the first four of which were built with support from UNESCO, Wade pledged to take schooling out of the towns and into the villages where the most disadvantaged children could be reached. There are now some 400 *cases* in Senegal.

The *cases* were to take a holistic approach to education and needed to address socio-economic concerns as well as pedagogical issues so as to be able to provide care and education for children from birth to six years of age when they could begin primary school. Taking a global view of early childhood development, the *case* hoped to provide nutrition for pregnant and nursing mothers and crèche-like facilities for very small children so that older girls, often required to look after younger siblings, could be liberated to attend school themselves. In an effort to combat childhood malnutrition, the *cases*, in conjunction with the World Food Programme, aspire to deliver one meal a day for each child, however, this has not, so far, proven possible.[7] The *cases*, therefore, were conceived as spaces of transition between home and school life and, as such, placed emphasis on the use of local languages, the integration and dissemination of local traditions and on a replication of the cultural environment.

The building is designed to be highly visible and recognisable, to act as a monument to the community's investment in its young people. In a bottom-up approach, leaders of the village or urban *quartier* must contact the state to voice their interest in providing a *case* and, through a series of negotiations including the nomination of a management committee and a setting of fees appropriate to the context, the viability of the project is discussed. It is a significant undertaking for a community since, although the building is provided by the state, much of the cost, in the initial period, falls to the community. Community leaders identify the people responsible for the care and teaching of the children; the teachers should be women educated to at least the fourth year of secondary school and, as the *cases* are intended to cater for approximately sixty children, communities should provide teachers at a ratio of 1:30. These women attend a training course and are supervised by the *Agence Nationale de la Case des Tout-Petits* during the first two years of their employment. During this time, they are paid by their own community but if, after the probation, they prove successful, their salary will be henceforth paid by the state. The community has autonomous control over the *case* and will decide the amount and means of payment for attendance but must also provide the funding for the childcare, cooking and cleaning of the *case*. Not all *cases* are as elaborate as those found in Dakar but they are each built to a uniform model, designed to reflect the family compounds from which the children come.

The structure is hexagonal and houses several rooms around a central space intended to mirror the traditional layout of Senegalese compounds where circular huts surround a communal open area. The giraffe shaped beam that holds the roof is meant to represent the ideals of the *case* as prescribed in the official publication by the *Agence Nationale de la Case des Tout-Petits* (2007), a strong rootedness in traditional values and an opening towards the larger world.[8] Inside it includes classrooms, a food storage area, a room for nursing mothers, and a kitchen. In a physical relocation of the traditional, the central space is used for storytelling, in which a person, usually an elder, is again nominated by the village or urban *quartier* to share local history and cultural values with the children through the use of popular tales.

Fig. 3. *La Case des Tout-Petits* at Douta Seck Cultural Centre, Dakar.[9]

Senegalese Storytelling Traditions

Storytelling is an integral part of Senegalese culture; from the epic sagas of the official griot or public storyteller, to the everyday tales or *contes* told within the household or in more communal village settings. The griot's stories perform particular social functions and are the preserve of this endogamous group about which a growing body of literature exists.[10] *Contes*, on the other hand, can be told by anyone in the community and are usually passed down from one generation to the next. They are usually shorter stories with a clear moral message and, while many of them can be found in versions told by almost all the ethnic groups in Senegal, recounted in their own languages, they are sometimes geographically and culturally specific and refer to recognisable villages and practices. The stories follow the patterns common to many traditional folktales with formulaic openings, repetition, audience participation and question and answer forms. They are peppered with proverbs and sayings and rely on stock character types. It is these stories that are told in the *Cases des Tout-Petits* and that are, increasingly, being collected, anthologised, translated and studied.[11]

Storytelling has, as one would expect, struggled to compete with new media in Senegal and has been marginalised but is now seeing a resurgence of interest and a repositioning in society through projects such as the *Case des Tout-Petits* to which it is central. Doua Diallo, the regional co-ordinator of the *Agence Nationale de la Case des Tout-Petits* in Matam recognises this shift in his article for *Tuut Tank*. As a result of urbanisation, changes to the configuration of the family and an introduction of new types of work and enter-tainment, storytelling has, he acknowledges, been side-lined, and school has become the new location for the trans-generational dissemination of cultural heritage:

> *Autrefois, le conte dans la société traditionnelle se faisait le soir, sur la place du village ou autour du feu avec les grands parents.*
>
> *De nos jours, avec l'éclatement de la grande famille en familles nucléaires, avec les nouveaux espaces de travail, avec l'avènement de nouveaux moyens d'éducation, de formation et de divertissement, le conte ne tient plus la place privilégiée qu'il tenait. C'est la raison pour laquelle, devant le recul des structures de la société traditionnelle, l'école a pris le relais pour perpétuer les vertus du conte en l'utilisant comme un instrument privilégié de développement global* (Diallo, 2006, p. 8).[12]

Therefore, the grandparents, or village elders, are brought into the school environment and stories are shared with the children in their local language. So important is this practice to the pre-school programme that it is publicised as the second of the two objectives of the *Case des Tout-Petits*. While the first focuses on the use of games and technology in early years education, the second is:

> *recevoir chaque jour le grand-père ou la grand-mère du village qui vient leur [aux enfants] raconter une légende africaine qui les ancre dans leur milieu culturel. Si l'on sait que chaque conte africain comporte l'enseignement d'une morale derrière les animaux qui en sont les personnages, la Case des Tout-Petits maintient l'enfant dans sa culture et ses traditions* (Diallo, 2006, p. 23).[13]

Recognising the intellectual and pedagogical worth of these stories and their effectiveness in developing attention, creativity and skills of abstraction and deduction, the emphasis is, nonetheless, on their function as vehicles for the teaching of local social norms and moral values.[14] Many of these positive traditional values were not, according to Wade, taken into account by colonial or even postcolonial education systems but are, he suggests, important for the development of Senegal.[15] Exactly what these traditional values may be is not outlined in any of the documentation but, if they are to be found in and translated through the stories themselves, then it is to the stories we should turn.

La belle histoire de Leuk-le-lièvre[16]
The best known collection of tales and the most widely available and read because written and published in French by Léopold Sédar Senghor and Abdoulaye Sadji in 1953, the *Leuk-le-lièvre* stories were intended not only to introduce

school children to written French, but also to African culture and traditions. By translating the familiar stories into French, Senghor hoped to lessen the cultural divide between the children's home environment and the French-language school system, thereby integrating the traditional into the progressive. As Birahim Thioune writes, « *L'intention des auteurs de ce livre de contes se traduit par une initiative pédagogique qui part d'une tradition de type oral* » (Thioune, 2009, p. 1).[17] The stories follow the adventures of the eponymous hare, the cunning Leuk who, though declared the most intelligent of animals by the king Gäindé the lion, has many lessons to learn. He embarks on a voyage across the brush and forest, encountering danger and difficulty and learning from the different animals he meets along the way. He faces his enemy, Bouki the hyena and eventually adopts a young human, Samba, who becomes his companion on his journey of discovery. The distance between the oral version, recounted in Wolof, and the written French, is symbolically bridged in the names given the animals which are French approximations of the Wolof nouns: Leuk is from the Wolof for hare, *lëk*; *Bouki* is the Wolof term for hyena; *Gäindé* the Wolof for lion and so on. As with Aesop's Fables in Europe, moral choices are illustrated in brief dilemmas and animals embody virtues or vices and obey their character traits to predictable ends. In this way a model of acceptable behaviour is sketched:

> *Toute l'initiation culturelle proposée dans cette fiction tient dans le savoir de Leuk, vérifié dans sa propre pratique, et les éléments d'éducation donnés à Samba. Ainsi, se dégage un profil d'homme idéal construit par le texte, dans la confrontation des différents personnages et de leurs parcours. La fiction de La Belle Histoire de Leuk-le-Lièvre peut se lire comme un ensemble d'événements construisant une image de l'élève idéal* (Thioune, 2009, p. 3).[18]

While Leuk's adventures teach him about the ways of the forest and the natural order of things, they also depict him as the solitary hero of the story and overlook one of the most central values of Senegalese society, communitarianism. In fact his craftiness and pride run counter to the principles of solidarity expounded in most traditional tales. A study of the other *contes* told, some of which are collected in the works of Mamadou Cissé and Lilyan Kesteloot and Chérif Mbodj, reveal recurrent themes of respect for elders, courteous behaviour, peaceful resolution of conflict and generosity to those less fortunate. « *Je ne t'ai pas vu à Mbaaw* » for example, a story now referenced in everyday conversation, recounts the terrible sickness that strikes the fishing village when the inhabitants butcher and divide a sperm whale without sharing it with the surrounding villages.[19] This relationship between the minority and the whole can be distilled into the underlying value present in most teachings around traditional society, the responsibility of the individual to the group.

In her book on the *Les griots wolof du Sénégal*, Isabelle Leymarie explains that Wolof culture includes the individual in a vast network and that:

> *l'individu wolof, est toujours perçu comme un membre de la communauté. Cette conscience aigüe d'un contexte familial élargi facilite le processus de socialisation. Les droits et les devoirs d'une personne sont définis par rapport au groupe familial* (Leymarie, 1999, p. 43).[20]

This tight alliance between the individual and his/her group is not only horizontal but vertical, across a long history of ancestral relationships. It is for this reason that memorising complicated genealogies forms part of the training of the public griot and for this reason too that stories passed down from generation to generation are seen as weaving an essential part of the societal fabric in Senegal. However, this cultural connection has led to both successes and failures for the *Case des Tout-Petits*. On the one hand, the community, by erecting the *case*, is providing care for its infants in accordance with traditional values of shared responsibility but, since traditional society already has a system of extended family to fulfil this function, some communities have rejected the interference of the state in community life. The socialisation and education of the child are considered a duty for the entire community, which teaches the child the principles, customs and knowledge that would enable him/her to live by the values of his society.[21] Therefore, the relocation of these traditional values in the school system of the *Case des Tout-Petits* may be patronising and unnecessary and the values foregrounded may, in fact, ignore positive social evolutions. The strength of the social system that has endured through colonisation and independence is still apparent and, some critics would argue, has resisted external influences. Lilyan Kesteloot, in discussing the role of the community in the education of the Wolof child in *Du Tieddo au Talibé* writes:

> *Ce système ingénieusement conçu fut d'une très grande efficacité puisque durant des siècles cette société conserva ses structures, et cette stabilité fut telle que ces structures perdurent encore aujourd'hui, malgré 100 ans de mise en cause par les idées occidentales de démocratie, égalitarisme, individualisme etc.* (Kesteloot and Dieng, 1989, p. 18).[22]

The world depicted in the majority of stories told is pre-colonial, structured around kingdoms and rulers for whom Gaïndé the lion is the legendary model. It is a period of strict social order in which the caste system was very much alive, and a time when animism was still widely practised, so that these stories predate the Islamic influence on Senegal and give voice to customs that are now weakened or hidden. Therefore, the set of values the educational programme in the *Case des Tout-Petits* refers to is, potentially, both chronologically and culturally remote.

This interval between the time of the stories and the time of their telling can be explained, in part, by the fact that many of them are ancient tales retold down the generations and, therefore, speak not only of but from that time. In the introduction to *Contes et mythes wolof* (Kesteloot and Mbodj, 2006, p. 12), Kesteloot refers to the principle that mental representation evolves more slowly than socio-economic structures but this ignores the wealth of newer stories and the evolution of older ones that have found something to say about contemporary realities through the use of anterior imagery. It also ignores the power of nostalgia and the political project of using pre-colonial foundations for the rebuilding of a nation after independence. Here too the choice of oral literature marks a return to a creative form that is vernacular and pre-colonial and opposed to written, French literature. While Senghor and Sadji's translation of *La belle histoire de Leuk-le-lièvre* tried to bridge the gap between national culture and the colonial language and education system by bringing familiar stories into the French-speaking classroom, current trends see a shift in the opposite direction, publishing *contes* in Wolof, Pular and other national languages, often in bilingual editions so as to introduce readers of French to the original stories (Senghor and Sadji, 1953). With language so closely associated with ethnic culture and customs, the recounting of these stories in their original language is seen as a step closer to the traditional. The production of literature in national languages in Senegal both written and orally is, increasingly, a conscious choice among authors who, in a process of linguistic re-appropriation, are keen to assert their identity and express themselves and their reality in the most appropriate voice. This move is still considered by some as a negrification of literature and is seen as a political act rather than a creative one in which oral literature is regarded as a valid contemporary form of world literature and an acknowledgement of the linguistic diversity of Senegal. The programme of the *Case des Tout-Petits* maintains the *contes* in their oral form and uses the local language for their telling, thereby integrating the cultural environment into the school system and recognising the value of the local language. This linguistic approach has met with mixed success and similar initiatives in other West African countries have confronted comparable challenges.

Language Learning

As part of its mission to provide a transition between home and school, the *Case des Tout-Petits* needs to negotiate the shift from local language to French and does this through the stepped introduction of French through the three stages of the *case*. After the crèche-like facilities for the youngest infants, children enter a more formal class sequence structured as in the French pre-school system on the *petite section, moyenne section* and *grande section*, catering for children from the ages of three or four to six when they begin primary school. In replicating the home environment, classes in the *petite section* are conducted in the local language; French is introduced in songs and games in the middle section and employed almost entirely in the final year of nursery school so as to facilitate progression into primary education. This is a familiar practice in other bilingual or multilingual contexts and one supported by UNESCO reports on the acquisition of second language in education.[23] Also familiar are the problems that arise, the lack of teachers trained in the local language and the paucity of educational resources in the local language.

Burkina Faso introduced a linguistic policy similar to that of the *Case des Tout-Petits* in their primary education sector in late 1970s and early 1980s.[24] Faced with the difficulty of choosing which of some sixty spoken languages to teach, three languages were initially designated for the pedagogical experiment; mooré, jula and fulfuldé. These languages were chosen because of their geographical sweep and because, taken together, they cover about 70% of the population. They are also the most codified of the national languages, having written grammars and attendant literatures. As in the *Case des Tout-Petits*, children started learning in the national language with French introduced orally in the second year of primary education and used more consistently in the third year. There was a split too in the subjects taught in the different languages with history and geography taught in the local language and the science subjects taught in French. The project was abandoned in 1984 because of a disappointing enrolment on the programme, with only 168 schools and fewer than 20,000 pupils taking part. Initial results were also poor and reports suggested that students displayed weak linguistic abilities in both the local language and French.

Ten years later the project was resurrected as a programme of satellite schools. These schools which again cover the first three years of primary education were, Abou Napon writes, conceived as a way of bridging the distance between the child and school and were intended to improve school attendance among girls.[25] As with the *Case des Tout-*

Petits, the satellite schools place emphasis on the child's environment:

> *Pour donc éduquer l'enfant en tenant compte de sa réalité sociale, il a été décidé de transmettre le savoir faire, le savoir être aux apprenants en s'appuyant sur les langues nationales (langues d'intégration au groupe) et le français (langue d'ouverture au monde extérieur)* (Napon, 2003, p. 149).[26]

Again, unfortunately, mixed results collected by UNICEF suggest that students did not have good written or oral skills in French and had quickly forgotten what they had learnt in the national language. Napon argues that the project has failed because of a lack of clear state-led policy, meagre educational materials and a persistent attachment to French as the language of social achievement. While acknowledging the advantages of French as a common language for the development of West Africa, he highlights the importance of local languages in promoting national cultures; « *le recours aux langues permettait d'une part, de valoriser les langues locales et d'autre part, de sauvegarder l'identité culturelle des enfants.* » (Napon, 2003, p. 147)[27]

Another project, started in Ivory Coast in 2001 is the *Projet École Intégrée*, again a primary-level initiative targeting rural communities and following the same principle of beginning education in the local language before introducing French.[28] In an effort to link home and school, the project also supports literacy programmes for parents and agricultural training for the children in order to reaffirm the importance of the local environment and its production. Piloted in only ten village schools, it has confronted the common challenges of a plurilingual society with inadequate teacher training and the prevalence of non-standard spoken French outside and often inside the classroom. More significantly, the civil conflict suffered by the country since 2002 halted the experiment in five of the ten villages chosen. However, results published for 2006–2007 and 2007–2008 show higher numbers of students succeeding in the *Projet École Integrée* schools compared to classic primary schools and higher numbers being accepted into secondary school. These results are, of course, based on an extremely small group of pupils and the programme has again been interrupted through lack of funding and renewed conflict in the country.

What Senegal is doing differently to both the Ivory Coast and Burkina Faso is adding to the current school system rather than trying to alter it. It has not replaced French as the language of instruction from primary school onwards but has tried to improve literacy and learning skills pre-primary in order to give pupils, particularly those in rural areas, an advantage which should see better achievement at primary and post-primary level.[29] French is still considered by many to be imperative for achieving success within West Africa and for relationships with Europe and the wider world; however, in Senegal, French is losing ground to the most widely spoken national language, Wolof, which is becoming a *de facto lingua franca* and, in so doing, could threaten other Senegalese languages.

Wolofisation, A Threat?
As the evidence referred to in this article suggests, more work has been done on Wolof society, culture, language and literature than on the other Senegalese languages. Wolof, understood by 70–80% of the population and used in the neighbouring countries of The Gambia and Mauritania, is quickly becoming the unofficial first language of the country. A language of trade during, and before, colonial times, Wolof is now spreading into domains usually reserved for French

including government and education. It is also, as the language of the Islamic Mouride brotherhood, the language of one of Senegal's most influential religious groups. As populations move to cities such as Dakar, Kaolack and Touba, Wolof is becoming the unifying language for groups of diverse ethnic backgrounds living together in urban districts. For the same reason, most *Cases des Tout-Petits* in Dakar and in other urban centres, choose Wolof as the local language even though this may not be the mother tongue of all the children in the school. In this way a double displacement is at play with the child learning a second language at nursery school before acquiring French and being further distanced from their family language and, potentially, their traditional culture. As more funds are directed into the development of teaching materials in Wolof, it becomes the obvious choice for schools in mixed language areas. Thus a new generation of Wolof-speaking children is being educated in the cities, further removed from the roots Wade intended to preserve. In a country where language has, until recently, been closely linked to ethnic group and its inherent culture, a new linguistic group is emerging that, though multicultural in background and not ethnically Wolof, identifies itself as Wolof.

The Wolof increasingly being spoken in cities and by new groups of people can be identified as an urban Wolof as distinct from pure Wolof. It is the language of the street and the schoolyard and often the language of families of mixed ethnic origin. It is characterised by frequent borrowings from French and Fallou Ngom identifies it as a "convergence" language. "Unlike 'pure' Wolof, 'urban' Wolof is a 'convergence language' with no ethnic significance, as more and more 'uprooted' members from other ethnic groups regard themselves as Wolof" (Ngom, 2004, p. 95). Due to migration and urbanisation, the population of Senegalese cities is increasingly ethnically diverse and Wolof serves to unite people linguistically, if not culturally. Ngom credits the relative stability of the country to this "de-ethnicization" of urban Wolof which allows speakers of the language to identify themselves as Wolof while not belonging to that ethnic group. There is, however, growing resistance to Wolofisation from other ethnic groups, most specifically among the Pular people in the north of the country, in particular around Saint Louis, and among the Joola in the south where, as part of a larger struggle for a distinct identity, Wolof is seen as representative of North Senegal from which the people wish to distance themselves. Fiona McLaughlin agrees that Wolofisation is forcing a reconfiguration of identity in which certain groups are reasserting their differences through their ethnic traditions and language in response to the threat of new domination.

The spread of Wolof as an urban language may entail changes in ethnic identification. In Dakar, as in many other urban centres, first generation inhabitants sometimes consider themselves Wolof regardless of their parents' ethnicity because that is the only language they speak. Linguistic Wolofisation thus poses an overt threat to other ethnic groups for whom linguistic acculturation entails ethnic acculturation. (McLaughlin, 1995, pp. 153–154)

It would appear that, in an organic evolution away from the language of the coloniser and in an effort to unite behind a national language, the spread of Wolof has become a very real threat to other national and regional languages.

Relocating the Traditional
Fifty years after independence, Senegal is manifesting a general shift away from French language and culture with a

re-centring of oral literatures and national and regional languages. New literature, both written and oral, is being produced in national languages and critical attention is being paid to the pedagogical benefits and cultural significance of popular stories told in domestic and communal situations. Literacy programmes are being developed in many of the regional languages and the tension between oral and written forms remains in the necessity to codify and transcribe the languages in order to validate and teach them. Within this context, the *Case des Tout-Petits* proposes a reassertion of cultural values as perceived in traditional stories that promote ideas of respect, generosity and solidarity. In offering an extension of Senegalese communal life and providing a bridge between home and school, it attempts to integrate practices that are viewed as important for the development of the child but are recognised as suffering from influences of contemporary and increasingly urban existence. The growth of Wolof as the language of daily communication, particularly in urban areas, is bringing about changes to social structure in which language and ethnic group are no longer inextricably linked. While this may harbour a threat for individual languages and may cause conflict and a reassertion of ethnic differences, it could also be seen as an inevitable transformation in a multicultural society and a statement of independent national identity. People are beginning to identify themselves as Wolof-speakers and, as part of a multi-ethnic mix in cities such as Dakar, may, in fact be moving further from the cultural roots Wade, in his education programme, wishes to reinforce. Potentially traditions are being displaced from fixed communities into cultural expressions such as the *contes*, many of which are shared across the country, across ethnic and linguistic boundaries.

Notes

1. The terms national, regional and local languages are used interchangeably in the text to refer to the diverse languages spoken in Senegal. These are opposed to the official language of education, French. Not all national languages in Senegal are recognised officially as such and the term "local language" is employed here to mean to the language spoken by the rural or urban community being discussed.

2. Translated in publicity material as "Little Children's Homes" or as the "Hut for Little Children", the *Case des Tout-Petits* is a pre-school built on the model of the traditional family compounds. In the article it will be referred to in French and, sometimes, abbreviated to the *case* meaning the house or, in this context, the school.

3. French was recommended as the exclusive language for education in the colonies at the 1944 Brazzaville Conference.

4. The six national languages declared in 1971 have been codified and transcribed using Latin letters. The constitution of 2001 states, however, that any indigenous language that has been codified can be regarded as an official national language.

5. For further information on the *Case des Tout-Petits*, including a virtual tour of the building and access to the journal *Tuut Tank*, Wolof for *le tout-petit* or little one, visit the website at http://www.case-toupetit.sn/

6. Interview with Madiop Ka, interim director of the *Agence Nationale de la Case des Tout-Petits* in Dakar, 29 July 2009.

7. Although Senegal has one of the lowest levels of malnutrition in West Africa, it was ranked 144th out of 169 on the 2010 UNDP Human Development Index.

8. The programme is designed as « *une orientation alliant l'enracinement aux valeurs culturelles du terroir et l'ouverture aux apports fécondants du monde moderne* », *Les Cahiers de l'Agence de la Case des Tout-Petits* (Fall, 2007, p. 11).

9. Photograph taken by the author in July 2009.

10. See, for example, Thomas Hale's *Griots and griottes* and Isabelle Leymarie's *Les griots wolof du Senegal.*

11. For collections of tales from the Wolof language and tradition see Lilyan Kesteloot and Chérif Mbodj, *Contes et mythes wolof* and Mamadou Cissé's bilingual edition *Contes wolof modernes*. Bassirou Dieng and his master's students at the Université Cheikh Anta Diop in Dakar are currently undertaking a project to record and tran- scribe stories in Senegal. Most of these stories, as evident from the works cited here, are from the Wolof tradition but collections of, for example, Pular tales have also been published. As well as collecting the stories themselves, work is also being done, by the *Institut fondamental d'Afrique noire*, UCAD and the Senegalese *Association des contours*, in conjunction with the National Agency for the *Case des Tout-Petits,* on storytelling practice, related pedagogy and the development of educational materials.

12. "In traditional society storytelling happened in the evening, in the village square or around the fire with the grandparents. Today, with the splintering of the extended family into nuclear families, with new work spaces, the advent of new means of education, training and entertainment, stories no longer hold the privileged place they once enjoyed. This is the reason why, faced with the weakening of traditional societal structures, school has taken up the preservation of the virtues of these stories by using them as a privileged instrument in global development."

13. "To welcome a grandfather or grandmother from the village every day to tell an African legend that will anchor (the children) in their cultural environment. If we know that each African tale holds a moral in their animal characters, the *Case des Tout-Petits* maintains the child in his/her culture and traditions."

14. « *Grâce aux contes, devinettes, proverbes et belles histories, les grands parents, les tantes développent l'attention, la créativité, le pouvoir d'abstraction et de généralisation, autant d'aptitudes intellectuelles permettant à l'enfant d'appréhender les normes, valeurs et croyances de son univers culturel et social.* » *Les Cahiers de l'Agence de la Case des Tout-Petits* (Fall, 2007, p. 18). "Thanks to the tales, riddles, proverbs and stories, the grandparents and aunts [in this context the women who look after the children] develop the attention, creativity, powers of abstraction and gene-ralisation, all these intellectual skills that allow the child to understand the norms, values and beliefs of his/her social and cultural universe."

15. In his introduction to the first *Cahier de l'Agence de la Case des Tout-Petits*, Abdoulaye Wade writes: « *Dans les sociétés traditionnelles africaines, l'enfant est un trésor, une richesse qu'il importait de préserver. Sa socialisation, de même que son éducation sont considérées comme l'affaire de toute la communauté chargée de lui transmettre principes, usages et connaissances à même de promouvoir un type d'homme incarnant les valeurs de sa société. Pourtant, beaucoup de ces valeurs traditionnelles positives ne furent guère prises en compte aussi bien par l'école coloniale que postcoloniale* » (Wade, 1989, p. 11). "In traditional African societies, the child is precious, a treasure that must be preserved. His/her socialisation and education are considered the business of the whole community charged with passing

on principles, behaviours and knowledge and promoting the model of a person embodying the values of that society. However, many of these positive traditional values were not taken into account by the colonial or postcolonial school system." For further discussion of the importance of traditional values for the future of Africa see Wade, *Un destin pour l'Afrique*.

16. *The adventures of Luke the hare.*
17. "The intention of the authors of this book of stories can be seen as a pedagogical initiative, born from an oral tradition."
18. "The cultural initiation proposed in this story resides in Leuk's knowledge, verified by his own practice, and the educational elements passed on to Samba. In this way, the profile of an ideal man is constructed by the text, in the confrontation between different characters and their journeys. The story of *La belle histoire de Leuk-le-lièvre* can be read as a collection of events constructing the image of the ideal pupil."
19. "Did I not see you in Mbaaw?" in Cissé's *Contes wolof modernes* (1994, p. 51).
20. "The Wolof individual is always perceived as a member of the community. This acute conscience of the extended family context facilitates the process of socialisation."
21. See note 13.
22. "This ingeniously conceived system was very effective because for centuries the society conserved its structures, and this stability was such that the structures have endured, despite being challenged for 100 years by Western ideas of democracy, egalitarianism and individualism etc."
23. See *Education in a multilingual world* (UNESCO, 2003).

24. Senegal's first experiment with national language education also took place around this time with Wolof being introduced in pre-schools in regional capitals. However, the programme was short-lived and failed because of lack of materials, teachers and clear objectives.

25. « *Conçues pour approcher l'école de l'élève et surtout faciliter l'accès et la frequentation des filles, les écoles satellites font partie intégrante du système primaire. Elles constituent le premier maillon de ce système dans les villages où il n'existe pas encore une école primaire classique* » (Napon, 2003, p. 148).

26. "In order to educate the child while taking into account his/her social reality, it was decided that knowledge should be transmitted to the pupils using the national languages (languages of social integration) and French (a language opening out to the wider world)."

27. "the use of these languages allowed, on the one hand, the valorisation of local languages and, on the other, the protection of the children's cultural identity".

28. For further explanation of the Integrated School Project see Clémentine Brou-Diallo (2011).

29. A comprehensive evaluation of the *Case des Tout-Petits* has not yet been undertaken but a survey of selected primary schools conducted in 2007 suggested that the top fifteen pupils in each school had come through the *Case des Tout-Petits*. (Interview with Mamadou Ka, 2009).

References

Brou-Diallo, C. (2011) *Le Projet École Intégrée* (PEI), un embryon de l'enseignement du français langue seconde (FLS) en Côte d'Ivoire, *Sudlangues*, 15. http://www.sudlangues.sn/

Chumbow, B. S., & Bobda, A. S. (2000). French in West Africa: A sociolinguistic perspective, *International Journal of the Sociology of Language*, *141*, 39–60.

Cissé, M. (1994). *Contes wolof modernes*. Paris: Editions L'Harmattan.

Diallo, D. (2006). Le conte au préscolaire, *Tuut Tank*, *9*, novembre-décembre.

Dieng, B. (2010). L'amitié dans le conte ouest-africain comme instrument de régulation et d'intégration, *Ethiopiques*, 84, http://ethiopiques.refer.sn/

Fall, B. (Ed.). (2007). *Les Cahiers de l'Agence Nationale de la Case des Tout-Petits*, numéro. 1, mars. Dakar: UCAD.

Hale, T. A. (1998). *Griots and griottes*. Bloomington and Indianapolis, IN: Indiana University Press.

Kesteloot, L., & Dieng, B. (1989). *Du tieddo au talibé*. Paris: Présence Africaine.

Kesteloot, L., & Mbodj, C. (2006). *Contes et mythes wolof*. Dakar: IFAN.

Leymarie, I. (1999). *Les griots wolof du Sénégal*. Paris: Maisonneuve & Larose.

McLaughlin, F. (1995). Haalpulaar identity as a response to Wolofization. *African Languages and Cultures*, *8*(2), 153–168.

Napon, A. (2003). La problematique de l'introduction des langues nationales dans l'enseignement primaire au Burkina Faso, *Sudlangues*, 2. http://www. sudlangues. sn/spip.php?article59

Ngom, F. (2004). Ethnic identity and linguistic hybridization in Senegal. *International Journal of the Sociology of Language*, *170*, 95–111.

Senghor, L. S., & Sadji, A. (1953). *La belle histoire de Leuk-le-lièvre*. Paris: Hachette.

Thioune, B. (2009). Traditions narratives et initiation culturelle de l'écolier africain dans *La belle histoire de Leuk-le-lièvre*, *Ethiopiques*, 83.

UNESCO. (1953). *The use of vernacular languages in education.* Paris: UNESCO.

UNESCO. (2003). *Education in a multilingual world.* Paris: UNESCO.

Wade, A. (1989). *Un destin pour l'Afrique.* Paris: Karthala.

PART 4
CONTESTING THE FUTURE:
POSTCOLONIALITY AND CULTURAL PRODUCTION
IN FRANCOPHONE AFRICA

CHAPTER 7

THE DIALECTICS OF *NÉGRITUDE* IN FRANCOPHONE AFRICAN FILM: MANSOUR SORA WADE'S *"NDEYSAAN"*

Alice Burgin

Using the case study of Mansour Sora Wade's *Ndeysaan* (*The Price of Forgiveness*, 2001), the following chapter examines the presence of *négritude* aesthetics and ideology in the film as a means of restoring the integrity of African heritage in a new form of national film language. Then, taking into account the contemporary charges against both cultural nationalism and essentialism in *négritude* philosophy, as well as the film's transnational production and reception context, it highlights some related issues and problematics connected to the association of *négritude* with a national cinema in the twenty-first century.

This chapter draws on Mansour Sora Wade's *Ndeysaan* to explore the multiple dialectics of *négritude* and the complicated politics of representation in contemporary Senegalese cinema. Beginning with Manthia Diawara's premise that *négritude* aesthetics are contributing to the development of a new national film language in Senegalese cinema (Diawara, 2010), it suggests that both the contemporary criticisms of *négritude* and the transnational nature of the Senegalese film industry produce unintended and contradictory forms of cross-cultural exchange that problematise reading this cinema purely in terms of national identity. In doing so, the following pages consider both the importance of *négritude* as a movement challenging colonial hegemony, and its criticisms of cultural nationalism and strategic essentialism, in an attempt to determine whether such a choice is indeed one of cultural affirmation or anachronistic nativism.

Négritude and *Ndeysaan*: Ideology and Aesthetics

In his book *African Cinema: New Forms of Aesthetics and Politics* (2010), Diawara writes that in Senegal a "revival" of *négritude* aesthetics is producing a new popular film language that "brings together all the artistic elements of rhythm, emotion, color and architecture, as elements of popular culture defined by Senghor" (Diawara, 2010, p. 146). Turning then to Wade's film, *Ndeysaan*, Diawara describes it as "perhaps the Senegalese film most grounded in the philosophy of *négritude*" (Diawara, 2010, p. 147). Diawara is referring here to the philosophical movement founded in the 1930s by three Francophone poets of African descent, Léopold Sédar Senghor, Aimé Césaire and Léon Damas, which evolved into a valorisation of African race and heritage through the affirmation of positive values and particularly on blackness as "a vibrant cultural force" (Petty, 2008, p. 54). As the name itself suggests, *négritude* functioned as a means of legitimising the derogatory term *nègre*, an attempt to rehabilitate African culture and history in the wake of colonial ideology and, particularly, its inscription of inferiority. In this sense the term worked as "an act of reclaiming and validating blackness in the face of systemic alienation" (Petty, 2008, p. 55), or what Jacques Chevrier describes as « *une attitude à l'égard du monde ... qui se définit essentiellement par opposition à la culture blanche* » (Chevrier (2004b, p. 44). For this reason, as F. Abiola Irele explains, *négritude* as an ideology, whilst symbolic, played an important role in reversing the negative associations of blackness by producing a cultural affirmation through new values that had previously been denied (Irele, 2011, p. 83).

Diawara's reading of *Ndeysaan* as an expression of *négritude* philosophy, and particularly of Senghorian poetics is indeed accurate. The film shares many of the key elements of *négritude* philosophy as well as many themes and motifs explored in the literary criticism dedicated to *négritude* poetry. The film delves into the distant past to recount a magical and tragic story concerning the complicated love triangle between a pair of young lovers, the beautiful Maxoye and Mbanick, and Mbanick's best friend, Yatma, who is himself in love with Maxoye. As Diawara suggests, such a setting recalls Senghor's own recurrent motif, the *retour au royaume d'enfance*, or return to the kingdom of childhood. Championing African cultural heritage that had previously been negated by French colonial ideology, Senghor glorifies the African past by romanticising the primitive society and the traditions of black cultures. The prominence of what Jean-Paul Sartre described in his seminal essay on *négritude*, "Black Orpheus" (Sartre and McCombie, 1964, p. 18) as an "anti-racist racism" is present, with the Hegelian dialectics associating blackness with a negative value inverted through the reinstating of African cultural values and traditions to produce "a consciousness brought about more particularly by those of African descent" (Jeanpierre, 1965, p. 871).

The film begins with a griot's narration, claiming, "yesterday is not today, once there was a village here ... where I was born", an opening that deliberately displaces the narrative from any specific moment in time, drawing on familiar fairy-tale conventions that set the scene for a fable. At the same time, the griot's presence as *témoin*, a witness to the events about to unfold creates the sense that what is to be recounted will blur the boundaries of reality and imagination. The film then dissolves into fog, which transports the viewer back to a primeval setting of a coastal fishing town where villagers are in the process of making a ritual offering to the ancestors to lift the fog hanging over the village, which has made the fish disappear from the ocean and is preventing the fisherman from being able to go to sea. Right from this early scene, ancestor worship is introduced, a second element of *négritude* identified by Sartre, with the presence of totems, ancestors and ritual infusing the narrative through the lives of the main characters (Sartre and MacCombie, 1964, pp. 21, 29, 30, 40).

Mbanick's father, Baye Sogui, the village's spiritual leader, is dying, and is therefore too weak to chase the fog away. Mbanick, we learn, has rejected his inherited destiny as the town's saviour and the wisdom of Baye Sogui. However, at the death of his father, possessed by the spirit of Baye Sogui, he builds a canoe and sails out to sea to chase the fog away. On his return, the fog lifted and the sea plentiful, he becomes the town hero and wins the heart of Maxoye. Yet Yatma, jealous of his best friend's relationship and new-found status within the town, murders Mbanick and dumps him in the sea, notable because, as we learn earlier, Mbanick's totem is the shark, and Yatma, the lion. Whilst the whole town is aware of what happened to Mbanick, the influence of Yatma's powerful father keeps Yatma himself safe. What's more, his father asks Maxoye to marry his son, which she agrees to. It is only on their wedding night that Yatma realises that Maxoye will not be a good wife, but rather, has married him to punish him. He learns too, that she is expecting Mbanick's child, and that he will raise the child with the knowledge of what he has done. As years go by, Yatma does his best for redemption. Eventually, Maxoye forgives him, but it is clear that the spirit of Mbanick has not. When Yatma goes out fishing, he becomes aware that a shark is waiting for him, and that his crime will not go unpunished.

Whilst warned not to go out to sea for twelve moons, Yatma decides to face his destiny, accepting his fate and disappears into the ocean. Fortunately, he too has left Maxoye with a son, and thus, the cycle of life continues.

However, it is only via the death of Baye Sogui and his possession of his son Mbanick that we see the ancestral world enter into the everyday reality of the village. It is from this point that the magical is infused into the narrative. Mbanick's transformation into his totem, the shark, which takes place after his murder, is what French film critic Catherine Ruelle describes in an interview with the filmmaker, the recognition of « *une autre réalité* », a comment that director Wade is quick to agree with (Ruelle, 2002, n.p.). Wade also creates unusual breaks in the narrative, with characters' direct address to the audience, large deliberate lapses in the diegetic time, and the use of mixed-media and special effects, for example during the story telling sessions and the scene where Mbanick chops down the tree under which his father is buried. These conventions, whilst designed to rupture the suspension of disbelief, also work to create a type of surreal rupture from the everyday, and in this sense, are closely aligned to what Senghor defines as a spiritual sub-reality (*surréalité*) that exists beyond the surface level of the everyday, creating in the film a duality within the Lébou universe (Senghor, 1964, p. 203). Aesthetically, Wade recreates this *surréalité* by blurring the boundary between worlds on a visual level. In a break from the film's overall style, the story of Mbanick and Yatma's totems' origins are narrated through shadow puppetry, using geometric rod puppets that are borrowed from Chinese puppetry. This mixed-media approach is unconventional, allowing the film to produce a secondary universe, different from, but connected with, those telling their ancestral stories. The film works at these moments to posit a dual reality, or an opposition between appearance and *surréalité*, a metaphor embodied in the very art of shadow puppetry itself. This engagement with a *surréalité* binds the film not only with Senghor's own work, but with that of the surrealists, who both influenced and supported the *négritude* movement, and recalls Breton's own powerful statement in the *Manifestes du Surréalisme*, « *Je crois à la résolution future de ces deux états, en apparence si contradictoires, que sont le rêve et la réalité, en une sorte de réalité absolue, de surréalité, si l'on peut ainsi dire* » (Breton, 1962, p. 23–24). The setting in the distant, ahistorical past, and this duality of worlds, one of the ordinary and one of the extraordinary, reinforces *négritude*'s desire for rediscovery of traditional African culture, creating "a mystique with a definite social aim: to create out of a community of experience and feeling a new community of values and destiny" (Irele, 2011, p. 83). This is part of the process of cultural legitimation, producing a narrative of self-differentiation that is marking the particularity of cultural heritage and, in the process, repositing Lébou culture as a source of pride, Sartre's anti-racist racism.

Yet, other connections between *négritude* as a philosophy, its aesthetics and the film can be made. In a ritual ceremony, Yatma performs his totem, the lion, to a circle of onlookers, including Maxoye. At the end of the ritual, with Yatma on all fours, Maxoye moves into the circle where she says "griot, don't add any more, it's tasty enough, we like it that way". She then proceeds to dance in front of Yatma, to the beat of a drum that, combined with the dance, expires an energy that is both emotionally and sexually charged. The film cuts to Yatma, still on all fours, who, remaining true to his totemesque bestiality, looks like a lion ready to devour his prey. This is the turning point in the relationship between the couple. As Yatma lifts himself from the ground and responds, in a dance equally erotic, the film makes multiple cuts to Maxoye's smiling face, her emotions visibly softening towards her husband. The next scene, which takes place at night in their hut, is the moment Yatma is finally forgiven for his crime, and finally permitted to satiate his desire for her body. The connection made in these scenes between the rhythmic performance of sexual desire, forgiveness and satiation is important, as it connects rhythm, via the dance, to life and rebirth, resonating with Sartre's third and fourth elements of *négritude*, rhythm (Sartre and MacCombie, 1964, pp. 35, 43) and sexual conception (Sartre and MacCombie, 1964, p. 42). The next time we see Maxoye, she has given birth to a second son this time, the son of Yatma. In relation to *négritude* aesthetics, the scene draws on a notion of rhythm in art as an ordering life force as described in Senghor's "What the black man contributes" (Senghor, 1964).[1]

Diawara draws the connection between the film's own primeval setting in the small, traditional African village, and concepts of a nostalgia and *douleur*, via the narrative that is fictional, but drawing visually on the everyday practices of village life, a key element in the restoring of identity back into the African consciousness. Wade's determination to draw faithfully upon his own traditional culture as a Lébou tribesman is another way of reading nostalgia and its accompanying sense of loss within the film. His choice to adapt the novel came from what he describes as the rigorous observation undertaken by the author on the Lébou community, whereby the director was impressed with the novel's detail to describe local customs as well as ancestral and animist practices. According to Wade, Baye Sogui, the village mystic, is « *un personnage qui a réellement existé ... il connaissait les secrets de la mer et a eu des pouvoirs mystiques* » (cited in Ruelle, 2002, n.p.). In Senghor's own writing this notion of loss is often present, accompanied by nostalgia for another time before the European upheaval of African communities, via the return to *le royaume d'enfance*, embodied in the film's pre-colonial setting. The return is not only to familial heritage, embodied in the love triangle and themes of family, but also literally through the griot, who is both the storyteller in the present day and the child, Amul Yaakar, within the story. Amul Yaakaar, like Mbanick, does not want to follow his father's footsteps as a griot, but, rather, wants to be a fisherman. Thus the nostalgia for the kingdom of childhood produced in the film is connected not only to childhood in general but also to that of a pre-colonial Africa, or Africa-as-child. It is poignant then that the name Amul Yaakaar – a creation of Wade who does not exist in the book – means "without hope" (*sans espoir*) in Wolof.

According to Irele, the motif of rediscovery, embodied in returning to Africa as a source of pride and the glorification of an African past, is one of the key thematics of *négritude* aesthetics. He writes: "This opening up of the African mind to certain dimensions of its own world which Western influence had obscured appears to be in fact the most essential and the most significant element in the literature of *négritude* … giving new meaning to the traditional African worldview" (Irele, 2011, pp. 50–51). However, whilst imbued with a Senghorian worldview, there are also elements of alienation, another dominant theme attributed more closely to writers such as Césaire, as a means of reflecting the violent rupture experienced by the colonial subject forced to enter modernity. This is embodied in the testimony of the griot, who, whilst a minor player in the story, is also the contemporary narrator spanning the fractured temporalities. The film's connection to *négritude* as an ideology is present in this figure of the griot upon whom, according to the narrative, colonial oppression is directly inflicted.

In addition, Wade can be read as engaging with *négritude* as an ideology, not just as style. Just as for Senghor *négritude* aesthetics were entwined in a philosophical response to mechanistic and dehumanising European epistemologies, Wade asserts a similar position:

> *Malgré mon éducation occidentale, je fais mon devoir, qui est de participer, de donner [aux ancêtres]. Il y a eu un moment dans ma vie où j'ai pensé et agi autrement. J'étais assez mal, désemparé. Quand mon cousin m'a dit qu'il fallait faire un sacrifice, je l'ai fait. Je me suis 'retrouvé' et je crois que je le dois aux ancêtres!* (Cited in Ruelle, 2002, n.p.)

In this sense, *négritude* in the film mirrors the way *négritude* poetry "retraces a collective drama as well as a spiritual adventure, involving the quest for self" (Irele, 2011, p. 52) and it is equally in this sense of collectivism that the final element of *négritude* as identified by Sartre emerges in *Ndeysaan* (Irele, 2011, p. 44). As Diawara writes, "In the film we learn that breaking this contract [of friendship and love between tribes and clans] in this primeval setting can lead to the destruction of the whole society" (Diawara, 2010, p. 149). In a similar way, the character of Maxoye, who agrees to marry Yatma despite him killing her lover, can be read in two different ways; firstly, she embodies the passive resistance that is an attribute of *négritude* highlighted by Sartre. Here, she symbolises the recurring construct of African women in *négritude* philosophy as "a motivational force constructed not in the active tense but in the passive" (Ajayi, 1997, p. 39); secondly, as she learns to forgive Yatma for his crime, Maxoye transforms into an embodiment of Mother Africa, whereby "[i]n the *négritude* construct, she is the antidote of colonialism and what it stands for, domination and the destruction of African values" (Ajayi, 1997, p. 40). This African woman, untouched by colonialism, who is natural and nurturing, is a recurring thematic construct in *négritude* philosophy, articulated in works such as Senghor's *"Femme noire"* (Senghor, 1990, p. 16).

Considering this, it is clear that *Ndeysaan* is a text actively engaging with the primary goal of *négritude* as an ideology, which, as Trica Keaton argues, "entails the restoration of the full integrity of a denigrated Africa and its peoples deemed inherently subhuman by strands of Enlightenment and post-Enlightenment thought presented to the world as modernity" (Keaton, 2010, p. 114). Keaton's emphasis of restoration is important, as it also draws attention to the notion of the loss, or "almost" loss that Wade is referring to above. Here, we see how, as Césaire claims, « *le mouvement de la négritude affirme la solidarité de la diaspora avec le monde africain* » (cited in Beloux, 1969, n.p.), reflecting the cultural nationalism of pan-Africanism that united the three poets, despite their different origins, whilst providing Senegal with its own popular film language.

Cultural Nationalism

Diawara draws on the connection between *négritude* and *Ndeysaan* to illustrate his main argument that *négritude* offers filmmakers a means of accessing a new popular film language through the use of popular African culture. He does not, however, further explore this relationship, leaving the ramifications of such an association open to interpretation by the reader. Yet, in an era of globalisation, in an industry of transnationalism, and at a point in history where, in the words of Stanislas Adotévi, "Negritude is dead" (cited in Jules-Rosette, 1998, p. 71), it seems that there are certain contradictions that such an association produces in the twenty-first century that are worth exploring. What does it mean to make a film entrenched in the aesthetics of *négritude*, of cultural nationalism, and romantic nostalgia for the tribalism of an African past today? And, taking into account the film as a transnational production with European funding and an international audience, how does such strategic, racial essentialism of *négritude* philosophy reinforce the way Africa is consumed in Europe?

Such questions explore the complex nature of represent-tation in an era that, according to Ella Shohat and Robert Stam, sees issues of self-representation "fraught with personal and political tensions about who speaks, when, how and in whose name" (Shohat and Stam, 1994, p. 342). Attempting to move away from traditional binaries of em-powered/disempowered and oppressor/oppressed, they recognise the "wide spectrum of complex relationalities of domination, subordination and collaboration" and suggest that "individuals are traversed by dissonance and contra-diction, existing within a constantly shifting cultural and psychic field in which the most varied discourses exist in evolving multivalenced relationships, constituting the sub-ject, like the media, as the site of competing discourses and voices" (Shohat and Stam, 1994, p. 343).

Indeed, the *négritude* movement at its inception was transnational in nature, developing as a response to Euro-pean prejudices experienced by its founders in Paris, which was home to a large expatriate international community, who were in turn forced to confront the realities of their own alienation and racism in response to these prejudices. The founders of the movement drew their inspiration from both a notion of pan-Africanism, as well as the influences of the Harlem Renaissance (coming out of the US) and the resistance to colonialism in Haiti in order to reflect upon their own racial and cultural identity. Importantly, this was facilitated by the emergence of modernism and the challenges this posed to colonial ideology within the European intellectual community, garnering the support of Breton and Sartre, who helped launch the movement into the limelight. Thus, *négritude* developed out of an intercultural exchange, with foundations in the black diaspora of Paris, and spread throughout the colonies. This *négritude*, in this sense, had less to do with creating a particularly nationalist identity (although it was appropriated to embody and justify nationalism in post-colonial African states), but was intended as a means of embodying a black African consciousness, that traversed the boundaries of the nation, be it in Africa or Europe. In this sense, the intentions of the movement can be understood as a means of developing a common consciousness that is not limited to national loyalties.

However, despite this transnational heritage, *négritude* became closely aligned to the politics of cultural nationalism and became connected to the aesthetic and ideological manifestation of an imagined pan-African cultural heritage, what Lilyan Kesteloot describes as « *le patrimoine culturel, les valeurs et surtout l'esprit de la civilisation négro-africaine* » (Kesteloot, 2001, p. 106). Whilst the *négritude* founders did not see this essentialism in absolutist terms, the ideology of *négritude* paved the way for a cultural nationalism that was grossly misinterpreted to justify abuses of power around the continent, rather than facilitate the entrance of African nation-states into modernity in the postcolonial era. Denis Ekpo argues that this *négritude*, what he labels "official Negritude", created a myth of Africa that was so oppositional to Europe that it meant that African nation-states could not enter into modernity in the way that they would have liked to. Rather, this type of cultural nationalism created an incommensurability which not only prohibited African nation-states from developing but also used *négritude* and its promotion of anti-European cultural nationalism to revert to a tribalism ("Africanised modernity") that in his words "became the abattoir for disposing of the last remnants of the heritage of modernity in Africa, including the state, the economy, reason and humanity" (Ekpo, 2010, p. 180). By the 1980s, *négritude* had become the chagrin of African Studies, a result of what Ekpo describes as "the sheer inanity of its postulations on race, Africanicity and emotivity; partly as a result of the grave errors of a purely cultural-nationalistic self-understanding and apprehension of modernity" (Ekpo, 2010, p. 178). Kenneth Harrow continues with a succinct overview of what Ekpo is referring to:

> The 1980s saw the general deterioration of economic conditions, the relative impoverishment of African societies, especially *vis-a-vis* the West, the commensurate increase of state corruption and oppression, the large scale violation of human rights, the general expansion of military rule, of police-state conditions, and the expropriation of national resources by multinational corporations with the connivance of ruling elites (Harrow, 1999, p. xvii).

It is for these reasons that Nwachukwu Frank Ukadike was confident enough to outline that whilst "Pan-Africanism and *négritude* are the two great philosophies invoked by African leaders ... today these movements have proven inadequate to the profound challenges of independence" (Ukadike, 1994, p. 67). It is in this context of post-pan-Africanism that *Ndeysaan*, with its subtle critique of colonialism and its romantic nostalgia for the primeval pre-colonial era, can be understood as expressing what Ekpo berates as "the anachronistic nativism of postcolonial art", which he sees as "Africa's major route to entanglement in the cross-cultural complications of modernity" (Ukadike, 1994, p. 186).

Racialised Essentialism

Conversely, a second problem with reading *Ndeysaan* through a national paradigm is that it ignores the transnational production context and the subsequent process of cross-cultural spectatorship that the film must negotiate. Of particular importance is the role of France, the co-producing country, who is both the major financial donor and consumer of the film. The accumulation of funds that financed *Ndeysaan* can be categorised as follows: 62% from France, 28% from Europe (including a fund from the EU, of which France is its most generous donor) and 10% from Senegal (Fig. 4), with the majority of the French money coming from the French Ministry's aid programme, *Fonds*

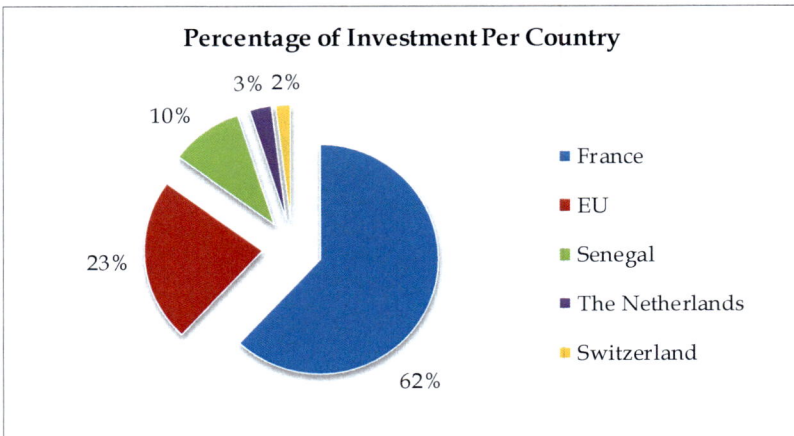

Fig. 4. Distribution of funds invested in *Ndeysaan* by percentage by nation, as outlined by budget proposal submitted to the Institut Français.

Sud Cinéma, the *Organisation internationale de la Francophonie* (*OIF*) and the French satellite television company TPS Star (which merged with Canal+ in 2007 to become CanalSat) (Fig. 5). The investment by TPS Star confirmed the rights to screen the film on satellite television in France after its theatrical release.

For most West African filmmakers, the motivation for participating in a transnational co-production is clear. As Ukadike explains, "[t]he primary reason that some African

Funds Distribution

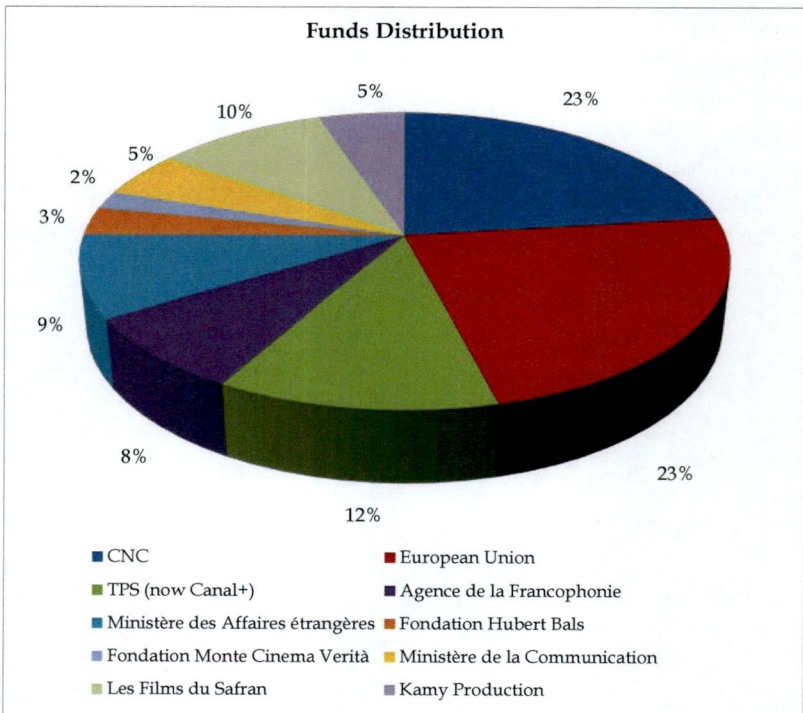

Fig. 5. Distribution of funds invested in *Ndeysaan* by percentage by investor, as outlined by budget proposal submitted to the Institut Français.

filmmakers opt for co-production extends far beyond the *raising* of capital. The *recuperation* of that capital and the *generation of profit* for reinvestment into another film project is [*sic*] essential" (Ukadike, 1994, p. 136). Whilst this explains the necessity for co-productions from the African perspective, motives for European investment in West African cinema, generally an unprofitable venture, are more complicated, with companies/organisations tending to invest in films that express certain core-values of the company/organisation itself. An example is the commitment to promote and preserve cultural diversity; an agenda shared by *Fonds Sud*, the OIF, and the EU program that funded *Ndeysaan*. The form of cultural diversity articulated within these policies addresses the struggle for non-European minority cultures to maintain a sense of cultural identity in relation to the homogenising forces of the global north through the creation of their own cinema, with the intention « *que toutes les voix puissent se faire entendre à une époque où la mondialisation des échanges a plutôt tendance à standardiser toutes les formes de consommations culturelles* » (Cayla, 2006, n.p.). However, as I have argued elsewhere, these European cultural policies are shaped primarily by internal political factors, and generally share a fear of US cultural exports as a form of cultural imperialism that undermines European integrity (Burgin, 2006). For this reason, the approach to the formation of cultural identity is developed in a way that Cris Shore describes as "a dualistic and oppositional process", whereby cultural policies remain committed to constructing a homo-genous dominant culture that is formulated around shared European assumptions (Shore, 2001, p. 118). Secondly, TPS Star's investment guarantees the film a European public, which introduces the notion of a transnational audience that must challenge what Mari Maasilta describes as "the dominant emphasis" which considers transnational films as "belong[ing] to the body of national cinema of that particular country", rather than taking into account the effects of globalised modernity on the way films are shaped (Shore, 2001, p. 21). Both of these ideas raise questions pertaining to the notion of the film's cultural guardianship, suggesting instead that we privilege concepts of cultural hybridity and interstitiality over cultural authenticity or cultural nationalism as fundamental to the successful reception of the film on two continents.

The inherent transnationalism of the film, whose funding, production and reception sees it reliant upon, and answerable to, the Franco-Parisian centre of cultural production, encourages us to think about how *négritude* aesthetics and ideology circulate outside Senegal, and predominantly in Paris, where the film garnered a ten-week theatrical release in 2002. Whilst Diawara argues that *négritude* aesthetics provide filmmakers a way of creating a national cinema, the presence of cultural hybridisation, the imbalance of power within the transnational exchange, and the consumption site being primarily European all produce what Will Higbee and Song Hwee Lim describe as "the continual negotiation between the global and the local that often extends beyond the host/home binary" (Higbee and Lim, 2010, pp. 9–10) and thus challenge claims to any pure national cinema (Diawara, 2010, p. 10)

Whilst it is impossible to speak of any essential spectator, it also seems impossible not to recognise that different forms of meaning-making will be produced in the *art et essai* cinemas in Paris as well as the historical role Paris played in the formation of *négritude* and its association with racialised essentialism which developed in opposition to French culture. Because of its confrontation of white supremacy through racial polemics, one of the greatest criticisms pertaining to *négritude* today has been aimed at its inversion of racial ideology, rather than its eradication. As Wole Soyinka states, "Negritude stayed within a pre-set system of Eurocentric intellectual analysis both of man and society and tried to re-define the African and his society in those externalised terms" (Soyinka, 1976, p. 136). In his own reading of Senghor's poetry, Diawara is aware of this contradiction:

> [I]t can be argued that [Senghor] had no choice but to speak in an appropriated discourse that could recognize the African only as other. Even his categories of the black as warm, rhythmic, musical, and emotional come from a well-established source in French literature ... The *négritude* of Senghor, because it was only addressed to French People, and because it was removed from Africa, constituted a black that never existed except as the unconscious of the French (Diawara, 1997, p. 460).[2]

Whilst Senghor's intention in the 1930s was to legitimise the concept of Blackness, seventy years of social and political advancement have seen the tenets of *négritude* become out-dated, embarrassing even, as scholars began to problematise the essentialist discourse of *négritude* as reinforcing clichés that reduce African identity to anti-modernity. Such representation, which posits Black culture in direct opposition with European culture, drawing on European stereotypes in order to define black identity, and associating *négritude* with a worldview that is exclusive of Europe, arguably contradict the empowerment sought by such cultural affirmation.

Considering the film's circulation beyond any national borders, it becomes part of what Arjun Appadurai describes as a transnational *mediascape* that transmits images and ideologies around the globe. For Appadurai, this introduces certain notions of fantasy that are useful for thinking about the consumption of the local within the global sphere. He writes:

> The lines between the realistic and the fictional landscapes ... are blurred, so that the farther away these audiences are from the direct experience of modern life, the more likely they are to construct imagined worlds that are chimerical, aesthetic even fantastic objects, particularly if assessed by the criteria of some other perspective, some other imagined world ... [T]hey help to constitute narratives of the Other and protonarratives of possible lives, fantasies that could become prolegomena and the desire for acquisition and movement" (Appadurai, 1996, pp. 35–36).

Whilst much of Appadurai's work focuses on the desire of movement from global south to north, increasingly, work in the sociology of tourism suggests that such fantasies work in a reverse order, although desire for movement is less entrenched in economic disparity and more closely connected to what can be understood as a form of escapism. Studies by Scott Lash and John Urry (1987), Dean MacCannell (1976) and Ian Munt (1994) all suggest that the desire for movement from the global north towards the south is representative of a ritualistic quest for the authentic in response to post-modernity's risks and dissonances, including wholesale commodification and disorganised capitalism. This resonates with the work of Dominique Wolton on the production of ethnic stereotypes in representations in France, which he describes works like a virtual tourism:

> [N]ous voulons « voir » le mythe et non le réel. Ainsi acceptons-nous d'être manipulés, car nous le voulons. Cela nous rassure sur un monde que nous croyons connaître et dont nous voulons qu'il soit comme nous l'imaginons et non comme il est ... Nous

apprenons à voir le réel à travers le virtuel et nous sommes conscients, aujourd'hui, de ce qu'est le « virtuel » (Wolton, 2008, p. 667).

Drawing from this idea of African cinema as a type of virtual tourism, *Ndeysaan* employs specific tropes that Nicolas Bancel found omnipresent in his research on *le tourisme ethnique*, whereby travel narratives « *s'impregnent sans préjugés de la culture et des mœurs de l'Autre* » (Bancel, 2008, p. 685). The recurring features discussed by Bancel include *une absence de temporalité* or what Bancel describes as a déhistoricisation of the Other, « *autorise à valider le mythe des sociétés circulaires* » (Bancel, 2008, p. 687). Bancel also notes that the recurrence of the tribal figure as a signature of this ahistoricity, and the presence of the griot produces a temporal immobility that relentlessly replays « *le théâtre d'ombres du retour aux sources* » (Bancel, 2008, p. 687). *Ndeysaan* exhibits all these narrative and aesthetic tropes. The film begins and ends with the monologue of the griot, the guardian of the memories, who addresses the audience directly. This narrative is circuitous, the griot's own monologue book-ending the film to create a sense of repetition, whilst simultaneously remaining ahistorical, which draws attention to the anxiety of contemporary modernity as oppositional to an earlier, simpler time.[3]

For Bancel, such narratives appeal to certain concerns about modernity and desires for exotic travel, appealing to both « *l'angoisse de "bougisme"* », « *de la transformation de la segmentation et de la fuite du temps des sociétés postmodernes* » as well as « *le ressourcement* » or « *l'inclination à retrouver – ne serait-ce que fugitivement – du sens dans la contemplation rassurante de sociétés fondées sur des valeurs stables* » which he argues « *s'opère par la quête de l'authenticité de l'Autre et l'appropriation symbolique d'une nature inviolée* » (Bancel, 2008,

p. 688). We can see this even in comments made to Wade by Ruelle, such as « *L'être africain est resté très attaché à la nature* » (Ruelle, 2002, n.p.), which echo same tenets of essentialist identity in *négritude* philosophy. Graham Huggan illustrates that this "interpellation of the authentic *other*" can be read as a perceived desire to invoke "a necessary antidote to a Western culture rendered inauthentic by its attachment to material excess" (Huggan, 2001, p. 158). *Ndeysaan* could thus be charged as working to reaffirm particular European fantasies through the consumption of an authentic African culture untouched by modernity. Considering the investment by European organisations in the film then, the *négritude* aesthetics in *Ndeysaan*, whilst perhaps conforming to a particular national film language, are also ideal for producing a consumable text within a transnational framework by appealing to desires to consume particular images of the exotic African other.

Conclusion

Whilst Diawara is correct in asserting the film's *négritude*, I have argued that it is problematic to draw from this an argument for a pure national cinema. Firstly, this association between *négritude* and cultural nationalism has been severely criticised for its perpetuation of an anti-modernity. Secondly, such claims ignore the transnational nature of the film's own production and reception context and the effects of this transnationalism on the film's overall thematic and stylistic choices. As David Murphy argues, "Africa and the West are not mutually exclusive worlds that possess their own authentic and unchanging identities: they are hybrid entities that influence and modify each other, and this process of exchange applies to cinema (Murphy, 2000, p. 241). Whilst a cinema engaged in the philosophical and aesthetic characteristics of *négritude* may in some ways work to reify a history lost through the trauma of the colonial project, this cultural nationalism and strategic essentialism also risk reinforcing a "defensive cultural protectionism" and "victim's mien" that pander to stereotypes of Africanness that exist in complete opposition not only to Europe, but to the contemporary globalised modernity of the twenty-first century (Ekpo, 2010, p. 186).

Notes

1. Senghor writes, "[t]his ordering force that constitutes Negro style is rhythm. It is the most sensible and the least material thing. It is the vital element *par excellence*. It is the primary condition for, and sign of, art, as respiration is of life – respiration that rushes or slows down, becomes regular or spasmodic, depending on the being's tension, the degree and quality of the emotion" (Senghor, 1964).

2. Thus, as Diawara claims, "the result of such a discourse is not only the impossibility of beautifying the other – that is of making it exotic and French – but also the impossibility of speaking of Africa without reasserting the superiority of the West over it" (Diawara, 1997, p. 461).

3. The griot did not appear in the novel from which the film was adapted, but was added by Wade because « *[i]l m'a semblé indispensable, pour me rapprocher de la structure narrative du conte* » (cited in Ruelle, 2002, n.p.).

References

Ajayi, O. (1997). Negritude, feminism, and the quest for identity: Re-reading Mariama Bâ's *So Long a Letter*,

Women's Studies Quarterly: Teaching African Literatures in a Global Literary Economy, 3/4, 35–52.

Appadurai, A. (1996). *Modernity at large: Cultural dimensions of globalization*. Minneapolis; London: University of Minnesota Press.

Bancel, N. (2008). Tourisme ethnique : une reconquête symbolique? (1961–2006). In P. Blanchard, S. Lemaire, & N. Bancel (Eds.), *Culture coloniale en France : De la Révolution française à nos jours*. Paris: CNRS Éditions.

Beloux, F. (1969). *Aimé Césaire: un poète politique*, http://www.magazine-litteraire.com/content/hommage/article?id=8774, accessed 24 November, 2011.

Breton, A. (1962). *Manifestes du surréalisme*. Paris: J. J. Pauvert.

Burgin, A. (2011). From cultural protection to national protectionism: Reading contradictions of France's Cultural Diversity Agenda in Abderrahmane Sissako's *Bamako* (2006), *Bulletin of Francophone Postcolonial Studies*, 2, 8–16.

Cayla, V. (2006). *Les 25 ans du Fonds Sud Cinéma*. Retrieved on 20 November 2010 from : http://www.cnc.fr/CNC_GALLERY_CONTENT/DOCUMENTS/publications/plaquettes/Plaquette_25ansFdsSud.pdf

Chevrier, J. (2004b). La littérature négro-africaine en langue française de 1921 à nos jours. *La littérature nègre*. Paris: Armand Colin, 14–158.

Diawara, M. (1997). Reading Africa through Foucault: V. Y. Mudimbe's reaffirmation of the subject. In A. McClintock, A. Mufti & E. Shohat (Eds.). *Dangerous liaisons: Gender, nation and postcolonial perspectives*. Minneapolis, MN: University of Minnesota Press.

Diawara, M. (2010). *African film: New forms of aesthetics and politics*. Munich: Prestel.

Ekpo, D. (2010). Introduction: From negritude to post-Africanism, *Third Text: Critical Perspectives on Contemporary Art and Criticism*, 24(2), 177–187.

Harrow, K. W. (1999). Introduction. In K. W. Harrow (Ed.), *African cinema: Postcolonial and feminist readings*. Trenton, NJ: Africa World Press.

Higbee, W., & Lim, S. H. (2010). Concepts of transnational cinema: Towards a critical transnationalism in film studies, *Transnational Cinemas*, 1(1), 7–21.

Huggan, G. (2001). *The postcolonial exotic: Marketing the margins*. London: Routledge.

Irele, F. A. (2011). *The negritude moment*. Trenton, NJ: Africa World Press.

Jeanpierre, W. A. (1965). Sartre's Theory of "Anti-Racist Racism" in his study of negritude, *The Massachusetts Review*, 6(4).

Jules-Rosette, B. (1998). *Black Paris: The African Writers' landscape*. Urbana, IL: University of Illinois Press.

Keaton, T. (2010). The politics of race blindness, *Du Bois Review*, 7(1), 103–131.

Kesteloot, L. (2001). *Histoire de la littérature négro-africaine*. Paris: Karthala, AUF.

Lash, S., & Urry, J. (1987). *The end of organized capitalism*. Cambridge: Polity Press.

Maasilta, M. (2007). *African Carmen: Transnational cinema as an arena for cultural contradictions*. Unpublished doctoral thesis, Tampere, University of Tampere.

MacCannell, D. (1976). *The tourist: A new theory of the leisure class*. London: Macmillan.

Munt, I. (1994). The "Other" postmodern tourism: Culture, travel and the new middle classes, *Theory, Culture & Society*, 11(3), 101–123.

Murphy, D. (2000). Africans filming Africa: Questioning theories of an authentic African cinema, *Journal of African Cultural Studies, 13*(2), 239–249.

Petty, S. J. (2008). *Contact zones: Memory, origin, and discourses in black diasporic cinema.* Detroit, MI: Wayne State University Press.

Ruelle, C. (2002). Le « souffle des ancêtres » est une morale de vie: entretien de Catherine Ruelle avec Mansour Sora Wade, *Africultures: Islam, croyances et négritude dans les cinémas d'Afrique, 47.*

Sartre, J.-P., & MacCombie J. (1964). (trans.), Black Orpheus, *The Massachusetts Review, 6*(1).

Senghor, L. S. (1964). *Liberté I: Négritude et humanisme.* Paris: Seuil.

Senghor, L. S. (1990). *Œuvre poétique.* Paris: Seuil.

Shohat, E., & Stam, R. (1994). *Unthinking Eurocentrism: Multiculturalism and the media.* London: Routledge.

Shore, C. (2001). The cultural policies of the European Union and cultural diversity. In Tony Bennett (Ed.), *Differing diversities: Transversal study on the theme of cultural policy and cultural diversity.* Strasbourg: Council of Europe.

Soyinka, W. (1976). *Myth, literature and the African world.* Cambridge: Cambridge University Press.

Ukadike, N. F. (1994). *Black African cinema.* Berkeley, CA: University of California Press.

Wolton, D. (2008). Des stéréotypes coloniaux aux regards post-coloniaux: l'indispensable évolution des imaginaires. In P. Blanchard, S. Lemaire & N. Bancel (Eds.), *Culture coloniale en France: De la Révolution française à nos jours.* Paris: CNRS Éditions.

CHAPTER 8

NEGOTIATING POSTCOLONIALITY IN FRANCOPHONE AFRICAN LITERATURE

Sarah Burnautzki

While the French literary field has changed over past decades offering up space for new literary positions, economic interests and power relations still occupy a key position in this system. In the absence of sufficient awareness of these factors, the current hype surrounding *métissage* and hybridity in France could serve to obfuscate the political and economic interests that lie hidden beneath the contemporary entanglement of "differentialist" discourses. By subjecting so-called Francophone African literature to a materialist critique, we uncover how these new positionings are controlled by established power structures, indicating that literary domination – as it impacts upon Francophone African writers – has regrouped along highly ambivalent multiculturalist conflict lines.

Contemporary Francophone "African" literature as it presents itself today is a product of a latent process of literary "ethnification"[1] that scholars and critics, especially in France, mostly fail to account for. For a long time in France neither public nor academic discourses were receptive to "communitarian" conceptual categories when accounting for the sociocultural reality of ethnic minorities in France. Rather, ethnic categories were perceived in France as a product of US-American social specificity that counteracted the French republicanist tradition of universalism. For this reason, "literary communitarianism" in the field of Francophone literature might be considered a theoretical blind spot: whilst remaining hidden behind an ideological tradition of colour blind French republicanism postulating equality for all, it fails to account for the very real inequalities and forms of literary domination within Francophone literature itself. Yet according to Pascale Casanova, French literary universalism is one of the most normative traditions. As she notes,

> ... this immense realm, a hundred times surveyed yet always ignored, has remained invisible because it rests on a fiction accepted by all who take part in the game: the fable of an enchanted world, a kingdom of pure creation, the best of all possible worlds, where universality reigns through liberty and equality. It is this fiction, proclaimed throughout the world, that has obscured its real nature until the present day. In thrall to the notion of literature as something pure, free and universal, the contestants of literary space refuse to acknowledge the actual functioning of its peculiar economy ... (Casanova, 2004, p. 11).

Moreover, as Casanova explains in a historical perspective, Paris claims to be the "city endowed with the greatest literary prestige in the world" (Casanova, 2004, p. 24), which is why, in the French literary field, actual inequalities and forms of domination remain mostly concealed behind the maxim of literary universalism.

With the development of Pierre Bourdieu's analysis of the social determinisms of possibilities for literary forms, the sociology of literature has come to provide critical tools to challenge the French tradition of immanent textual inter-pretation. In the context of basic literary relations of domination due to the minimal autonomy within the literary field, I would like to focus on a more specific form of literary domination in the French literary field. Precisely that so-called Francophone "African" literature is not produced and consumed under the same rules of art as national French literature. Instead, I would argue that another rule – that of radical "othering" – and reduction of authors and texts to a few ethnic attributes takes place when it comes to certain writers and their texts. Thus so-called African literature results not only from objective positioning and aesthetic oppositions in the field of literary possibilities, but is also determined by different practices of cultural "othering" and "ethnification"[2] brought forward by publishers, promoters and consumers of texts.

If these processes of literary "ethnification" are not easily distinguishable in the Francophone context, this may be due to the fact that they are embedded in a more general field of power in which symbolic capital is unequally distributed while several general processes of marketing, legitimation and reception are already taking place without necessarily meeting the criteria of ethnic discrimination. By describing the aesthetic phenomena, not only through a textual approach but also through an external contextualisation (that is, highlighting the specific context of textual production and consumption itself), the following pages focus on the social parameters that make possible the emergence of certain aesthetic forms within the field of "African" literature.

Theoretical Principles of Literary Domination

When we study the literary domination so-called Francophone African writers face in the field of literature, we find some helpful elements in Bourdieu's exploration of the social determinism of possibility in this kind of literature. According to Bourdieu, the structure of the literary field is based on the opposition between dominant and dominated positions. While representatives of the dominant pole stand for an established and consecrated definition of literature, defining the criteria of legitimacy, they regulate access to recognition. At the same time their competitors are representatives of the dominated pole, engaging with vanguard or heretical forms of literature and fighting for new definitions. However, according to Bourdieu, these opposing camps actually accredit the same literary game.

> It is engendered in the fight between those who have already left their mark and are trying to endure, and those who cannot make their own marks in their turn without consigning to the past those who have an interest in stopping time, eternalizing the present state; between the dominants whose strategy is tied to continuity, identity and reproduction, and the dominated, the new entrants, whose interest is in discontinuity, rupture, difference and revolution. *Faire date* is at once *to make a new position exist* beyond established positions, *ahead [en avant]* of those positions, *en avant-garde*, and in introducing difference, to produce time itself (Bourdieu, 1996, p. 154).

That is, the game of legitimation is reproducing itself steadily through transformations and aesthetic "revolutions" that become a part of the history of literature, before being replaced by new forms of literary legitimacy. Consequently aesthetic forms of "heresy" or resistance are to be understood as constitutive of the continuity of the field in its historical change. However, resistance and heresy fail to challenge the rules of the literary game since these heretical forms, when they are once accepted and recognised, become themselves the new normative form. Therefore, according to Bourdieu, a dependency of the literary field on the field of power remains present, with political relations continuing to determine the literary "Space of Possibles" (Bourdieu, 1996, p. 234). Each literary innovation has to be enabled preceded by a shift in power relations. He writes,

> If the permanent struggles between possessors of specific capital and those who are still deprived of it constitute the motor of an incessant transformation of the supply of symbolic products, it remains true that they can only lead to deep transformations of the symbolic relations of force that result in the overthrowing of the hierarchy of genres, schools and authors, when these struggles can draw support from external changes moving in the same direction (Bourdieu, 1996, p. 127).

Bourdieu identifies this as a "dialectic of distinction" (Bourdieu, 1996, p. 157), a principle that enables new entrants or dominated writers to represent and purport a new definition of literature by means of distinction from the former definition.

> [O]ne can understand the role given to marks of distinction, which, in the best of cases, aim to pinpoint the most superficial and visible of the properties attached to a set of works or of producers. Words, names of schools or groups, proper names – they only have such importance because they make things into something: distinctive signs, they produce existence in a universe where to exist is to be different, "to make oneself a name", a proper name or a name in common (that of a group) (Bourdieu, 1996, p. 157).

However, distinction as a principle of implementation of aesthetic innovations by differentiation and demarcation from older forms is of little help when it comes to so-called Francophone African writers. Within the existing power relations, due to both a perceived lack of symbolic capital, and because of an attitude of exoticism on the part of legitimating instances (as publishers, journalists and critics for instance), a certain "difference" is being *a priori* ascribed to those writers. Dominated authors are though constrained to negotiate and merchandise their own presumed difference and it is not primarily to the aesthetical difference of their texts but often to themselves that some value is granted; whilst performing for better or worse an identitarian masquerade, many authors rely on exoticising their novels as well, as I will further demonstrate. Thus they cannot easily liberate themselves from over-determination. Furthermore, this determinism is primarily reductive – but not heretic in a Bourdieusian sense. By means of an aprioristic ascription of difference that most of the time comes along with a lack of symbolic capital, Francophone "African" literature is perceived as being inferior to the dominant norm and thus cannot deploy any heretic or resistant potential.

In addition, Casanova outlines the problem of literary domination with regard to international dimensions: as the international arena of literature represents in many cases the same contours as the political arena, which is shaped by economic dependencies, the same dependencies are repro-duced on a literary level. Former colonised regions and particularly Francophone ones, remain, to this day depen-dent on the power of consecration of the former metropolis. Thus it is still Paris that represents the dominant pole, deciding on the legitimate definition of literature for almost all Francophone regions (with the exception of Canada). Paris still maintains a monopoly on the most powerful areas of consecration, such as academic institutions, publishing houses, a broad readership with purchasing power and literary prizes. This indicates that a specific literary domina-tion continues to take place within the Francophone "African" literary arena. If some forms of consecration and canonisation are indeed possible for these authors, they can only take place within a framework that remains controlled by power structures with a highly ambivalent process of reception. If the entire process of literary communication from the moment of production until the final reception is thus exposed to the field of power, we have to account for any vanguard emancipation by Francophone "African" authors ending up in aporia. What is more, there remains an illusion of emancipation through the production of a conservative, literary aesthetic that is consolidated and presented as characteristic of the coherent, marketable genre of Francophone "African" literature.

Globalisation of Power Relations and a Paradigm Shift in France

In order to develop a deeper understanding of the historical process behind the emergence of contemporary Francophone "African" literature in France, it is necessary to consider this process within a broader context of French and Francophone cultural theory within an era of globalisation. For a long time in France, cultural theories and identity models served as an opposing model to what is considered in France as the threat of US cultural imperialism. Indeed, the dominant model of self-conception of the French nation defines itself by the ideals of the French Revolution, particularly French universalism (Schor, 2001, p. 43) – as expressed in the principle of equality – and republicanism, holding any French citizen as equal. Therefore the French identity model is regarded as colour blind in contrast to the multicultural, differentialist and colour conscious US Model and struggles hence to account for any cultural, religious or ethnic differences in official discourses. Together with universalism and republicanism, French self-conception is also defined by a cultural self-awareness expressed in the idea of cultural exceptionalism. Initially intended as a means of cultural protectionism, the politics of French cultural exceptionalism served equally to marginalise France to a degree in the international dialogue of theories (Compagnon, 2000, pp. 41–44). To this effect, quite a few paradigm shifts, such as the cultural or the postcolonial turn, did not take place in the French field of literary studies (Murphy, 2002, p. 175). Papa Samba Diop asks for instance why Francophone literary critics and academics have, for a long time resisted any engagement with the concept of postcolonialism: « ... *hormis quelques exemples au sein de l'espace francophone, la majorité des écrits sur le postcolonialisme, pour l'instant sont publiés en anglais et il serait intéressant de savoir pourquoi il en est ainsi* » (Diop 2002, p. 17). (... except some examples in the Francophone zone, a majority of texts on postcolonialism are presently published in English and it would be of some interest to know why.) As François Cusset has shown in his study of the impact of French poststructuralism in the intellectual and academic field of the United States that inspired since the 1980s the developing field of postcolonial studies, there was not, until recently, any significant re-importation of post-colonial theory to France (2003). Thus what resembles a French embargo of Anglophone theory finds a pronounced expression in the delayed translation of seminal postcolonial texts (such as Bhabha, 2007 and Spivak, 2006). An interesting and significant exception from that rule is the case of Francophone Caribbean writers. In fact, cultural theorists and writers such as Édouard Glissant (1981; 1997; 2009), Patrick Chamoiseau, Raphael Confiant and Jean Bernabé (1990), Francophone Caribbean successors of the *négritude* movement, have promoted cultural theories and identity models reminiscent of American cultural differentialism. These writers thus act as mediators between the oppositional camps of Francophone universalism and Anglophone multiculturalism (their regional proximity to the Americas perhaps playing a role in this mediation).

While Francophone Caribbean theory has promoted a multiculturalist cultural theory in the Francophone world since 1989 through the notion of "creoleness", French resistance to American cultural theories remains. Though the inherent contradictions of French universalism have long been criticised (Césaire, 1995 [1955]; Fanon 2002 [1961]), it is in part due to the effects of an ongoing global immigration process that the official discourse is beginning to change, and precisely because of this ongoing process of transformation has precipitated a crisis in the current prevalent model of French national identity. After the decline of the colonial empire, generations of people from former colonies have continued to immigrate to France, highlighting a social reality of permanent change and continuous social inequality in the *Hexagone*, which the official discourse of republican universalism can no longer coherently account for. In this current crisis of French republicanism, postcolonial theories can establish themselves much more easily. But still, as Laetitia Zecchini points out, the French reception of postcolonial theory is not only discrepant in time but also attests to several academic misunderstandings occurring during transfer (Zecchini, 2011, p. 2). Moreover the early writing-back idealism of the 1990s (Ashcroft et al., 2002, p. 11–12), which predicted that the former colonised subjects would engage in a counter-hegemonic dialogical relation with the colonial metropoles and rewrite Eurocentric historiography, reveals itself to be a misapprehension, especially in the case of Francophone literature. Even when French critical discourses on literature engage with postcolonial theory today, the persisting patterns of literary domination often contribute to the reduction of any supposed subversive or counter-hegemonic momentum to reactionary rhetoric, accounting for instance for hybridity in the text or simply ascribing it to the text without any critical analysis of that highly conflicting notion. Therefore the underlying problem of postcolonial theory in the French literary field is the lack of commitment to a critical materialist revision of postcolonial theory as it took place in the Anglophone world two decades ago.

Graham Huggan's materialist critique of "the postcolonial exotic" is very useful for disentangling the complex correlation between Francophone literature, post-colonial theory and the field of power, thus providing a better understanding of how literary dominance is con-figured in a highly globalised, late-capitalist French society. Scrutinising "the sociological dimensions of postcolonial studies" as Huggan explains,

> [p]ostcolonial studies ... has capitalised on its perceived marginality while helping turn marginality itself into a valuable intellectual commodity. Meanwhile, postcolonial writers, and a handful of critics, have accumulated forms of cultural capital that have made them recognized – even celebrity – figures despite their openly oppositional stance (Huggan, 2001, p. vii).

In other words, whereas the academic discipline of postcolonial studies succeeds in becoming recognised and even institutionalised, the theory itself remains deprived of its counter-hegemonic and subversive potential, while inevitably merging with the global late-capitalist system. There, postcolonial theory becomes an intellectual commo-dity serving the logic of production and consumption mainly for the interest of a dominant and global consumer public (Huggan, 2001, pp. vii–xvi). As Huggan suggests, "the term [postcolonialism] circulates as a token of cultural value; it functions as a sales-tag in the context of today's globalised commodity culture." (Huggan, 2001, p. ix). Yet the very same logic of commodification and de-politisation of cultural difference becomes noticeable in the Francophone world, which, he argues, is equally "bound up in a late-capitalist mode of production – a mode in which such terms as "marginality", "authenticity" and "resistance" circulate as commodities available for commercial exploitation, and as signs within a larger semiotic system: the postcolonial exotic" (Huggan, 2001, p. xvi).

This is seen even in a reportedly universalist France, where a booming "alterity industry" (Huggan, 2001, p. vii) and a symbolic market for cultural difference exists not-withstanding universalism. It is therefore almost impossible to account for positive possibilities of subversive and counter-hegemonic positioning in the field of literature, which would not be immediately appropriated by the new multicultural, yet depolitising French postcolonial main-stream. As Marwan Kraidy explains "[m]ainstream public discourse" frames processes of hybridisation and *métissage* as "benign and beneficial" (Kraidy, 2005, p. 148) and points out that the assumption of a genuine counter-hegemonic hybridity is highly misleading. What is more, praise for hybridity in public discourses generally hides the "causal link between politico-economic power" and "unequal inter-cultural relations" (Kraidy, 2005, p. 148). Indeed, when we reconsider the case of Francophone, and especially "African" writers in France, it seems that contemporary multicultural and *métissage*-discourses can actually work, paradoxically, to produce new exclusions: in 2007, forty-four French and Francophone authors (among them several Francophone "African" authors such as Nimrod, Alain Mabanckou and

Abdourahmane Wabéri) signed a manifesto published in *Le Monde* entitled *Pour une littérature-monde en français* celebrating the literary emancipation of supposedly marginalised authors from French literature's domination by acclaiming *métissage*, creolisation and hybridity as legitimate distinctive characteristics of a new definition of literature. Promoted by Michel Le Bris, a French publishing entrepreneur whose interests encompass adventure novels and literature from Francophone non-French writers in France, suspicion has arisen that *littérature-monde*, without using the word, is part of a complex merchandising strategy of a new kind of "ethnic literature" in France. Avoiding terms and definitions of Anglophone postcolonial theory, Le Bris is nevertheless recycling the very postcolonial discourse of a self-emancipating writing-back of marginalised writers to the former colonial empire in a French and Francophone literary context. However he fails to reflect on the material conditions of production and consumption of Francophone literature that he himself contributes to, customising and exploiting it for a primarily European readership. Hence, in analysing carefully the economic interests hidden behind the *littérature-monde* project, it appears that a certain complicity is taking place in the production and consumption of cultural difference and postcolonial cultural management. As a matter of fact, an ambivalent tendency to homogenise a set of very different authors having in fact different (historical) relationships to French language and universalism, and of writings emanating from historically and politically different literary traditions (Sall and Kesteloot in *Le Monde des livres*, 6 avril 2007) to one federating project has produced a criticism that *littérature-monde* reasserts the very universalism it claims to challenge (Kleppinger, 2010, p. 82). Symbolic value is ascribed to authors like Maryse Condé, Didier Daeninckx or

Brina Svit for instance to account for their common denominator which is supposed to be cultural hybridity. Thus, just as Kien Nghi Ha explains in his critique of hybridity hype in late-capitalism, by extinguishing the historical connotation of hybridity, the act of reframing it positively so as to produce it as a harmless, apolitical and playful condition is intrinsic to the very transformation process aimed at producing an enjoyable consumption of difference (Ha, 2005, p. 61). Thus at the same time Jeanne Garane demonstrates how, contradictorily, each contribution of an essay to the manifesto is followed by a notice indicating the "ethnic origin" of every author (Garane, 2010, p. 232), which reinforces the idea that the point of difference is of symbolic value in the marketplace of alterity. In addition, some critics have stressed the fact that *littérature-monde* does not engage in any political way with either a colonial past, or with present social inequalities, notwithstanding an ambient politicised discourse denouncing social exclusions. In fact, whilst bringing to the metropolitan centre of the symbolic market (represented by Editions Gallimard, one of the most renowned Parisian publishing houses) supposed "marginal" literatures from outside the French *Hexagone* (but on closer inspection well-established, legitimised authors such as Édouard Glissant, Dany Laferrière, Alain Mabanckou and even J. M. Le Clézio), the manifesto acts tacitly to exclude another French minority, namely "Beur" literature, more familiar, more political but less exotic and thus less marketable than the non-French texts (Reeck, 2010, pp. 259, 270).

Finally, the economic interests of *littérature-monde* are revealed when considering the broader literary enterprise headed by Le Bris that is also affiliated with the literary festival *Étonnants-Voyageurs*. As Jean-Xavier Ridon has demonstrated, the marketing strategy of the festival is based on an exotic exaltation staged in Saint-Malo[3] in an ahistorical and depoliticised manner, silencing for instance the colonial past of Saint-Malo. Silencing likewise the ideological commitment of travel and adventure writing of the late nineteenth and early twentieth centuries with the colonial ideology and the anticolonial genealogy that especially postcolonial Francophone writers can lay claim to, Le Bris designs *littérature-monde* as emerging from the genre of Western travel writing (Hargreaves et al., 2010, p. 6). This strategy helps to legitimise the festival whilst giving a forum to writers from the putative periphery, which in turn take on an exotic discourse and exculpates the event from "importunate" ideological suspicion (Ridon, 2010, p. 200).

Processes of Literary Production under the Sign of Self-Formatting

Considering these reconfigurations within the field of Francophone literature, it is also useful to note how contemporary "African" writers negotiate their position in the field as well as how they contribute to the process of production and marketing of Francophone "African" literature as an aesthetically well-defined genre. For instance, Francophone writer and critic Abdourahmane Wabéri[4] supports the notion of « *enfants de la postcolonie* » (Wabéri, 1998, p. 7) and insists on the hyphenated identity of what he sees as the contemporary generation of Francophone "African" writers. A few years later literary scholar Jacques Chevrier argues for the notion of "migritude" in opposition to *négritude*, pointing to the migration experience as being the definitional characteristic of French "African" contemporary writings (Chevrier, 2004a, p. 85). Efforts are made to create the illusion of an emergent, coherent literary movement by

242

means of classification, through a discourse of emancipation, and indeterminate, even absolute "literariness". Yet these propositions fail to account for the very postcolonial-exotic marketing strategies relying precisely on a differentialist "alterity industry" that are inevitably at stake when Francophone "African" writers try to enter the literary mainstream.

In order to account for some of the strategies Francophone "African" writers deploy to accumulate symbolic capital today, it is helpful to bear in mind the theoretical reflexions on late-capitalist mechanisms of production and consumption of cultural alterity. Having said this, we can observe that self-exoticisation, depolitisation, universalisation and cultural industrial domestication are often at stake when it comes to position-taking and self-mediatisation of many Francophone "African" writers. Appropriating for example the notion of cultural hybridity as a token of symbolic value in moments of public self-representation is a strategy to be observed when Leonora Miano, a Francophone-Cameroonian writer, declares « *Je suis une hybride culturelle totalement transversale* » (I am a totally transversal cultural hybrid) (Miano, interviewed in January 2008). Miano likewise explains in an article for *Le Monde Magazine*: « *Identité frontalière. C'est par ce terme que je définis habituellement ma propre identité ... Etre un Africain, de nos jours, c'est être un hybride culturel* » (Miano, *Le Monde Magazine*, 4 décembre 2010) (Hyphenated identity. It is by this notion that I usually define my own identity ... To be an African, today, means to be a being of cultural hybridity). Hybridity and hyphenated identities are also implicitly at stake when Wabéri defines his understanding of the present generation of "African" writers as defined by being « *Franco-quelque chose* » (Wabéri, 1998, p. 7) (French-something). Furthermore the strategic moment of these positionings in the field of literature becomes all the more evident when authors do not see any contradiction, subscribing to disparate branches, affirming for example some generational linkage to culturalist yet essentialist *négritude* authors, whilst at the same time claiming in a universalist manner to be just a "writer full stop". Gaël Ndoumbi Sow writes on behalf of Alan Mabanckou:

> *Alors que ses œuvres s'inscrivent toujours dans une perspective africaine, il refuse d'être considéré comme « un écrivain africain », se proclamant « écrivain » tout court. Le paradoxe qui s'installe est cette prise de distance par rapport au continent africain, en même temps que la confirmation d'un lien avec le lieu d'origine* (Sow, 2009).

> (While his works are always inscribed in an African perspective, he refuses to be considered as an "African writer", claiming to be a "writer" full stop. The paradox that arises consists in that distanciation from the African continent and simultaneously the confirmation of a linkage with the location of origin.)

Such almost apolitical performances of identity construction and marketing inform the postcolonial-exotic production and consumption process legitimising Francophone "African" literature as being at the same time of exotic difference and as well of non-specific inoffensiveness, which are prerequisites of commercialisation and consumption. In fact, Alain Mabanckou is expressing his consciousness of the importance of strategic positionings and identity as alterity politics in the Francophone literary industry when he states:

> [C]*'est maintenant qu'il faut être écrivain africain. Après il sera trop tard. Parce que si maintenant tu n'es pas écrivain africain, après il sera trop tard, puisque tu seras banalisé ; il n'y aura plus de carte de visite « écrivain africain ». C'est maintenant ou*

jamais qu'il faut réclamer qu'on est écrivain africain. Il faut savoir goûter ce statut d'écrivain africain.[5]

Mabanckou has produced a self-staging as a « *sapeur* » (referring to the Congolese « *sape* » trend of placing a particular importance upon vestimentary appearances), with his newsboy cap serving a personal trademark. Moreover he stages himself, in an aesthetic of valuable cultural difference, as a « *sapeur* » referring to the « *sapeurs* » populating his fiction from *Bleu-Blanc-Rouge* (1998) to *Black Bazar* (2009), engaging in a playful mirroring between fiction and reality, a reminder of the exoticist desires for cultural authenticity from "African" fiction requested by a European readership. Although Mabanckou masters the management of his public image as an "African", yet also postcolonial and cosmopolitan, writer to his own benefit, his self-staging is performed in conformity with certain Euro-American reader expectations. As Ndoumbi Sow states, Mabanckou's oscillation between differentiation and renunciation of specific categorisations are part of a strategy of exoticism that accumulates a specific symbolic capital in the field of Francophone literature (Sow, 2009). Still in competition for literary recognition, the postcolonial-exotic (thus essentialist) stake grants the highest symbolic exchange for Francophone "African" writers. "Strategic exoticism", as we can observe in the case of Mabanckou, is, according to Huggan,

> an option, then, but …, it is not necessarily a way out of the dilemma. Indeed, the self-conscious use of the exoticist techniques and modalities of cultural representation might be considered less as a response to the phenomenon of the postcolonial exotic than as a further symptom of it (Huggan, 2001, pp. 32 ff.).

Ultimately when it comes to aesthetic strategies, which narrative forms and what kind of subjects are most eligible to provide recognition for an "African" author in the French literary field? Most of the time an exotic and easily marketable aesthetic is deployed by these writers. In regard to literary exoticism I do not define any intrinsic criteria for texts (Huggan, 2001, p. 13), I would rather argue alongside Huggan that a text is to be considered as aesthetically exotic when it engages in an exotic mode of perception with the Euro-American reader thereby presenting itself as different (Huggan, 2001, p. 13). Thus exoticism is construed as style, as (stereo)typical yet dehistorised themes and particular topographic elements that establish a hierarchical relationship through a suggested alterity. When contemporary Francophone "African" texts produce fictional scenarios they often hark back to Africa or a migration experience in France, but particular motives such as state corruption, the violence of civil wars and child soldiers appear most frequently in an essentialist, dehistorised manner and respond to a prejudicial attitude and exotic mode of perception by the Euro-American reader that predesigns and facilitates the literary communication process in as much as writers adapt their writing to the reader's expectation. "African" literature becomes by those means an accessible consumer product. Nevertheless there are many different stylistic registers that might transport an exotic reception process. Yet "[the] arrival of the exotic in the "centre" cannot disguise the inequalities – the hierarchical encodings of cultural difference – through which exoticist discourses and industries continue to function." (Huggan, 2001, p. 15). While most of the texts engage with a realistic mode of narration (exalted by Le Bris in his *littérature-monde* essay), some writers also deploy non-referential narratives. In fact, every aesthetic mode of narration permitting the representation of alterity from the perspective of the "Occident", in a more or less essentialist manner, can serve as an exotic mode of perception and consumption. Thus we rarely encounter aesthetic innovations that are in the vanguard of aesthetic norms as defined by the Parisian "centre", which is why it is to be assumed that in the literary field, Francophone "African" authors are still perceived as too different to be measured by the same aesthetic framework as national French authors, although still familiar enough to earn symbolic value for their performance of cultural difference. Therefore, it seems that the current boom of *métissage* and hybridity discourses in France only work to reproduce hierarchies, albeit through new forms of exclusions that consolidate an old literary domination.

Homology Between the Space of Authors and the Space of Consumers

To conclude, it seems possible to argue that there are not any absolute or essential similarities that can justify the classification of a group labelled contemporary Francophone "African" writers, despite the fact that these writers are often considered as a coherent group and do themselves often conform to this label to produce texts that correspond to the public expectation. Such a situation resonates with what Bourdieu describes as a structural and functional homology between the space of the author and the space of the consumer. He explains that the social structure of the space of production *corresponds* to the expectations that consumers have of literary products.[6] That is to say, these same expectations dictate the production and the reception of literary texts.[7]

In 1957, Francophone Malagasy writer Jacques Rabemananjara stated that « *[l]e temps n'est pas encore né où [les Africains] auraient loisir de ... s'adonner au culte de l'art pour l'art »* (1957, p. 29). (Time has not yet arrived where [African writers] have the luxury of ... devoting themselves to the cult of art for art's sake.) Today, it seems that the position of "African" writers in the French field of literature has scarcely improved. There remains a homology between the expectations of consumers – marked by prejudicial attitudes and stereotypical preconceptions – and the predetermined structure of literary production that makes it almost impossible for a writer perceived as "African" to invalidate this powerful mechanism of literary domination.

Notes

1. Mindful of the fact that conceptual structures, as for instance 'ethnification', reduce a mutifaceted reality to one ideological interpretation, I would like the notion to be understood as a critical tool to describe phenomena of literary domination. Therefore it must not be understood as a stipulation of putative intrinsic qualities.
2. I would like to highlight that non-French authors are not only 'othered' but that constructed differences are assigned with recourse to essentialist attributes as ethnical origin and monolithic cultural identity.
3. "As Hindson notes, the Saint-Malo to which Le Bris refers is the town of Chateaubriand and pirates and not the French port that was amongst the most active in the slave trade (Hindson, 2008, p. 41). The decision to erase this aspect of the town's history forms part of the exoticisation of the festival's location which in turn recalls the very literature it promotes by becoming a place of desires, of dreams or an elsewhere that prompt flights of imagination. At the same time, this allows for the creation

of a new cultural centre that offers a counterpoint to Parisian dominance." (Ridon, 2010, p. 199.)

4. Co-initiator of the manifesto *Pour une littérature-monde*, as well as Alain Mabanckou and Jean Rouaud and as such closely related to Le Bris.

5. From a discussion with Mongo Mboussa at the *Musée du Quai Branly*, Paris.

   Authors translation: "Now is the moment one must be an African writer. Afterwards it will be too late. Since if you miss being an African writer today, after it will be too late, you will be perceived as banal; There won't be any more "African Writers" business cards. It is now or never we must claim that we are African writers. We have to know how to value the status of being an African writer."

6. Bourdieu, Pierre: "The structural and functional homology between the space of authors and the space of consumers (and of critics) and the correspondence between the social structures of spaces of production and the mental structures which authors, critics and consumers apply to products (themselves organised according to these structures) is at the root of the coincidence that is established between the different categories of works offered and the expectations of different categories of the public." (Bourdieu, 1996, p. 162.)

7. Bourdieu, Pierre: "The objective structures of the field of production are the basis of the categories of perception and appreciation which structure the perception and appreciation of the different positions offered by the field and its products." (Bourdieu, 1996, p. 164.)

References

Ashcroft, B., Griffiths, G., & Tiffin, H. (2002) [1989]. *The Empire writes back: Theory and practice in post-colonial literatures*. London; New York: Routledge.

Bhabha, H. K. (2007). *The location of culture*. New York: Routledge. Trans. Françoise Bouillot, *Les lieux de la culture. Une théorie postcoloniale*. Paris: Payot (Original work published 1994).

Bourdieu, P. (1996). *The rules of art. Genesis and structure of the literary field*. Trans. S. Emanuel, Stanford, CA: Stanford University Press. Trans. of *Les règles de l'art. Genèse et structure du champ littéraire* (Original work published 1992).

Casanova, P. (2004).*The world republic of letters*. Trans. M. B. DeBevoise. Cambridge: MA: Harvard University Press. Trans. *La république mondiale des lettres* (Original work published 1999).

Césaire, A. (1995) [1955]. *Discours sur le colonialisme*. Paris: Présence Africaine.

Chamoiseau, P., Confiant, R., & Bernabé, J. (1990). In praise of creoleness, *Callaloo, 13*(4), 886–909.

Chevrier, J. (2004a). Afrique(s)-sur-Seine: autour de la notion de "migritude", *Notre Librairie, 155–156*, juillet-décembre, 85–89.

Chevrier, J. (2004b). La littérature négro-africaine en langue française de 1921 à nos jours. *La littérature nègre*. Paris: Armand Colin, 14–158.

Compagnon, A. (2000). L'exception française, *Textuel, 37*, 41–52.

Cusset, F. (2003). *French theory: Foucault, Derrida, Deleuze & Cie et les mutations de la vie intellectuelle aux Etats-Unis*. Paris: La Découverte.

Diop, P. S. (2002). Introduction. In P. S. Diop (Ed.) *Fictions africaines et postcolonialisme*. Paris: L'Harmattan.

Fanon, F. (2002) [1961]. *Les damnées de la terre*. Paris: La Découverte.

Garane, J. (2010). Littérature-monde and the space of translation, or, where is littérature-monde? In A. G. Hargreaves, C. Forsdick & D. Murphy (Eds.). *Transnational French studies: Postcolonialism and littérature-monde*, (pp. 227–239). Liverpool: Liverpool University Press.

Glissant, E. (1981). *Le discours antillais*. Paris: Gallimard.

Glissant, E. (1997). *Traité du tout-monde. (Poétique IV)*. Paris: Gallimard.

Glissant, E. (2009). *Philosophie de la relation*. Paris: Gallimard.

Ha, K. N. (2005). *Hype um Hybridität. Kultureller Differenzkonsum und postmoderne Verwertungstechniken im Spätkapitalismus*. Bielefeld: transcript Verlag.

Hargreaves, A. G., Forsdick, C., & Murphy, D. (2010). Introduction: What does littérature-monde mean for French, Francophone and postcolonial studies? In A. G. Hargreaves, C. Forsdick & D. Murphy (Eds.), *Transnational French studies: Postcolonialism and littérature-monde* (pp. 1–111). Liverpool: Liverpool University Press.

Hindson, K. (2008). *Pour une littérature voyageuse : Travel and identity in late twentieth century France*. Unpublished PhD thesis, University of Liverpool, 41.

Huggan, G. (2001). *The postcolonial exotic: Marketing the margins*. London: Routledge.

Kleppinger, K. (2010). What's wrong with the littérature-monde manifesto? *Contemporary French and Francophone Studies: SITES*, 14(1), 77–84.

Kraidy, M. (2005). *Hybridity, or the cultural logic of globalization*. Philadelphia, PA: Temple University Press.

Le Bris, M., & Rouaud, J. (Eds.). (2007). *Pour une littérature-monde*. Paris: Gallimard.

Mabanckou, A. (1998). *Bleu-Blanc-Rouge*. Paris: Présence Africaine.

Mabanckou, A. (2009). *Black Bazar*. Paris: Éditions du Seuil.

Miano, L. (2008). Interview at Librairie Imagigraphe in January 2008, Retrieved on 4 January 2012 from: http://www.frequency.com/topic/leonora+miano

Miano, L. (2010). Habiter la frontière, *Le Monde Magazine*, 4 décembre, retrieved on 4 January 2012 from: http://www.lemonde.fr/international/article_interactif /2010/12/04/huit-ecrivains-africains-racontent-l-afrique -qui-vient_1447623_3210_2.html

Mongo-Mboussa, B., Mabanckou, A., & Miano, L. (2011). Table ronde: Les positionnements des écrivains dans le champ littéraire contemporain, littératures noires ("Les actes"), 26 avril. Retrieved on 4 January 2012 from: http://actesbranly.revues.org/507

Murphy, D. (2002). De-centring French studies: Towards a postcolonial theory of Francophone cultures, *French Cultural Studies*, *13*, 165–185.

Rabemananjara, J. (1957). Le poète noir et son peuple, *Présence Africaine, Revue culturelle du monde noir*, *16*, octobre-novembre, 9–25, 12.

Reeck, L. (2010). The world and the mirror in two twenty-first-century manifestos: Pour une littérature-monde en français and Qui fait la France ? In A. G. Hargreaves, C. Forsdick & D. Murphy (Eds.) *Transnational French studies: Postcolonialism and littérature-monde* (pp. 258–273). Liverpool: Liverpool University Press.

Ridon, J.-X. (2010). *Littérature-monde*, or redefining exotic literature? In A. G. Hargreaves, C. Forsdick & D. Murphy (Eds.). *Transnational French studies: Postcolonialism and littérature-monde* (pp. 195–208). Liverpool: Liverpool University Press.

Sall, A. L., & Kesteloot, L. (2007). Un peu de mémoire, s'il vous plaît! *Le Monde,* 6 avril, 51.

Schor, N. (2001). The crisis of French universalism, *Yale French Studies*, *100*, 43–64.

Sow, G. N. (2009). Stratégies d'écriture et émergence d'un écrivain africain dans le système littéraire francophone. Le cas d'Alain Mabanckou, *Loxias, 26*(Doctoriales VI), retrieved on 4 January 2012 from: http://revel.unice.fr/loxias/index. html?id=3050

Spivak, G. C. (2006). Can the subaltern speak? Trans. J. Vidal: *Les subalternes peuvent-elles parler?* Paris: Éditions Amsterdam.

Wabéri, A. (1998). Les enfants de la postcolonie. Esquisse d'une nouvelle génération d'écrivains francophones d'Afrique noire, *Notre Librairie, 135*, septembre-décembre, 7–15.

Zecchini, L. (2011). *Les études postcoloniales colonisent-elles les sciences sociales?* Retrieved on 4 January 2012 from: http://www.laviedesidees.fr/Les-etudes-postcoloniales. html 27.01.2011

CONCLUDING REMARKS

As we move through the second half century since the French administrative, legal and military complex was dismantled in Africa, we have reason to suspect that at least some of the ties that bind France to Africa today will endure through the decades to come.

As this volume goes to print, France is withdrawing its troops from Mali in readiness for the handover to a UN multilateral peacekeeping force. Simultaneously France is increasing the deployment of military personnel around the uranium mines of its former colony, Niger, where over one-fifth of France's annual uranium requirements is extracted. While the economic imperatives driving the continued French presence in the former African colonies are trans-parent and part of a long-term national economic strategy, the future of France's cultural and linguistic roles in Africa and the Indian Ocean plays out through less predictable channels. It is not without some irony that France's political opponents in the recent conflicts in West Africa are globally known by the French acronyms given to their component parts. The *MUJAO, le mouvement pour l'unicité et le jihad en Afrique de l'Ouest,* occupied a key role in the uprising that brought four thousand French troops into northern Mali in early 2013 when France led the move to restore military order to the former Soudan. Likewise the *MUJAO*'s Tuareg ally, *le mouvement national pour la liberation de l'Azawad (MNLA),* operates across territorial borders drawn up by France following the Berlin Act of 1885 using the language of the former coloniser. Whether or not the term "Francophone Africa" continues to be used decades from now, a review of the political year 2013 provides ample evidence as to why we persist in attributing the adjective to several million square miles of the African continent. For the moment at least the global language of French endures as a potent *lingua franca* on the African continent and the surrounding islands.

The essays in the present volume testify to the complex and multi-dimensional nature of relations between France and its former colonies in Africa. Cultural dynamics still bear multiple and visible traces of French universalism, while other dimensions of the Franco-African legacy have moved into an identifiably "postcolonial" era. Social politics provide diminishing evidence of the norms and values of French family life imported into French Africa during colonial rule, while political relations between France and some of its former and current Indian Ocean possessions reveal a quite different and enduring imbrication between coloniser and colonised.

The aim of this book has been to add to the ongoing debate surrounding the legacy of France in Africa and, perhaps more ambitiously, to give a few tentative pointers of where these relations may be going over the next fifty years. The work presented here has sought to avoid the reductive perspective that casts France in the role of neocolonial villain and African postcolonial states as victims of exogenous hegemony and has chosen rather to illustrate, through a few examples taken from the region, how postcolonial societies are fundamentally complex, dynamic and unique pheno-mena. If the volume has also illustrated helpfully how transdisciplinary modes of analysis, inspired by postcolonial critical studies, serve well the purpose of illuminating the social, cultural and political complexities of the postcolonial world, then it will also have succeeded in contributing in some small measure to the methodological progress of historiography.

The fiftieth anniversary of independence from French colonial rule in Africa has generated a plethora of publications on the subject of France in Africa today. The challenge for this emerging literature and for the present volume is one of moving us as critics and analysts beyond traditional perspectives and colonial chronologies, enabling us better to grasp the uniquely hybrid and changing character of the dynamics that are driving postcolonial societies out of their past.

Claire H. Griffiths
29 May 2013

NOTES ON CONTRIBUTORS

Dr Alice Burgin has recently completed a double-badged doctoral degree in French Studies with the University of Melbourne and the Université de Paris X. Her PhD investigated the impact of French involvement in the production and circulation of Francophone West African films in the twenty-first century. She currently holds a research position on the University of Melbourne's AuSud Media Project. She is also co-authoring a book on African cinema, to be published in 2014.

Sarah Burnautzki is currently engaged in doctoral research at the École des Hautes Études en Sciences Sociales (Paris) and Ruprecht-Karls-Universität Heidelberg. In her thesis, which she began in 2009, she focuses on factors of social, cultural-political and structural domination operating in the French literary field. Over and above issues surrounding the aesthetic impacts of literary domination, questions and practices of identity negotiation performed by the authors themselves are the main interests of her research. She has published a number of articles in this field in French, including « *Repenser la négritude : le nihilisme dans le "monde noir" selon Célestin Monga* », which appeared in *Études littéraires africaines* in 2010 as well as in English, including "Yambo Ouologuem's struggle for recognition in the field of "African" literature in French", Special Issue: Postcolonial Studies and World Literature, published in the *Journal of Postcolonial Writing* in December 2012.

Jonathan Derrick has worked as a journalist and historian specialising in Africa, especially in the nineteenth and twentieth centuries. After working with the West Africa weekly magazine he worked for some years for Africa Books Ltd, publishers of reference books, and did wide-ranging freelance work for magazines in London and Paris and reference books. He worked in Nigeria in the 1970s, at Ahmadu Bello University and the University of Ilorin. He was awarded a PhD from the University of London for his thesis "Douala under the French Mandate, 1916 to 1936" (1979), co-authored with Ralph Austen *Middlemen of the Cameroons rivers* (1999), and published *Africa's "Agitators": Militant Anti-Colonialism in Africa and the West, 1919–1939* (2008).

Dr Martin Evans is a Senior Lecturer in International Development at the University of Chester and a Council Member of the African Studies Association of the UK. He has been conducting research on economic and political aspects of the Casamance conflict in Senegal for over a decade, including "war economies", transnational dynamics, the livelihoods of local people displaced or otherwise affected by violence, the rebel movement, and the articulations between international aid, insecurity and local politics in the return and reconstruction process. He has also published research on the role of diasporas in local development in Cameroon and Tanzania.

Brenda Garvey is a Senior Lecturer in French and Francophone studies at the University of Chester and a founding member of the University's Francophone Africa Research Group. She works on fiction and folktales, with a specific interest in West Africa and in oral and written literature by women. She has published on Annie Ernaux and Marie Darrieussecq and on storytelling performances in Senegal.

Dr Claire Griffiths is Professor of French and Francophone studies and head of the Department of Modern Languages at the University of Chester. Prior to joining the University of Chester in 2009–2010, she was senior research fellow in Francophone African Studies in the WISE Institute for the study of Slavery and Emancipation and taught French and Francophone Studies and postgraduate development studies at the University of Hull. Her most recent work is a project exploring contemporary visual discourses of development in Francophone Africa.

Dr Simon Massey is Senior Lecturer in International Relations and Politics at Coventry University, where he is also a core member of the African Studies Centre. He has conducted research on a wide range of political issues in Africa, particularly security and peacekeeping, democratisation and electoral processes in Francophone and Lusophone countries, extractive industries, and human trafficking. He has particularly focused on Chad, Guinea-Bissau and, recently, the Comoros islands.

Dr David Perfect is the co-author with Arnold Hughes of *A Political History of The Gambia, 1816–1994* (2006) and of the fourth edition of *Historical Dictionary of The Gambia* (2008). His most recent publications include an initial analysis of the 2011 Gambian presidential election (with Ebrima Ceesay), an overview of Gambian electoral politics between 1960 and 2012 (with Arnold Hughes) and an analysis of Gambian trade union history from the 1960s to the 1990s. He is a Visiting Research Associate at the University of Chester and works for the Equality and Human Rights Commission as a Research Manager.

BIBLIOGRAPHY

Africa Research Bulletin: Political, Social and Cultural Series. (2006). The Gambia: No idle boast, 43(10) (November), 16820C–16821B.

African Union. (2000). *Constitutive Act of the African Union adopted by the Thirty-Sixth Ordinary Session of the Assembly of Heads of State and Government,* 11 July, Lomé, Togo.

Ageron, C.-R. (1991). De l'empire à la dislocation de l'Union Française (1939–1956). *Histoire de la France coloniale, III – Le déclin,* (Part 2). Paris : Armand Colin.

Ajayi, O. (1997). Negritude, feminism, and the quest for identity: Re-reading Mariama Bâ's *So Long a Letter, Women's Studies Quarterly: Teaching African Literatures in a Global Literary Economy,* 25(3&4), 435–452.

Alwahti, A. (2003). Prevention of secessionist movements in a micro-state: The international mediation in the Comoros Islands, *International Affairs,* 13(1), 65–83.

Anderson, B. (1991). *Imagined communities.* (Revised ed.). London: Verso.

Appadurai, A. (1996). *Modernity at large: Cultural dimensions of globalization.* Minneapolis; London: University of Minnesota Press.

Ashcroft, B., Griffiths, G., & Tiffin, H. (2002) [1989]. *The empire writes back: Theory and practice in post-colonial literatures.* London; New York: Routledge.

Assié-Lumumba, N. T. & CEPARRED. (2001). Gender, access to learning and production of knowledge in Africa. In AAWORD, *Visions of gender theories and social development in Africa: Harnessing knowledge for social justice and equality.* Dakar: AAWORD.

Bâ, A. H. (1994). *Oui mon commandant ! : mémoires II.* Arles: Actes sud.

Bibliography

Baker, B. (2002). Political sensitivities in Gambian refugee policy, *Journal of Humanitarian Assistance*, posted online June 2002 at http://sites.tufts.edu/jha/

Bancel, N. (2008). Tourisme ethnique : une reconquête symbolique? (1961–2006). In P. Blanchard, S. Lemaire, & N. Bancel (Eds.), *Culture coloniale en France : De la Révolution française à nos jours*. Paris: CNRS Éditions.

Barbier-Wiesser, F.-G. (1994). *Comprendre la Casamance : chronique d'une intégration contrastée*. Paris: Karthala.

Barrows, L. C. (1976) Faidherbe and Senegal: A critical discussion, *African Studies Review*, 19(1), 95–117.

Barry, B. (1998). *Senegambia and the Atlantic slave trade*. Cambridge: Cambridge University Press.

Barthel, D. (1985). Women's educational experience under colonialism: Towards a diachronic model, *Signs, 11*(1), 137–154.

Bashir Salau, M. (2011). *The West African slave plantation: A case study*. Basingstoke: Palgrave Macmillan.

Beloux, F. (1969). *Aimé Césaire : un poète politique*, Retrieved on 24 November, 2011 from: http://www. magazine-litteraire.com/content/hommage/article? id= 8774

Bertho, E. (2011). Sarraounia, une reine africaine entre histoire et mythe littéraire (Niger, 1899–2010), *Genre et Histoire, 8*. Available at : http:// genrehistoire. revues. org/1218

Betts, R. F. (1961). *Assimilation and association in French colonial theory, 1890–1914*. New York: Columbia University Press.

Bhabha, H. K. (2007). *The location of culture*. New York: Routledge. Trans. Françoise Bouillot, *Les lieux de la culture. Une théorie postcoloniale*. Paris: Payot (Original work published 1994).

Biondi, J.-P., (1992) *Les anticolonialistes (1881–1962)*. Paris: Laffont.

Blackburne, Sir K. W. (1976). *Lasting legacy: A story of British colonialism*. London: Johnson.

Blackmon, D. A. (2012). *Slavery by another name: The re-enslavement of Black Americans from the Civil War to World War II*. London: Iccn Books.

Bourdieu, P. (1996). *The rules of art. Genesis and structure of the literary field*. Trans. S. Emanuel, Stanford, CA: Stanford University Press. Trans. of *Les règles de l'Art. Genèse et structure du champ littéraire* (Original work published 1992).

Bouya, A. (1994). Education des filles : Quelles perspectives pour l'Afrique subsaharienne au XXIème siècle, *Afrique et Développement, 19*(4), 11–34.

Breton, A. (1962). *Manifestes du surréalisme*. Paris: J. J. Pauvert.

Brou-Diallo, C. (2011). Le *Projet École Intégrée* (PEI), un embryon de l'enseignement du français langue seconde (FLS) en Côte d'Ivoire, *Sudlangues, 15.* http://www.sudlangues.sn/

Burgin, A. (2011). From cultural protection to national protectionism: Reading contradictions of France's Cultural Diversity Agenda in Abderrahmane Sissako's *Bamako* (2006), *Bulletin of Francophone Postcolonial Studies, 2*, 8–16.

Caminade, P. (2004). La France et l'Union des Comores : saboteur et protéger, *Multitudes, 3*(17), 119–122.

Casanova, P. (2004). *The world republic of letters*. Trans. M. B. DeBevoise, Cambridge: MA: Harvard University Press. Trans. *La république mondiale des lettres* (Original work published 1999).

Cayla, V. (2006). *Les 25 ans du Fonds Sud Cinéma*. Retrieved on 20 November 2010 from: http://www.cnc.fr/CNC_GALLERY_CONTENT/DOCUMENTS/publications/plaquettes/Plaquette_25ansFdsSud.pdf

Bibliography

Ceesay, E. & Perfect, D. (2011). The Gambia's Presidential Election, 2011, *African Arguments Online* (available at: http://africanarguments.org/)

Césaire, A. (1995) [1955]. *Discours sur le colonialisme*. Paris: Présence Africaine.

Chabal, P. (1983). *Amílcar Cabral: Revolutionary leadership and people's war*. Cambridge: Cambridge University Press.

Chafer, T. (2002a). Franco-African relations: No longer so exceptional? *African Affairs*, *101*(404), 343–363.

Chafer, T. (2002b). *The end of empire in French West Africa: France's successful decolonization?* Oxford: Berg.

Chafer, T. (2007). Education and political socialisation of a national-colonial political elite in French West Africa, 1936–47, *Journal of Imperial and Commonwealth History XXXV*(3), 437–458.

Chafer, T., & Sackur, A. (Eds.). (2002). *Promoting the colonial idea: Propaganda and visions of empire in France*. Basingstoke: Palgrave Macmillan.

Chamoiseau, P., Confiant, R., & Bernabé, J. (1990). In praise of creoleness, *Callaloo*, *13*(4), 886–909.

Chevrier, J. (2004a). Afrique(s)-sur-Seine: autour de la notion de "migritude", *Notre Librairie*, *155–156*, juillet-décembre, 85–89.

Chevrier, J. (2004b). La littérature négro-africaine en langue française de 1921 à nos jours. *La littérature nègre*. Paris: Armand Colin, 14–158.

Chumbow, B. S., & Bobda, A. S. (2000). French in West Africa: A sociolinguistic perspective, *International Journal of the Sociology of Language*, *141*, 39–60.

Cissé, M. (1994). *Contes wolof modernes*. Paris: Editions L'Harmattan.

Cohen, W. B. (1971). *Rulers of empire: The French colonial service in Africa*. Stanford, CA: Hoover Institution Press.

Comité Maorais. (2012). Déclaration du Comité Maorais: A bas le visa Balladur, 29 mai. Available at: http://mouroua.centerblog.net/21-declaration-du-comite-maore

Compagnon, A. (2000). L'exception française, *Textuel, 37,* 41–52.

CONGAD. (2000). *Répertoire des organisations non gouvernementales membres du Conseil des organisations non gouvernementales d'appui au développement.* Dakar: CID/CONGAD.

Conklin, A. L. (1997). *A mission to civilize: The republican idea of empire in France and West Africa, 1895–1930.* Stanford, CA: Stanford University Press.

Conklin, A. L. (1998). Colonialism and human rights. A contradiction in terms? The case of France and West Africa, 1895–1914, *The American Historical Review, 103*(2), 419–442.

Cooper, F. (1979). The problem of slavery in African Studies: Review article, *Journal of African History, 20*(1), 103–125.

Cooper, F. (2002). *Africa since 1940: The past of the present.* Cambridge: Cambridge University Press.

Cooper, F. (2005). *Colonialism in Question: Theory, Knowledge, History.* Berkeley: University of California Press.

Coquéry-Vidrovitch, C. (1991). La colonisation française 1931–1939. In C.-R. Ageron (Ed.), *Histoire de la France Coloniale, III – Le Déclin, (1ᵉ partie).* Paris: Armand Colin.

Coquéry-Vidrovitch, C. (1994). *Les Africaines : Histoire des femmes d'Afrique noire du XIXe siècle au XXe siècle.* Paris: Editions Desjonquères.

Cornwell, R. (1998). Anjouan: A spat in the Indian Ocean, *African Security Review, 7*(3), 57–58.

Crowder, M. (1968). *West Africa under colonial rule.* London: Hutchinson.

Cusset, F. (2003). *French theory: Foucault, Derrida, Deleuze & Cie et les mutations de la vie intellectuelle aux Etats-Unis*. Paris: La Découverte.

da Cruz, V., Fengler, W., & Schwartzman, A. (2004). *Remittances to Comoros*. Washington, DC: World Bank. Available at: http://www. worldbank.org/afr/wps/ wp75.pdf

Darbon, D. (1985). « La voix de la Casamance » … une parole diola, *Politique Africaine, 18*, 125–138.

de Jong, F. (1998). *The Casamance Conflict in Senegal*. The Hague: Netherlands Institute for International Relations.

Derrick, J. (1983). The "native clerk" in colonial West Africa, *African Affairs, 82*(326), January, 61–74.

Derrick, J. (2008). *Africa's "agitators": Militant anti-colonialism in Africa and the west, 1919–1939*. London: C. Hurst.

Deschamps, H. (1963). Et maintenant, Lord Lugard? *Africa xxxiii*(4), 291–306.

Dialla, B. E. (2003). *La Question foncière sur les périmètres hydro-agricoles du Burkina-Faso*. Available at: http:// www.capes.bf/ IMG/pdf/Question-fonciere.pdf

Diallo, D. (2006). Le conte au préscolaire, *Tuut Tank, 9*, novembre-décembre.

Diatta, O. (2008). *La Casamance : essai sur le destin tumultueux d'une région*. Paris: L'Harmattan.

Diawara, M. (1997). Reading Africa through Foucault: V. Y. Mudimbe's reaffirmation of the subject. In A. McClintock, A. Mufti & E. Shohat (Eds.). *Dangerous liaisons: Gender, nation and postcolonial perspectives*. Minneapolis, MN: University of Minnesota Press.

Diawara, M. (2010). *African film: New forms of aesthetics and politics*. Munich: Prestel.

Dieng, B. (2010). L'amitié dans le conte ouest-africain comme instrument de régulation et d'intégration, *Ethiopiques, 84,* http://ethiopiques.refer.sn/

Dimier, V. (2002). Direct or indirect rule: Propaganda around a scientific controversy. In T. Chafer & A. Sackur (Eds.), *Promoting the colonial idea: Propaganda and visions of empire in France* (Chapter 12). Basingstoke: Palgrave Macmillan.

Diop, C. A. (1960). *L'Afrique noire pré-coloniale : Étude comparée des systèmes politiques et sociaux de l'Europe et de l'Afrique noire, de l'antiquité à la formation des états modernes.* Paris : Présence Africaine.

Diop, P. S. (2002). Introduction. In P. S. Diop (Ed.). *Fictions africaines et postcolonialisme.* Paris: L'Harmattan.

Domenichini, J.-P. (1969). Jean Ralaimongo (1884–1943), ou Madagascar au seuil du nationalisme, *Revue Française d'Histoire d'Outremer, LVI*(204), 3ᵉ trimestre, 236–287.

Ekpo, D. (2010). Introduction: From negritude to post-Africanism, *Third Text: Critical Perspectives on Contemporary Art and Criticism, 24*(2), 177–187.

Ellis, S. (2001). Les guerres en Afrique de l'Ouest : le poids de l'histoire, *Afrique contemporaine, 198,* 51–56.

Etienne, M. (1983). Gender relations and conjugality among the Baule. In C. Oppong (Ed.), *Female and male in West Africa.* London: George, Allen and Unwin.

ETNGlobal Travel Industry, retrieved on 19 January 2013 from: http://www. eturbonews. com /30693/tourism-assessment-Indian-Ocean-Region

Evans, M. (2000). Briefing: Senegal: Wade and the Casamance dossier, *African Affairs, 99*(397), 649–658.

Evans, M. (2002). The Casamance Conflict: Out of sight, out of mind?, *Humanitarian Exchange, 20,* 5–7.

Evans, M. (2003). Ni paix ni guerre: The political economy of low-level conflict in the Casamance. In S. Collinson (Ed.),

Power, livelihoods and conflict: Case studies in political economy analysis for humanitarian action (pp. 37–52). Humanitarian Policy Group Report, 13. London: Overseas Development Institute.

Evans, M. (2004). *Senegal: Mouvement des forces démocratiques de la Casamance (MFDC)*. Africa Programme Armed Non-State Actors Project Briefing Paper, 2. London: Chatham House.

Evans, M. (2007). "The suffering is too great": Urban internally displaced persons in the Casamance Conflict, Senegal, *Journal of Refugee Studies, 20*(1), 60–85.

Evans, M. (2009). Flexibility in return, reconstruction and livelihoods in displaced villages in Casamance, Senegal, *GeoJournal, 74*(6), 507–524.

Evans, M., & Ray, C. (2013) Uncertain ground: The Gambia and the Casamance Conflict. In A. Saine, E. Ceesay and E. Sall (Eds.), *State and society in The Gambia since independence 1965–2012* (pp. 247–287). Trenton, NJ: Africa World Press.

Fall, B. (2002). *Social history of French West Africa*. Amsterdam and India: SEPHIS/CSSSF.

Fall, B. (Ed.). (2007). *Les Cahiers de l'Agence Nationale de la Case des Tout-Petits*, no. 1, mars. Dakar: UCAD.

Fall, R. (1994). *Femmes et pouvoir dans les sociétés Nord-Sénégambiennes*. Dakar: CODESRIA.

Fanon, F. (2002) [1961]. *Les damnées de la terre*. Paris: La Découverte.

Florence, S., Lebas, J., Parizot, I., et al. (2010). Migration, health and access to care in Mayotte Island in 2007: lessons learned from a representative survey, *Revue d'épidémiologie et de santé publique, 58*(4) 237–244.

Foroyaa. (2012). West Africa: Senegal–Gambia relations: Casamance and the bridge/dissidents and open borders,

Foroyaa newspaper online, 19 April, retrieved from: http://www.foroyaa.gm/

Foucher, V. (2002). Les « évolués », la migration, l'école : pour une nouvelle interprétation de la naissance du nationalisme casamançais. In M.-C. Diop (Ed.), *Le Sénégal contemporain* (pp. 375–424). Paris: Karthala.

Foucher, V. (2003). Pas d'alternance en Casamance? Le nouveau pouvoir sénégalais face à la revendication séparatiste casamançaise, *Politique Africaine,* 91, 101–119.

Foucher, V. (2007). Senegal: The resilient weakness of Casamançais separatists. In M. Bøås & K. C. Dunn (Eds.), *African guerrillas: Raging against the machine* (pp. 171–197). Boulder, CO: Lynne Rienner.

Foucher, V. (2011). On the matter (and materiality) of the nation: Interpreting Casamance's unresolved separatist struggle, *Studies in Ethnicity and Nationalism,* 11(1), 82–103.

Fouillet, Agnès (Director) (2007). *Comores: Un aller simple pour Maoré.* Les Films Bonnette et Minette.

Gailey, H. A. (1964). *A history of the Gambia.* London: Routledge & Kegan Paul.

Galli, R. E., & Jones, J. (1987). *Guinea-Bissau: Politics, economics and society.* London: Frances Pinter.

Garane, J. (2010). Littérature-monde and the space of translation, or, where is littérature-monde? In A. G. Hargreaves, C. Forsdick & D. Murphy (Eds.). *Transnational French studies: Postcolonialism and littérature-monde,* (pp. 227–239). Liverpool: Liverpool University Press.

Gardinier, D. E. (1985) The French impact on education in Africa, 1817–1960. In G. W. Johnson (Ed.). *Double impact: France and Africa in the age of imperialism* (Chapter 18, pp. 333–344). Westport, CT: Greenwood Press.

Bibliography

Gellar, S. (1995). *Senegal: An African nation between Islam and the West*. Boulder, CO: Westview Press.

Genova, J. E. (2004). *Colonial ambivalence, cultural authenticity, and the limitations of mimicry in French-ruled West Africa, 1914–1956*. New York: Peter Lang.

Ghorbal, S. (2008). Sambi sur le pied de guerre, *Jeune Afrique*, 2457, février.

Ginio, R. (2006). *French colonialism unmasked: The Vichy years in French West Africa*. Lincoln, NE: University of Nebraska Press.

Glissant, E. (1981). *Le Discours antillais*. Paris: Gallimard.

Glissant, E. (1997). *Traité du tout-monde. (Poétique IV)*. Paris: Gallimard.

Glissant, E. (2009). *Philosophie de la relation*. Paris: Gallimard.

Gray, Sir J. M. (1966). *A history of the Gambia*, (2nd ed.). London: Frank Cass.

Griffiths, C. H. (2005). Gender, education and literary output in Francophone Africa. In E. Makward, M. Lillelet & A. Saber (Eds.), *North-south linkages and connections in continental and diaspora African literatures* (pp. 388–403). Trenton NJ: Africa World Press.

Griffiths, C. H. (2006). Colonial subjects: race and gender in French West Africa. *International Journal of Sociology and Social Policy, 26*: (11–12, special issue), pp. 449–594.

Griffiths, C. H. (2010). *Globalizing the postcolony: Contesting discourses of gender and development in francophone Africa*. Lanham, MD: Lexington Books.

Ha, K. N. (2005). *Hype um Hybridität. Kultureller Differenzkonsum und postmoderne Verwertungstechniken im Spätkapitalismus*. Bielefeld: transcript Verlag.

Hailey, Lord (1957). *An African survey revised 1956* (p. 209). London: Oxford University Press.

Hale, T. A. (1998). *Griots and griottes*. Bloomington and Indianapolis, IN: Indiana University Press.

Hargreaves, A. G. (1981). *The colonial experience in French fiction: A study of Pierre Loti, Ernest Psichari and Pierre Mille*. Basingstoke: Macmillan.

Hargreaves, A. G., Forsdick, C., & Murphy, D. (2010). Introduction: What does littérature-monde mean for French, Francophone and postcolonial studies? In A. G. Hargreaves, C. Forsdick & D. Murphy (Eds.), *Transnational French studies: Postcolonialism and littérature-monde* (pp. 1–111). Liverpool: Liverpool University Press.

Hargreaves, J. D. (1963). *Prelude to the partition of West Africa*. London: Macmillan.

Hargreaves, J. D. (1974). *West Africa partitioned: The loaded pause, 1885–1889*. London: Macmillan.

Harrow, K. W. (1999). Introduction. In K. W. Harrow (Ed.), *African cinema: Postcolonial and feminist readings*. Trenton, NJ: Africa World Press.

Hausteiner, E. M. (2011). Review of *Empires in world history: Power and the politics of difference*, by J. Burbank & F. Cooper (Princeton, NJ: Princeton University Press, 2010), in *Ethics & International Affairs*, 25(4), 484–486.

Higbee, W., & Lim, S. H. (2010). Concepts of transnational cinema: Towards a critical transnationalism in film studies, *Transnational Cinemas*, 1(1), 7–21.

Hindson, K. (2008). *Pour une littérature voyageuse : Travel and identity in late twentieth century France*. Unpublished PhD thesis, University of Liverpool, 41.

Hodeir, C., & Pierre, M. (1991). *L'Exposition coloniale*. Brussels: Complexe.

[House of Commons] (1971). *British Parliamentary Papers Colonies Africa 56*. Shannon: Irish University Press.

270

Huggan, G. (2001). *The postcolonial exotic: Marketing the margins*. London: Routledge.

Hughes, A. (1992). The collapse of the Senegambian Confederation, *Journal of Commonwealth and Comparative Politics*, *30*(2), 200–222.

Hughes, A. (2004). Decolonizing Africa: Colonial boundaries and the crisis of the (non) nation state, *Diplomacy and Statecraft, 15*(4), 833–866.

Hughes, A., & Lewis, J. (1995). Beyond Francophonie? The Senegambia Confederation in retrospect. In A. Kirk-Greene & D. Bach (Eds.), *State and society in Francophone Africa since independence* (pp. 228–243). Basingstoke: Macmillan.

Hughes, A., & Perfect, D. (2006). *A political history of The Gambia*. Rochester, NY: University of Rochester Press.

Hughes, A., & Perfect, D. (2008). *Historical dictionary of The Gambia* (4th ed.). Lanham, MD: Scarecrow Press.

Hugon, A. (Ed.) (2004). *L'Histoire des femmes en situation coloniale*. Paris: Karthala.

Idowu, H. O. (1968). The establishment of elective institutions in Senegal, 1869–1880, *Journal of African History*, *9*(2), 261–277.

Indian Ocean Newsletter (2011), 1317, 1 October.

Institut national de la statistique et des études économiques (2011). Produit intérieur brut à Mayotte en 2009, *Mayotte Infos*, no. 55, novembre. Available at: http://www.insee.fr/fr/insee_regions/mayotte/themes/infos/infos55/infos55.pdf

Irele, F. A. (2011). *The negritude moment*. Trenton, NJ: Africa World Press.

Jawara, D. K. (2009). *Kairaba*. Haywards Heath: D. K. Jawara.

Jeanpierre, W. A. (1965). Sartre's Theory of "Anti-Racist Racism" in his study of negritude, *The Massachusetts Review*, 6(4).

Jeune Afrique. (2000). Wade: « Je n'ai pas changé, mais ... », *Jeune Afrique/L'Intelligent*, 23–29 mai.

Johnson, G. W. (1971). *The emergence of black politics in Senegal: The struggle for power in the Four Communes, 1900–1930.* Stanford, CA: Stanford University Press.

Johnson, G. W. (Ed.) (1985). *Double impact: France and Africa in the age of imperialism.* Westport, CT: Greenwood Press.

Jules-Rosette, B. (1998). *Black Paris: The African Writers' landscape.* Urbana, IL: University of Illinois Press.

Keaton, T. (2010). The politics of race blindness, *Du Bois Review*, 7(1), 103–131.

Kent, J. (1990). Regionalism or territorial autonomy? The case of British West African development, 1939–49, *Journal of Imperial and Commonwealth History*, 18(1), 61–80.

Kesteloot, L. (2001). *Histoire de la littérature négro-africaine.* Paris: AUF, Karthala.

Kesteloot, L., & Dieng, B. (1989). *Du tieddo au talibé.* Paris: Présence Africaine.

Kesteloot, L., & Mbodj, C. (2006). *Contes et mythes wolof.* Dakar: IFAN.

Klein, M. A. (1998). *Slavery and colonial rule in French West Africa.* New York: Cambridge University Press.

Kleppinger, K. (2010). What's wrong with the littérature-monde manifesto? *Contemporary French and Francophone Studies: SITES*, 14(1), 77–84.

Konings, P., & Nyamnjoh, F. B. (2003). *Negotiating an Anglophone identity: A study of the politics of recognition and representation in Cameroon.* Leiden: Brill.

Kraidy, M. (2005). *Hybridity, or the cultural logic of globalization.* Philadelphia, PA: Temple University Press.

Bibliography

Lambert, M. C. (1998). Violence and the war of words: Ethnicity *v.* nationalism in the Casamance, *Africa*, *68*(4), 585–602.

Lash, S., & Urry, J. (1987). *The end of organized capitalism.* Cambridge: Polity Press.

Lebeuf, A. M. D. (1963). The role of women in the political organisation of African societies. In D. Paulme (Ed.), *Women of tropical Africa.* London: Routledge & Kegan Paul.

Le Bris, M., & Rouaud, J. (Eds.). (2007). *Pour une littérature-monde.* Paris: Gallimard.

Le Populaire. (2000). Commentaires, 12, 13 et 14 décembre.

Leymarie, I. (1999). *Les griots wolof du Sénégal.* Paris: Maisonneuve & Larose.

Maasilta, M. (2007). *African Carmen: Transnational cinema as an arena for cultural contradictions.* Unpublished doctoral thesis, Tampere, University of Tampere.

Mabanckou, A. (1998). *Bleu-Blanc-Rouge.* Paris: Présence Africaine.

Mabanckou, A. (2009). *Black Bazar.* Paris: Éditions du Seuil.

MacCannell, D. (1976). *The tourist: A new theory of the leisure class.* London: Macmillan.

McLaughlin, F. (1995). Haalpulaar identity as a response to Wolofization. *African Languages and Cultures, 8*(2), 153–168.

Malango Actualité, 25 janvier 2009.

Marut, J.-C. (2010). *Le conflit de Casamance : ce que disent les armes.* Paris: Karthala.

Massey, S., & Baker, B. (2009). Comoros: External involvement in a small island state, *Chatham House Programme Paper*, June. Available at: http://www.chathamhouse.org/sites/default/files/public/Research/Africa/0709comorospp.pdf

MFDC. (1994). *La voix de la Casamance.*

MFDC. (1999). *Casamance Kunda : La voie de la liberté,* novembre-décembre.

MFDC. (2000) Letter from the Secretary-General to His Excellency the President of the French Republic, 15 November.

MFDC. (2001). Letter from Salif Sadio to the President of the Republic of Guinea-Bissau, 3 January.

Miano, L. (2008). Interview at Librairie Imagigraphe in January 2008. Retrieved on 4 January 2012 from: http://www.frequency.com/topic/leonora+miano

Miano, L. (2010). Habiter la frontière, *Le Monde Magazine,* 4 decémbre, retrieved on 4 January 2012 from: http://www.lemonde.fr/international/article_interactif /2010/12/04/huit-ecrivains-africains-racontent-l-afrique -qui-vient_1447623_3210_2.html

Michel, M. (2003). *Les Africains et la Grande Guerre : l'appel à l'Afrique, 1914–1918.* Paris: Karthala.

Mongo-Mboussa, B., Mabanckou, A., & Miano, L. (2011). Table ronde: Les positionnements des écrivains dans le champ littéraire contemporain, littératures noires ("Les actes"), 26 avril. Retrieved on 4 January 2012 from: http://actesbranly.revues.org/507

Mortimer, E. (1969). *France and the Africans 1944–1960.* London: Faber and Faber.

Mumford, W. & Orde Browne, G. St. J. (1936). *Africans learn to be French.* London: Evans Bros.

Munt, I. (1994). The "Other" postmodern tourism: Culture, travel and the new middle classes, *Theory, Culture & Society, 11*(3), 101–123.

Murphy, D. (2000). Africans filming Africa: Questioning theories of an authentic African cinema, *Journal of African Cultural Studies,* 13(2), 239–249.

Murphy, D. (2002). De-centring French studies: Towards a postcolonial theory of Francophone cultures, *French Cultural Studies*, *13*, 165–185.

Muselier, R. (2011). Rapport fait au nom de la Commission des Affaires étrangères sur le projet de loi, nᵒ. 3598, autorisant l'approbation de l'accord entre le Gouvernement de la République française et le Gouvernement de l'Union des Comores instituant un partenariat de défense, Rapport de l'Assemblée Nationale, nᵒ. 3979, 16 novembre.

Napon, A. (2003). La problématique de l'introduction des langues nationales dans l'enseignement primaire au Burkina Faso, *Sudlangues*, 2. http://www. sudlangues. sn/spip.php?article59

Ngom, F. (2004). Ethnic identity and linguistic hybridization in Senegal. *International Journal of the Sociology of Language*, *170*, 95–111.

Nguyen, V. K. (2010). *The republic of therapy: Tirage and sovereignty in West Africa's time of AIDS*. Durham and London: Duke University Press.

Nugent, P. (2007). Cyclical history in the Gambia/Casamance borderlands: Refuge, settlement and Islam from *c*.1880 to the present, *Journal of African History*, *47*(2), 221–243.

Ottenheimer, H. (2001). Spelling Shinzwani: Dictionary construction and orthographic choice in the Comoro Islands, *Written Language and Literacy*, *4*(1), 15–24.

Parker, R. (1991). The Senegal–Mauritania Conflict of 1989: A fragile equilibrium, *Journal of Modern African Studies*, *29*(1), 155–171.

Paulme, D. (Ed.) (1963). *Women of tropical Africa.* London: Routledge & Kegan Paul.

Perfect, D., & Hughes, A. (2013). Gambian electoral politics: 1960–2012. In A. Saine, E. Ceesay & E. Sall (Eds.), *State and society in The Gambia since independence: 1965–2012* (pp. 79–111). Trenton, NJ: Africa World Press.

Perham, M. (1967). *Colonial sequence 1930 to 1949.* London: Methuen.

Petty, S. J. (2008). *Contact zones: Memory, origin, and discourses in black diasporic cinema.* Detroit, MI: Wayne State University Press.

Phillips, L. C. (1991). The Senegambia Confederation. In C. L. Delgado & S. Jammeh (Eds.), *The political economy of Senegal under structural adjustment* (pp. 175–193). Westport, CT: Praeger.

Quinn, C. A. (1972). *Mandingo kingdoms of the Senegambia.* Evanston, IL: Northwestern University Press.

Rabemananjara, J. (1957). Le poète noir et son peuple, *Présence Africaine. Revue culturelle du monde noir, 16,* octobre-novembre, 9–25, 12.

Randrianja, S. (2001). *Société et luttes anticoloniales à Madagascar (1896 à 1946).* Paris: Karthala.

Reeck, L. (2010). The world and the mirror in two twenty-first-century manifestos: Pour une littérature-monde en français and Qui fait la France ? In A. G. Hargreaves, C. Forsdick & D. Murphy (Eds.) *Transnational French studies: Postcolonialism and littérature-monde* (pp. 258–273). Liverpool: Liverpool University Press.

Renou, X. (2006). *La privatisation de la violence.* Paris: Agone.

République du Sénégal. (1991). *Les faits en Casamance : le droit contre la violence.* Dakar: République du Sénégal.

République du Sénégal. (2005). *Situation économique et sociale régionale.* Ziguinchor: Service Régional de la Statistique et de la Démographie de Ziguinchor.

Richards, P. (1996). *Fighting for the rain forest: War, youth and resources in Sierra Leone.* Oxford: James Currey in association with International African Institute.

Ridon, J.-X. (2010). Littérature-monde, or redefining exotic literature? In A. G. Hargreaves, C. Forsdick & D. Murphy (Eds.). *Transnational French studies: Postcolonialism and littérature-monde* (pp. 195–208). Liverpool: Liverpool University Press.

Roche, C. (1985). *Histoire de la Casamance : conquête et résistance : 1850–1920.* Paris: Karthala.

Ruelle, C. (2002). Le « souffle des ancêtres » est une morale de vie: entretien de Catherine Ruelle avec Mansour Sora Wade, *Africultures: Islam, croyances et négritude dans les cinémas d'Afrique, 47.*

Sabatier, P. (1985). Did Africans really learn to be French? The Francophone elite of the École William Ponty. In G. W. Johnson (Ed.), *Double impact: France and Africa in the age of imperialism* (Chapter 9). Westport, CT: Greenwood Press.

Saindou, K. (2008). Edine, 'Polices des îles: le spectre des soldats négligés, *Kashkazi,* juin/juillet.

Saine, A. (2009). *The paradox of third-wave democratization in Africa: The Gambia under AFPRC-APRC rule, 1994–2008.* Lanham, MD: Lexington Books.

Saine, A., & Ceesay, E. (2013). Post-coup politics and authoritarianism in The Gambia: 1994–2012. In A. Saine, E. Ceesay & E. Sall (Eds.), *State and society in The Gambia since independence: 1965–2012* (pp. 151–184). Trenton, NJ: Africa World Press.

Sall, A. L., & Kesteloot, L. (2007). Un peu de mémoire, s'il vous plait ! *Le Monde,* 6 avril, 51.

Sartre, J. P., & MacCombie J. (1964). (trans.), Black Orpheus, *The Massachusetts Review, 6*(1).

Schmidt, E. (2005). *Mobilizing the masses: Gender, ethnicity, and class in the Nationalist Movement in Guinea, 1939–1958.* New York: Heinemann.

Schmidt, E. (2007). *Cold War and decolonization in Guinea, 1946–1958*. Athens, OH: Ohio University Press.

Schor, N. (2001). The crisis of French universalism, *Yale French Studies, 100*, 43–64.

Seneweb. (2010). Interdiction d'un livre sur la Casamance : la Raddho et Amnesty international dénoncent, *Senewebnews*, 14 octobre, http://www. seneweb.com/ news/Societe/ interdiction-d-un-livre-sur-la-casamance-la-raddho-et-amnesty-international-d-noncent_n_ 36292 .html.

Senghor, J. C. (2008). *The politics of Senegambian integration, 1958–1994*. Bern: Peter Lang.

Senghor, J. C. (2013). The 'Senegambia' experience: Twelve pointers for regional integration in Africa. In A. Saine, E. Ceesay & E. Sall (Eds.), *State and society in The Gambia since independence: 1965–2012* (pp. 215–245). Trenton, NJ: Africa World Press.

Senghor, L. S. (1964). *Liberté I: Negritude et humanisme*. Paris: Seuil.

Senghor, L. S. (1990). *Œuvre poétique*. Paris: Seuil.

Senghor, L. S., & Sadji, A. (1953). *La belle histoire de Leuk-le-lièvre*. Paris: Hachette.

Shohat, E., & Stam, R. (1994). *Unthinking Eurocentrism: Multiculturalism and the media*. London: Routledge.

Shore, C. (2001). The cultural policies of the European Union and cultural diversity. In Tony Bennett (Ed.), *Differing diversities: Transversal study on the theme of cultural policy and cultural diversity*. Strasbourg: Council of Europe.

Sow, F., Diouf, M. & le Moine, G. (1993). *Femmes sénégalaises à l'horizon 2015*. Dakar: Ministère de la Femme/The Population Council.

Sow, G. N. (2009). Stratégies d'écriture et émergence d'un écrivain africain dans le système littéraire francophone.

Le cas d'Alain Mabanckou, *Loxias, 26*(Doctoriales VI) retrieved on 4 January 2012 from: http://revel.unice.fr/loxias/index. html?id=3050

Soyinka, W. (1976). *Myth, literature and the African world.* Cambridge: Cambridge University Press.

Spivak, G. C. (2006). Can the subaltern speak? Trans. J. Vidal: *Les subalternes peuvent-elles parler ?* Paris: Éditions Amsterdam.

Stovall, T. (2003). Love, labor, and race: Colonial men and white women in France during the Great War. In T. Stovall & G. van den Abeele (Eds.), *French civilisation and its discontents – nationalism, colonialism, race.* Lanham, MD: Lexington Books.

Sudarkasa, N. (1996). The "status" of women in indigenous African societies. In R. Terborg-Penn & A. Benton Rushing (Eds.), *Women in Africa and the African diaspora – a reader.* Washington, DC: Howard University Press.

Swindell, K. (1982). *The strange farmers of The Gambia: A study in the redistribution of African population.* Norwich: Geo Books.

Thioune, B. (2009). Traditions narratives et initiation culturelle de l'écolier africain dans *La belle histoire de Leuk-le-lièvre, Ethiopiques*, 83.

Toliver-Diallo, W. J. (2005). "The woman who was more than a man": Making Aline Sitoe Diatta into a national heroine in Senegal, *Canadian Journal of African Studies*, *39*(2), 338–360.

Tomàs, J. (2005). « La parole de paix n'a jamais tort. » La paix et la tradition dans le Royaume d'Oussouye (Casamance, Sénégal), *Canadian Journal of African Studies*, *39*(2), 414–441.

Touray, O. A. (2000). *The Gambia and the world: A history of the foreign policy of Africa's smallest state, 1965–1995.* Hamburg: Institute of African Affairs.

Ugo Nwokeji, G. (2011). *The slave trade and culture in the Bight of Biafra.* Cambridge: Cambridge University Press.

Ukadike, N. F. (1994). *Black African cinema.* Berkeley, CA: University of California Press.

UNESCO. (1953). *The use of vernacular languages in education.* Paris: UNESCO.

UNESCO. (1993). *Le rôle des mouvements d'étudiants africains dans l'évolution politique et sociale de l'Afrique de 1900 à 1975.* Paris: Editions UNESCO/L'Harmattan.

UNESCO. (2003). *Education in a multilingual world.* Paris: UNESCO.

United Democratic Party/Gambia Moral Congress (2011). Final Report of the UDP–GMC Alliance on the Presidential Election held on 24 November. Available at: http://www.maafanta.com/UDPGMCFinalReport Elections2011.html

United Nations. (2011). *World population prospects: The 2010 revision,* New York: United Nations. Available at: http://esa.un.org/ unpd/wpp/ Documentation /pdf/ WPP2010_Volume-I_ Comprehensive-Tables.pdf.

Vaillant, J. G. (1990). *Black, French, and African: A life of Léopold Sédar Senghor.* Cambridge, MA: Harvard University Press.

Wabéri, A. (1998). Les enfants de la postcolonie. Esquisse d'une nouvelle génération d'écrivains francophones d'Afrique noire, *Notre Librairie, 135,* septembre-décembre, 7–15.

Wade, A. (1989). *Un destin pour l'Afrique.* Paris: Karthala.

Walker, I. (2007). What came first, the nation or the state? Political process in the Comoro Islands, *Africa*, *77*(4), 582–605.

Welch, C. E. Jr. (1964). *Dream of unity: Pan Africanism and political unification in West Africa*. Ithaca, NY: Cornell University Press.

Wolton, D. (2008). Des stéréotypes coloniaux aux regards post-coloniaux: l'indispensable évolution des imaginaires. In P. Blanchard, S. Lemaire & N. Bancel (Eds.), *Culture coloniale en France : De la Révolution française à nos jours*. Paris: CNRS Éditions.

Wyse, A. J. G. (1976). The Gambia in Anglo-French relations, 1905–12, *Journal of Imperial and Commonwealth History*, 4(2), 164–175.

Zecchini, L. (2011). Les études postcoloniales colonisent-elles les sciences sociales ? 27 January. Retrieved on 4 January 2012 from: http://www.laviedesidees.fr/Les-etudes-postcoloniales. html

INDEX